A TREATISE

ON THE

AMERICAN LAW

OF

ELECTIONS.

BY

GEO. W. McCRARY,

OF THE IOWA BAR, MEMBER OF THE HOUSE OF REPRESENTATIVES OF THE UNITED STATES, AND LATE CHAIRMAN OF THE COMMITTEE OF ELECTIONS OF THAT BOD'

KEOKUK, IOWA:
R. B OGDEN, PUBLISHER.
CHICAGO:
E. B. MYERS, LAW BOOKSELLER.
1875.

Entered according to the act of Congress, in the year 1875,
By GEO. W. McCRARY,
in the Office of the Librarian of Congress, at Washington.

TO THE HONORABLE

SAMUEL F. MILLER LL. D.,

ASSOCIATE JUSTICE SUPREME COURT UNITED STATES, THIS TREATISE IS MOST RESPECTFULLY DEDICATED.

HIS GREAT LEARNING AND ABILITY AS A LAWYER, AND AS A JUDGE; HIS HIGH CHARACTER AS A MAN AND AS A CITIZEN; AND THE LASTING OBLIGATIONS I AM UNDER TO HIM FOR GENEROUS AID AND INSTRUCTION AS MY TEACHER IN THE LAW, AND FOR AN EARNEST FRIENDSHIP CONTINUING THROUGH MANY YEARS, ALL COMBINE TO MAKE THIS RECOGNITION AND ACKNOWLEDGMENT BOTH A DUTY AND A PLEASURE, ON THE PART OF HIS FRIEND AND PUPIL.

THE AUTHOR.

PREFACE

The subject which I have imperfectly treated in the following pages is of great importance, especially to the people of the United States. In a country like ours, where all the powers of government reside with the people, and are delegated to representatives chosen by means of the ballot, and who serve only for short periods, making necessary a frequent appeal to the popular will; and where the decisions reached by this means are often so important, it is inevitable that controversies growing out of elections should be numerous. And it is manifest that it is a matter of great consequence, that the principles which are to control the determination of controversies of this character should be understood, not only by the legal profession, but also by the people generally.

Perhaps the most important purpose to be subserved by the publication of books of the law, is the prevention of litigation by informing the people as to their rights and duties; and it is hoped that this humble contribution to the law of elections may serve this purpose, by diminishing somewhat the number of election contests in the future, while at the same time affording some valuable aid and assistance in their proper decision, when they do arise. It has been my aim to bring together, in a convenient form, the adjudications of the Courts and other tribunals of this country, touching the subjects treated, among which are the following:

The qualifications of electors.

The qualifications, powers and duties of election officers.

The time, place and manner of holding elections.—Notice.

The *prima facie* right to an office.

Eligibility to office.—Tenure.

Practice and Evidence in contested election cases.

Imperfect ballots.

Violence and intimidation.

Fraud and illegal voting.

Prosecutions for violation of election laws.

Civil liability of election and registration officers, for a failure to discharge their duties.

The organization of legislative bodies, and the power and authority of such bodies over their members.

A considerable experience in the investigation of cases of contested elections, has caused me to feel the need of some such treatise as I have attempted to prepare. The law upon this subject, as determined by the courts and legislative bodies of this country, is only to be found scattered through many hundreds of volumes of reports, and the labor of collecting and examining them is necessarily very great. It has been my endeavor in the preparation of this volume, to state briefly and clearly the principles or rules which have been settled, and to cite the authorities where they will be found discussed more at length. I have myself entered into discussion only when considering unsettled or disputed points.

I have entitled this book *The* AMERICAN *Law of Elections*. The authorities cited are chiefly American authorities. Upon this subject we are, from the very necessities of the case, building up an American common law.

I do not say that English authorities are of no value upon this branch of the law. On the contrary, I have cited them freely whenever I have deemed them applicable and useful. I have, however, endeavored to keep steadily in view the fact that the genius of our institutions, the character of our political system, and the principles upon which the right of suffrage in this country is founded, all differ so radically from those of England, as to diminish very greatly the value of English precedents in election cases, and I have labored to show that our own tribunals have, by a long course of judicial decisions, settled the law of this country, as it relates to the questions I have treated, upon a firm and solid basis.

KEOKUK, IOWA, 1875.

THE AMERICAN LAW

OF

ELECTIONS.

CHAPTER I.

OF THE QUALIFICATIONS OF VOTERS.

§ 1. Subject to the limitation contained in the Fifteenth Amendment to the Constitution of the United States, the power to fix the qualifications of voters is vested in the States. Each State fixes for itself these qualifications, and the United States adopts the State law upon the subject, as the rule in Federal Elections, as will be seen by reference to Sec. II of Art. I of the Constitution, which provides as follows:

"The House of Representatives shall be composed of members chosen every second year by the people of the several States, *and the electors in each State shall have the qualifications required for electors of the most numerous branch of the State Legislature.*"

The qualifications of voters for presidential electors, are also to be fixed by the States, as will be seen by reference to Sec. I of Art. II of the Constitution, which provides that "each State shall appoint, *in such manner as the legislature thereof may direct*, a number of electors equal to the whole number of Senators and Representatives, to which the State may be entitled in the Congress."

Inasmuch as Representatives in Congress, and Presidential electors, are the only Federal officers to be chosen by popular ballot, it is manifest that all controversies concerning the right of individuals to vote, whether at a State or a Federal election, must be determined by reference to the local or State law upon this subject, provided, of course, that such local or State law is not in conflict with any provision of the Constitution of the United States.

§ 2. As already intimated, the power of the State government to prescribe the qualifications of voters, is limited by the terms of the Fifteenth Amendment to the Constitution of the United States, which provides as follows:

"The right of citizens of the United States to vote shall not be denied or abridged by the United States, or by any State, on account of race, color or previous condition of servitude.

"The Congress shall have power to enforce this article by appropriate legislation."

The effect of this constitutional provision most clearly is to render absolutely null and void all provisions of a State constitution or State law, which come in conflict with the amendment itself, or with any statute passed by Congress to enforce it, and which is appropriate for that purpose. In point of fact the adoption of this amendment abrogated certain provisions found in the constitutions and laws of most of the States, which provided, among other things, that all voters should be *white* male citizens.

In pursuance of the power conferred upon Congress by the latter clause of the Fifteenth Amendment, that body has enacted certain laws to protect the newly enfranchised voter in the exercise of his rights. These acts of Congress will be found in full in the appendix to this volume.

§ 3. The right of suffrage is not a natural right, nor is it an absolute, unqualified personal right. It is a right derived in this country from constitutions and statutes. It is regulated by the States, and their power to fix the qualifications of voters, is limited only by the provisions of the Fifteenth Amendment to the Constitution, which forbids any distinction on account of "race, color, or previous condition of servitude." *Huber vs. Reily*, 53 *Penn. State R.* 115. *Ridley vs. Sherbrook*, 3 *Cold*, 569. *Anderson vs. Baker*, 23 *Md.* 531. *Brightley's Election Cases*, 27. *See also* 1 *Story Const. Ch.* 9, *Sec.* 581, 582.

§ 4. The qualifications of voters are not uniform in all the States, but they are similar. Among those which are generally required, are the following:

1. Citizenship, either by birth or naturalization.
2. Residence for a given period of time in the State, County, and voting precinct.
3. Age. In all the States it is required that a voter shall have reached the age of twenty-one years.
4. In some States the payment of taxes, and in many States registration.
5. Freedom from the infamy of having been convicted of an infamous crime,
6. That no idiot or lunatic shall vote.

§ 5. The Legislature of a State cannot add to the

qualifications of an elector, as prescribed by the State constitution. Where the constitution prescribes the qualifications, whoever possesses them, has a constitutional right to vote, and of this right he cannot be deprived by legislative enactment. This rule has been applied in the construction of the constitution of Pennsylvania, which declares affirmatively that all persons possessing certain qualifications shall be entitled to vote. The Legislature of that State, in 1866, passed an Act, declaring, in substance, that no person should be permitted to vote, who, having been drafted into the Military Service, and duly notified, had failed to report for duty. But it was held by the Supreme Court of that State, that this was an attempt of the Legislature to disfranchise those to whom the constitution had given the rights of electors, and that the act was therefore unconstitutional and void. *McCafferty vs. Guyer*, 59 *Pa. State R.* 109, *Brightley's Election Cases*, 44.

§ 6. While the Legislature cannot add to, abridge or alter the constitutional qualifications of voters, it may, and should, prescribe proper and necessary rules for the orderly exercise of the right resulting from these qualifications. The Legislature must prescribe the necessary regulations as to place, mode, manner, &c. But such regulations are to be subordinated to the enjoyment of the right itself. *Page vs. Allen*, 58 *Pa. State R.* 338, 347, *vide also Patterson vs. Barlow*, 60 *do* 54.

It has been held under the authority of the rule in McCafferty vs. Guyer, that an act of the legislature declaring that a voter who has removed from his district within ten days of the election may vote in the district removed from, is unconstitutional and void. This, for the reason that the constitution requires, that the voter should have resided in the election district "ten days immediately preceding the election." *Thompson vs. Ewing*, 1 *Brewst.* 103. And in State vs. Adams, 2 Stewart 239, the Supreme Court of Alabama held that no department of the government, nor all of them combined, have the power to divest an individual of his constitutional right of suffrage.

§ 7. The power to provide for the orderly exercise of the right of suffrage, which we have seen belongs to the State legislature, includes the power to enact registry laws, and to prohibit from voting, persons not registered. It is now generally admitted that these laws do not add to the constitutional qualifications of voters, and are therefore not invalid. *Capen vs. Foster*, 12 *Pick* 485, *Brightley's Election Cases*, 51.

§ 8. But it is manifest, that under color of regulating the mode of exercising the elective franchise, it is quite possible to subvert or injuriously restrain the right itself. And a statute which clearly does either of these things, must of course be held invalid, on the ground that it seeks to deprive the citizen of his constitutional right.

For example, a registry act which should undertake to require a longer residence, prior to the time of voting, than that required by the constitution, or which should require the payment of taxes not required to be paid by constitutional provision, or which should impose upon a particular class of citizens, conditions and requirements not required of all others, would be void. The right to vote must not be impaired by the regulation. It must be regulation purely, and not destruction.

§ 9. It being conceded that the power to enact a registry law, is within the power to regulate the exercise of the elective franchise, and preserve the purity of the ballot, it follows that an election held in disregard of the provisions of a registry law must be held void. In Ensworth vs. Albin *et. al.*, 44 Mo. 347, an election was set aside upon the ground that there was no registration whatever, although the statute required registration as an indispensable pre-requisite to an election. It has been suggested, that this doctrine puts it in the power of the board of registration to defeat an election, by failing to meet, and refusing altogether to discharge their official duties. But it is hardly safe to attempt to test the validity of a statute by presupposing a case so extreme and so improbable as the refusal of a sworn officer of the law to act. Should such a case occur, of course a *mandamus* would lie to compel the recusant officer to discharge his duties, and severe penalties ought to, and it is believed generally do, follow any such failure to discharge an official duty so grave and important.

Upon this point the Supreme Court of Missouri, in Ensworth vs. Albin *et. al.*, say: "We are referred to no case where a law has been held unconstitutional for the reason that the officers required to execute it, had neglected their duty, or abused their trust, nor are we aware of any principle on which to base such a decision."

§ 10. A case may occur where a portion of the legal voters have, without their fault, and in spite of due diligence on their part, been denied the privilege of registration. In such a case, if the voter was otherwise qualified, and is clearly shown to have performed all the acts required of him by the law, and to have been denied registration, by the wrongful act of the registering officer, it would seem a very unjust thing to deny him the right to vote. In elections for State officers, however, under a constitution or statute, which imperatively requires registration as a qualification for voting, it may be that the voter's only remedy would be found in an action against the registering officer for damages. *People vs. Kopplekam,* 16 *Mich.* 342. *State vs. Stumpf,* 23 *Wis.* 630. *State vs. Helmantel,* 21 *Wis.* 566.

Where, however, a portion of the voters of a given precinct are thus unjustly denied the privilege of registration, and another portion, are duly registered, and permitted to vote, no doubt is entertained but that the entire poll should be rejected, if the votes of the former class cannot be counted, and if they are sufficiently numerous to affect the result.

§ 11. In the absence of any positive law making registration, imperative, as a qualification for voting, it is a very plain proposition that the wrongful refusal of a registering officer to register a legal voter, who has complied with the law, and applies for registration, ought not to disfranchise such voter. The offer to register in such a case is equivalent to registration. This would be held to be the law upon the well settled principle, that the offer to perform an act which depends for its performance upon the action of another person, who wrongfully refuses to act, is equivalent to its performance. The Congress of the United States has, however, provided against injustice of this kind by a positive statute, which must, of course, (if held valid,) control all federal elections. By the 3d Section of the Act of May 31st, 1870, (16 Stat. at Large, p. 140,) it is provided as follows :

"That whenever, by or under the authority of the constitution or laws of any State, or the laws of any territory, any act is, or shall be required to be done by any citizen as a pre-requisite to qualify or entitle him to vote, the offer of any such citizen to perform the act required to be done as aforesaid, shall, if it fail to be carried into execution by reason of the wrongful act or omission of the person or officer charged with the duty of receiving or permitting such performance, or offer to perform, or acting thereon, be deemed and held as a performance in law of such act, and the person so offering and failing as aforesaid, and being otherwise qualified, shall be entitled to vote in the same manner, and to the same extent as if he had in fact performed such act."

It is undoubtedly necessary that a person who, having been refused registration, seeks to have his vote counted under this statute, should prove that he actually and personally applied to the proper board or officer for registration, and offered to make such proof, or perform such acts as the law required of him ; that he was in fact legally qualified to vote and entitled to registration, and that registration was refused. In other words, it must appear that the voter did, or offered to do, all that the law required at his hands, and that his failure to be registered was the fault of the board or officer of registration.

Nor is it enough that he demanded registration of the proper officer or board, and was refused. It must also appear, before his vote can be counted as if cast, that he offered his vote at the proper time and place, or used proper diligence in endeavoring to do so.

§ 12. It has been held that the aforesaid act of Congress of 31st May, 1870, does not interfere with the laws of the several States, which prescribe the qualifications of voters, except so far as they are founded upon the distinction of race, color or previous condition of servitude. (*Exparte McIllwee*, 3 *American Law Times*, 251, *Brightley's Lead. Cases on Elections*, 65.) And the same doctrine was laid down by the District Court U. S. for District of Oregon, in the case of McKay vs. Campbell, 2 Abbott U. S. Rep. 120. It was determined in this latter case that in a proceeding to recover the penalty provided by the second section of said act, it must be averred among other things, that the denial of right was on account of the race, color or previous condition of servitude of the plaintiff.

§ 13. It is still, however, a disputed question, whether the act aforesaid should be so construed as not to afford relief to a citizen, who is deprived of his right to vote or to be registered, for a cause other than race, color or previous condition of servitude. Judge Jackson, of the District Court of the U. S. for the District of West Virginia, took the ground that said act was designed to protect all citizens without distinction in the right of suffrage, and he enforced this view as follows:

"The last clause of the 14th amendment to the

Constitution of the United States, provides that no one shall be denied the equal protection of the laws. In framing this act, Congress must have had this provision of the Constitution in view. It cannot be supposed that it would escape their attention; it must therefore be conceded, that all citizens are, under the fundamental law of the land, entitled to equal privileges, and the equal protection of the law; the latter right is embraced in the very words of the amendment. It is incredible to suppose that Congress intended, by the passage of this act, to do so vain a thing as to enact a law purely for the benefit of one class of citizens, to the manifest neglect and prejudice of another, thus attempting by legislation to deprive them of the equal privileges and the equal protection of the law, as guaranteed by the Fourteenth Amendment." (3 *Am. Law Times*, 254-5.)

§ 14. And this view is strengthened by an examination of the act itself. It would seem that its aim and purpose is to do more than protect persons of color, alone, in their right to vote. Thus by section 2 it is provided that, when "any act is required to be done as a pre-requisite or qualification for voting" the proper person or officer "shall give to *all citizens* of the United States the same and equal opportunity to perform such pre-requisite, and to become qualified to vote." This could hardly have been framed with a view to the protection of one class of citizens above another. The recent decision of the Supreme Court of the United States, in the Slaughter House cases, (16 *Wallace*,) is not necessarily in conflict with this view. This latter case presented the question whether an act of the legislature of

Louisiana, to regulate the business of slaughtering animals in and near the city of New Orleans, was in conflict with the 14th Amendment to the Constitution, because of the creation thereby of a monopoly. It is true that in the opinion of the Court delivered by Mr. Justice Miller, it is shown that the recent amendments to the constitution were intended especially, if not exclusively, for the protection of the rights of the freedmen, and doubt is expressed as to whether "any action of a State not directed by way of discrimination against the negroes on account of their race, will ever be held to come within the purview of this provision." It is also said that "the Fourteenth Amendment is so clearly a provision for the colored race, that a strong case would be necessary for its application to any other."

The point decided, however, was as to the power of the State Legislature to pass the act under discussion, and the question of the power of Congress to pass laws to protect the citizen in his right to vote, was of course not touched, because no such question arose in the case.

§ 15. The Fourteenth Amendment to the Constitution declares that "no State * * * shall deny to any person the equal protection of the laws," and gives Congress power to enforce this provision by appropriate legislation. It is yet an open question how far Congress may go in the enforcement of this provision, and any extended discussion of the subject in advance of its settlement by the Supreme Court, is perhaps not desirable. Very much will depend upon the meaning of the word "State," as used in the clause above quoted.

No *State* shall deprive any person, &c. Are we to understand this as prohibiting only such acts as are done by the complete State government, acting through all its departments? Clearly not. For, if so, a class of citizens or of persons, may be effectually deprived of the equal protection of the laws, by the action of some one of the departments of the State government, and no remedy can be had, because the act is not that of the State. If the word "State," means all the departments of the State government, then it is easy to see that the constitutional provision under consideration, may be rendered entirely nugatory. Thus the Legislature may fail to provide the necessary laws for the protection of a class of persons, or the judiciary may refuse to enforce such laws if enacted, or the executive may so administer them as to deny the equal protection guaranteed by the Constitution. It would seem, therefore, that whenever, by the action of any department or officer of the State, any person or class of persons are deprived of the equal protection of the laws, this clause of the Constitution is violated, and for any and all such cases Congress may provide a remedy. The State must be held to have denied the equal protection of the laws, when her officers, servants or agents have done so.

§ 16. It must be conceded that the question of the nature and extent of the power of Congress under the Constitution, as recently amended, to enact laws to protect and enforce the right to vote in the several States, is one of great importance, and of considerable difficulty. As we have seen, this question has not yet been settled by a decision of the Supreme Court, although the decision of that Court in the Slaughter House cases, certainly indicates that the Court is inclined to construe the recent amendments to the Constitution, as conferring power upon Congress to protect only the newly enfranchised people, and not as authorizing Congress to legislate generally for the regulation and enforcement of the right of suffrage in the States. And this view is fully sustained by the very recent decision of the Circuit Court of the United States for Louisiana. (*The United States vs. Cruikshank*, 13, *Am. Law Reg.* (*N. S.*) 630.) In this case a very learned and elaborate opinion was pronounced by Mr. Justice Bradley, of the Supreme Court, and as this is the latest and most authoritative exposition of the law upon this subject, it will doubtless be generally adopted and followed, unless it shall be reversed or modified hereafter by the Supreme Court. (a)

§ 17. By the fourth section of the first article of the Constitution, Congress is empowered to make "regulations" concerning the "times, places and *manner* of holding elections for Representatives in Congress." If the power to provide for a fair registration and election for Representatives in Congress, is not derived from the Fourteenth Amendment, may it not be found here? Everything which pertains to the *manner* of holding such elections, is included within the power here conferred, and no sound reason is perceived why a statute requiring that all legal voters at such elections shall be en-

---

(a) This case was one arising upon an indictment framed under the Act of Congress of May 31, 1870, commonly called the enforcement act.

titled to registration, and to be permitted to vote upon equal terms, is not a regulation of the manner of conducting the election.

This question of the power of Congress to pass laws to prevent or punish frauds *in an election for Representatives in Congress,* is not discussed in any of the cases to which we have referred. It would seem that the government of the United States, like all other governments, should possess the power to protect itself against frauds and crimes aimed at the purity of its legislative department.

§ 18. By the 21st section of the Act of Congress, approved March 3d, 1865, it was provided that "in addition to the other lawful penalties of the crime of desertion from the military or naval service of the United States, all persons who have deserted the military or naval service of the United States, who shall not return to said service or report themselves to a Provost Marshal within sixty days after the proclamation hereinafter mentioned, shall be deemed and taken to have voluntarily relinquished and forfeited their rights of citizenship, and their right to become citizens, and such deserters shall be forever incapable of holding any office of trust or profit under the United States, *or of exercising any right of citizens thereof.*" The constitutionality of this act was brought in question before the Supreme Court of Pennsylvania, in the case of Huber vs. Riely, (53 *Pa. State Reports,* 112, *Brightley's Election Cases,* 69.) The case was that of a citizen whose vote was refused by the judges of election, upon the ground that having been regularly drafted, he had failed and refused to report, and never did report for muster.

The constitutionality of the act was assailed, upon these grounds, viz:

1. That it was an *ex post facto* law, imposing additional punishment for an offense committed before its passage.

2. That it was an attempt on the part of Congress to regulate suffrage in the States, or to impair it.

3. That the act proposed to inflict pains and penalties upon offenders without a trial and conviction by due process of law, and that it was therefore prohibited by the bill of rights.

Upon the first point it was held that the penalty of forfeiture of citizenship, imposed upon those who had deserted the military or naval service, prior to the passage of the act, was not a penalty for the original desertion, but for persistence in the crime, and a refusal to report for muster and duty when commanded so to do. Upon the second point, the court held that the act was not an attempt to regulate suffrage in the States, but simply an exercise on the part of Congress of its power to "deprive an individual of the opportunity to enjoy a right that belongs to him as a citizen of a State," which was held to be a different thing from taking away or impairing the right itself. The Federal Government, in an exercise of its right to imprison a citizen of a State for crime, or to impress him into the military service, and remove him from the State, may deprive him of the opportunity to vote, and no doubt the forfeiture of citizenship, and of all its rights, may be affixed as a penalty, for the commission of a crime against the United States.

Upon the third point the Court held that the act

could not be upheld as constitutional, if it did in fact impose penalties, before and without a trial by due process of law; and by due process of law is meant "the law of the particular case administered by a judicial tribunal, authorized to adjudicate upon it," and the Court say that "a judge of elections, or board of election officers, constituted under State laws, is not such a tribunal." The Court, however, conclude that the act of Congress was intended to apply, and does apply, only to those cases of desertion, in which there has been a conviction by court martial, and that thus construed, it is constitutional. To the same effect is *State vs. Symonds*, 57 *Maine*, 148.

§ 19. The punishment of disfranchisement is not a cruel and unusual one, and it is competent for the legislature, unless restrained by the State constitution, to inflict it as a penalty for crime. But when the constitution provides, that a law may be passed, excluding from the right of suffrage, persons who have been or may be convicted of *infamous* crimes, it would seem that it is not in the power of the legislature to inflict this penalty for any other than infamous offenses. (*Barker vs. People*, 20 *Johnson*, 457.)

§ 20. In the case last named, it was held that the right of voting, and being voted for, are not convertible terms. It is there said that "a great class of voters are not required to be free holders, and yet it is necessary (in New York) to the qualification of a Senator or a Governor, that he should be a free holder, and with respect to the Governor, he must be a native citizen of the United States, thirty years of age, and a resident within the State for five years. The right of suffrage is therefore distinct from the right of being elegible to an office." And it was accordingly held that an act of the Legislature of New York to suppress dueling, passed in 1816, and which declared that any person convicted of sending or accepting a challenge to fight a duel "shall be incapable of holding or being elected to any post of profit, trust or emolument, civil or military, under this State," is constitutional. And a conviction and judgment of disqualification under it, are legal and valid. But in the same connection the Court discuss the question whether the legislature are not restrained from excluding from the right of suffrage, persons convicted of a crime which is not infamous, within the legal signification of that term, and the conclusion is that it is only upon the conviction for an infamous crime that a voter can be disqualified. Infamous crimes are treason, felony, and every species of the *crimen falsi*, such as perjury, conspiracy and barratry.

Sending or accepting a challenge to fight a duel is not, therefore, an infamous crime, but inasmuch as the right of suffrage does not necessarily imply the right of being voted for, it was held that the latter right might be forfeited by conviction for a crime not infamous, if so provided by statute.

§ 21. In a contested election case, where it is alleged that certain aliens voted illegally, without having been naturalized according to law, parol evidence is admissible to show that naturalization papers were fraudulently issued, or fraudulently procured. Thus in Wisconsin it has been held that where oaths (or affirmations,) in the form required for aliens, declaring their intention to become citizens, were signed in blank, by the Clerk of a Circuit Court, and so delivered by him to a Justice of the Peace; to be by him filled out, with the date and names of the persons subscribing them, &c., and the oath was in fact administered by the Justice, and not (as it purported to have been) by the Clerk, these facts might be shown by parol, and the votes of such aliens must be rejected. [*State vs. Stumpf*, 23 *Wis.* 630.) It is very true, that the judgment of a Court of competent jurisdiction, in the matter of the naturalization of a citizen, is as conclusive as its judgment in any other matter within its jurisdiction. But it is always competent to show that the parties were not within the jurisdiction of the Court, and if the act of pretended naturalization was in fact the act of the Clerk alone, and not in any proper sense the act of the Court, it would be a monstrous doctrine to hold that the certificate bearing the Clerk's signature and seal is conclusive. Such a rule would permit the party who committed the fraud to protect himself by his own fraudulent certificate.

§ 22. In some of the States it is provided by constitutional provision, that to entitle a man to vote, he must, as a pre-requisite, have paid, within two years next preceding the time of the election at which he claims a right to vote, a State or County tax. In Massachusetts it has been held under a provision of this character, that the payment of a State tax within the proper period of time, by one who is in other respects a qualified voter, entitles him to vote, although such tax was illegally assessed upon him. (*Humphrey vs. Kingman* 4, *Metcalfe* 162.)

§ 23. Though a tax which is assessed upon one

person, is paid for him by another, without his previous authority, yet if he recognizes the act, and repays or promises to repay the amount on the ground that such person acted as his agent, he thereby acquires the same right to vote, as if he had paid the tax with his own hand. (*ib. and see Draper vs. Johnson, Clark & Hall,* 702.)

§ 24. Where A., who was taxed for land, denied, when called on for payment, that he was rightfully taxed, or that he owned the land, and directed the collector to call on B., the true owner, and the collector thereupon called on B.'s wife, in the absence of B., and she paid the tax, and where A. afterwards not believing himself rightfully assessed, or that B. had any claim on him, repaid the amount, merely for the purpose of securing the right to vote, *Held,* that it was not such a payment as entitled him to vote. *ib.*

§ 25. Under a constitutional provision, requiring as a qualification for voting, the payment of a tax which had been *assessed* at least six months before the election, it has been held that an assessment upon the voter individually, six months before the election, was necessary, and that it is not enough that it be laid upon the County of which he is a resident. It seems, however, that it is not necessary that it be a personal or poll tax. It is sufficient if it be a tax assessed either upon his person or his property within the time required. (*Cather vs. Smith,* 2 *Sergeant & Rawle,* 267.)

§ 26. In Massachusetts it has been held, that persons who have the requisite qualifications as to residence, but who have been exempted from taxation on account of their poverty two successive years before their arrival at the age of seventy years, are not entitled to vote, under that clause of the Constitution of that State, which gives the right of suffrage to persons otherwise qualified, and who "shall be by law exempted from taxation." (*Opinion of Judges* 5, *Metcalfe* 591. *See also* 11 *Pick.* 538.)

§ 27. An action cannot be maintained against assessors by an individual who is liable to taxation for their omission to tax him, whereby he loses his right to vote at an election, unless it be shown affirmatively that they omitted to tax him wilfully, purposely, or with design to deprive him of his vote. [*Griffin vs. Rising*, 11 *Pick.* 339.]

§ 28. The Constitution of Massachusetts in force in 1837, vested the right to vote "in every male citizen otherwise qualified, who shall have paid, by himself or his master, parent or guardian, any State or County tax, which shall within two years next preceding the election in question, have been assessed upon him in any town or district in this commonwealth." Under this clause it was held that after any general assessment of a tax has been made by the assessors of a town, and committed to the proper officer for collection, and before another tax is committed to the assessors to assess, they have no authority to assess a poll or other tax on any person, for the purpose of enabling him to vote at an election, nor is any person on the payment of a tax so assessed upon him, qualified to vote, under the above constitutional provision. [*Opinion of Judges*, 18 *Pick*, 575.]

§ 29. Where a State has ceded a given tract of land to the United States for a navy yard, arsenal, or the like, and where there is no reservation of jurisdiction to the State other than the right to serve civil and criminal process on such lands, persons who reside upon such lands do not acquire any elective franchise, as inhabitants of such State. [*Opinion of Judges*, 1 *Metcalfe*, [*Mass.*] 580. *Sinks vs. Reese*, 19 *Ohio State*, 306, *Commonwealth vs. Clary*, 8 *Mass.* 72.]

§ 30. "But this rule does not apply to persons residing upon a tract of land in a territory of the U. S., which has been reserved or set apart by the executive for military purposes. It was so held in *Burleigh vs. Armstrong*, 42*d Congress*, in which case the committee said in their report:

"But with regard to the election held within the military reservations of Fort Sully and Fort Randall, [or the Ellis precinct,] the committee have reached the conclusion that there is nothing in the terms of the organic act, nor in the general policy of the law, forbidding an election to be held at such places. The contestants have insisted that the rule which disqualifies persons from voting within any State, who reside within forts or other territory to which the title and jurisdiction has been ceded by the State to the Federal Government, applies to the military reservations which have been designated by the Executive within the Territories belonging to the United States. But forasmuch as there is no conflict of sovereignty between the Government and the Territory, and the latter holds all its jurisdiction in subordination to the controlling power of Congress, and the military reservations are not permanently severed from the body of the public lands, but are simply set apart and withheld from private ownership by an executive order to the Commissioner of the Land Office, and may be and often are restored to the common stock of the public domain, when the occasion for their temporary occupancy has ceased, at the pleasure of Congress, and which requires no concurrent act of any State authority to give it efficacy, the residents upon such reservations, although abiding thereon by the mere sufferance of the United States authorities, do not in any just sense cease to be inhabitants or residents of the Territory within which such military reserve may be situate. Such residents seem to the committee to have that same general interest in the welfare of the community in which they live, and the same right to vote there, as any of the workmen at the arsenal or navy yard in Washington City, who may be allowed to sojourn within their limits, have to vote at elections within the District of Columbia for officers of its territorial government, or for a Delegate in Congress from that District."

§ 31. It seems to be settled that a State, in the exercise of its power to prescribe the qualifications of its electors, may require a test oath to be taken by every voter, at the polls. This is not a violation of the Constitution of the United States.

The Amended Constitution of Missouri required such an oath to be taken as a pre-requisite to exercising the right to vote, as well as to the exercise of the duties of certain callings in life, such as that of Attorney at Law, Minister of the Gospel, &c. In *Cummings vs. Missouri*, (4 *Wall* 277,) the Supreme Court of the United States, by a bare majority of the Judges, held this provision of the Constitution of Missouri to be void, as being in the nature of pains and penalties, so far as it related to the oath required to be taken by Ministers of the Gospel.—Mr. Justice Miller, however, for the minority of the Court, delivered a dissenting opinion which has been well characterized as "an opinion which for ability, logic, and admirable judicial criticism has rarely been excelled even in that august tribunal." The question of the validity of this test oath, as applied to voters, came before the Supreme Court of Missouri in *Blair vs. Ridgely*, (41 *Missouri*, 63,) and that Court in an elaborate and able opinion held it valid.

§ 32. This decision was not in conflict with Cummings vs. Missouri, *supra*. In the latter case the Supreme Court of the United States held that the right to adopt and follow the calling or avocation of a preacher, or minister of the gospel, was a natural right; a right absolute and vested, and that it was therefore not within the power of the State to prescribe a test oath to be taken, as a condition precedent to its enjoyment. But the right to vote is not a natural right; it is not such a right as belongs to man in a state of nature. It follows that the reasoning of the Court in Cummings vs. Missouri does not apply to the question of the validity of the test oath as applied to a voter. And it also follows, that inasmuch as the right to vote is derived from and regulated by the State Constitution and laws, it is competent for the State to prescribe loyalty as a qualification, and to enforce the requirement by exacting of every voter an oath of loyalty.

§ 33. This question arose in the House of Representatives of the United States in *Birch vs. Van*

Horn, (2 *Bartlett* 205,) and the decision of the committee, and of the House, was in accordance with the view just expressed. The committee use the following language in their report:

"The ninth section of the same article provides that after sixty days from the time the constitution takes effect, no person shall be "permitted to practice as an attorney or counselor-at-law, nor after that time shall any person be competent as a bishop, priest, deacon, minister, elder, or other clergyman of any religious persuasion, sect, or denomination, to teach or preach, or solemnize marriages, unless such person shall have first taken, subscribed, and filed said oath."

Under this ninth section of the constitution arose the case of Cummings vs. The State of Missouri, (4 *Wallace*, 277,) in which it was held by a majority of the Supreme Court of the United States that this provision, having the effect to deprive persons of the right to practice professions and pursue avocations lawful in themselves, in consequence of acts done prior to the adoption of the constitution, could only have been intended as punishment for such acts, and was therefore in essence and substance an *ex post facto* law, and therefore forbidden by the Constitution of the United States. The contestant claims that the same application of principles requires the same decision in relation to voters; that the virtual disfranchisement of persons who were voters under the previous Constitution and laws of the State, but who are prevented from voting under the new Constitution, by reason of their inability to take the oath it requires, can only be regarded as a punishment for the act which stands in the way of taking the oath, and that the Constitution of the United States prohibits the infliction of punishment by subsequent legislation.

If such disfranchisement must be regarded as established for the purpose of punishing the persons thus deprived of the right of voting, it must be admitted to come entirely within the reasoning by which the above cited judgment of the Court is supported.

Your committee believe that the provisions of the new Constitution of Missouri may be supported, so far as they require this oath of voters, without at all trenching upon the decision of the Supreme Court.

Each of the States of the Union have hitherto regulated suffrage within their own limits for themselves, and in such a manner as the people of the State deemed most conducive to their own interests and welfare. Suffrage is a political right or privilege which every free community grants to such number and class of persons as it deems fittest to represent and advance the wants and interests of the whole. No State grants it to all persons, but with such limitations as the interests of all and the interest of the State require.

When once granted it is not a vested, irrevocable right, but it is held at the pleasure of the power that gave it, and the State may, by a change of its fundamental law, restrict as well as enlarge it. When, therefore, the State of Missouri, in changing its constitution, saw fit to declare that the interests of the State and of the people of the State would be promoted by withholding the right of voting from all persons who could not take the prescribed oath, they exercised no greater or higher power than exists in every State."

§ 34. It was held by the Supreme Court of Mass. in 1814, that a person having a permanent home in one town within that State, and being a legal voter in such town, is not disqualified by a temporary absence in another town, and being there admitted to vote. (*Lincoln vs. Hapgood*, 11 *Mass.* 350.) The general doctrine laid down in this case is doubtless correct. If a person is clearly a resident of, and a legal voter, in one place, and is improperly and illegally permitted to vote at another, that fact alone will not disqualify him from continuing to vote at the place of his actual residence. But it is proper to observe in this connection, that if there is any doubt as to which of two places is the home, or residence of a voter, the fact that he has within a recent period voted at one of such places, would be very strong evidence that he had decided for himself to make his home where he cast his vote. And if a person is residing at a particular place, and there is doubt as to whether he is residing there temporarily, and claiming another place as his house, if he claims and exercises the right to vote at the place where he is for the time residing, that fact ought to be regarded as evidence well nigh conclusive that he has abandoned his former residence, and determined to make his home where he claims his vote. The question of residence or domicil is a question largely of intention, and the fact of voting is very strong evidence of the voter's intention to claim a domicil at the place of voting.

§ 35. A certificate of naturalization in due form,

issued by a Court possessing the jurisdiction to grant the same, is *prima facie* evidence of naturalization, and an election officer cannot go behind it. If a voter could be obliged to bring proof *aliunde* to sustain such a certificate, and the judges of election could be obliged to hear evidence *pro* and *con*, the value of the boon of citizenship, which we confer upon foreigners who come to our shores, would be greatly lessened. Besides, in many localities where the number of naturalized voters is very large, this mode of proceeding would be impossible, since a few cases would consume the whole of the day of election, and the many would remain unheard. (*Commonwealth vs. Lee*, 1 *Brewster*, 273. *Commonwealth vs. Sheriff*, *ibid*, 183. *Commonwealth vs. Leary*, *ibid* 270.)

§ 36. In the case of *Williams vs. Whiting*, (11 *Mass.* 424,) the question was as to when the plaintiff ceased to be a resident of Roxbury, and became a resident of Dedham. On the 28th day of October, 1811, being then a resident of Roxbury, "he received," says the Court, "an appointment which rendered it convenient, if not necessary, for him to dwell in Dedham ; and he then began to prepare for his removal; from that time until the 12th of November, he passed almost every day in Dedham, where he transacted his business, and returned to his family each night, except three, on which he slept in Dedham, rather by accident than design ; he had also on the 29th of October, engaged a house in Dedham, but he did not occupy it until the 12th of November, on which day he removed his family and became domiciled in Dedham." And the Court held upon these facts that he remained an inhabitant of Roxbury *until the day of his removal with his family.*

In the same case it is held that under the statute of Mass., to entitle a person to vote for a Representative in Congress, he must have resided one whole year previous to the election in the town where he offers to vote, and that it made no difference, that the person offering to vote had removed, inside of a year, from another town in the same congressional district. The Constitution of the United States requires that the electors for Representatives in Congress shall have the qualifications requisite for electors of the most numerous branch of the State Legislature, and one of these qualifications in Massachusetts was one year's residence in the place of voting.

§ 37. A person who removes with his family from one town to another, does not retain the right to vote in the former, until he acquires it, in the latter. (*McDaniels Case*, 3 *Pa., L. J.* 310. *Thompson vs. Ewing*, 1 *Brewst.*, 103.)

§ 38. For a thorough and able discussion of the question of residence, as applied to voters, see the Report of the committee of Elections in the House of Representatives of the 42d Congress, in the case of *Cessna vs. Myers*, to be found in full in the appendix to this volume. This Report presents forcibly and clearly the important consideration that no definition of " residence " or " domicil " can be made sufficiently comprehensive to apply to all conceivable cases and circumstances. Tests which are satisfactory in some cases cannot be applied as inflexible rules in all. Thus it is a *general* rule that in order to gain a residence in a particular place, a man must fix his domicil there with the intention of remaining an indefinite time, and with no fixed purpose of making that place a temporary abiding place only. But there are persons whose lives are necessarily migratory, whose business is to travel from place to place. As for example a Methodist minister, who, by the law of his church, cannot remain permanently and pursue his calling in any one place; or a school teacher who resides wherever he can get employment, and removes when his business requires it; or a laborer who lives where there is an iron furnace, or a coal mine, or a railroad in process of construction, to furnish him employment and a livelihood, and when these fail him in one place, goes to another. With reference to these and other similar classes a different rule must be applied. As to what that rule is, nothing need be added to what is said in *Cessna vs. Myers*; and let it be understood that the authorities cited in this chapter upon the general question of residence, are to be read with reference to the qualifications expressed in that report.

§ 39. Residence, within the meaning of the Constitution of Pennsylvania, as applied to the qualification of an elector, means the same thing as domicil, the place where a man establishes his abode, makes the seat of his property, and exercises his civil and political rights. (*Chase vs. Miller*, 41 *Penn. State R.* 404.) Such residence must have been with intent to become a citizen of the State, and to abandon the citizenship he may have had in another State. Mere residence for the purpose of business or pleasure, unaccompanied with an intention to abandon the former citizenship, is not sufficient. To constitute residence there must be an intention to remain, but this intention is entirely consistent with a purpose to remove at some future indefinite time. (*Miller vs. Thompson*, 1 *Bartlett*, 118 *Pigott's Case, ibid*, 463.)

§ 40. Domicil or residence in a legal sense, is determined by the intention of the party; he cannot have two homes at the same time; when he acquires the new home, he loses the old one; but to effect this change there must be both act and intention. (*State vs. Frost*, 4 *Harrington*, 558 *McDaniel's Case*, 3 *Penn., L. J.* 310.)

When a man removes with his family into a county with the intention to make that his residence, that is the county where he should vote so long as his family remains there, though he may himself pass his time, and engage in business, or work, in another county. (*People vs. Holden*, 28 *Cal.* 124.) Residence once acquired, by birth or habitancy, is not lost by a temporary absence for pleasure or business, with an intention of returning. (*State vs. Judge, &c.*, 13 *Ala.*, 806, *Lincoln vs. Hapgood*, 11 *Mass.* 350.)

§ 41. The fact that an elector is a soldier in the army of the United States, does not disqualify him from voting at his place of residence, but he cannot acquire a residence so as to qualify him as a voter, by being stationed at a military post whilst in the service of the United States. (*People vs. Riley*, 15 *Cal.* 48; *Hunt vs. Richards*, 4 *Kansas* 549; *Biddle vs. Wing, Clark & Hall*, 504.) As to the right of a student at a college, being of age, and otherwise qualified to vote, see *Cessna vs. Myers, supra*, and also see *Putnam vs. Johnson*, 10 *Mass.* 488, *Farlee vs. Runk*, 1 *Bartlett*, 87, *Opinion of Judges*, 5 *Met.*

587, *Cushing's Election Cases*, 436. It will be found from an examination of these authorities, and from a full consideration of the subject, that the question whether or not a student at college is a *bonafide* resident of the place where the college is located must in each case depend upon the facts. He may be a resident and he may not be. Whether he is or not depends upon the answer which may be given to a variety of questions, such as the following. Is he of age? Is he fully emancipated from his parent's control? Does he regard the place where the college is situated as his home, or has he a home elsewhere to which he expects to go, and at which he expects to reside? In a word, it is necessary from a survey of all the facts to determine whether while at college he is at his home, his residence, or temporarily absent from it.

§ 42. In the absence of statute regulations, the general rule seems to be that a pauper abiding in a public almshouse, locally situated in a different district from that where he dwells when he becomes a pauper, and by which he is supported, does not acquire a residence in the almshouse for the purpose of voting. (*Monroe vs. Jackson*, 1 *Bartlett*, 98; *Covode vs. Foster*, 2 *Bartlett*, 600; *Taylor vs. Reading*, 2 *Bartlett*, 661.)

But see *Cessna vs. Myers*, *supra*, from which it would seem that this is not entirely settled.

§ 43. In several of the States the elective franchise is given by Constitutional provision to "all male *inhabitants* above the age of twenty-one years" having resided in the State for a given period. An important question has arisen as to whether unnaturalized aliens, otherwise qualified, have the right to vote under a provision of this character. The controversy is as to the meaning of the term "inhabitant," when used in this connection. Does it embrace the idea of citizenship? In *Spragins vs. Houghton*, [3 *Ill.* 377,] it was held that the question of citizenship does not enter into the qualification of a voter in such a case, and the question is there discussed at great length and with much ability. And this doctrine is sustained by the Supreme Court of Pennsylvania, in *Stewart vs. Foster*, [2 *Binn.* 110.]

§ 44. In *Howard College vs. Gore*, [5 *Pick* 370,] the Supreme Court of Massachusetts express a different view of the meaning of the word inhabitant. The question there was as to what constitutes an inhabitant of a county, within the meaning of the statute for taking the probate of Wills and granting administration on the estates of persons deceased "being inhabitants of or residents in, the same county at the time of their decease." And the Court in construing this statute say: "The term inhabitant, as used in our laws and this statute, means something more than a person having a domicil It imports citizenship and municipal relations, whereas a man may have a domicil in a county to which he is alien, and where he has no political relations." And see *opinion of Judge Cushing's Election Cases*, 120 *Malden's Case ib*, 377

§ 45. Notwithstanding the conflict of authority above referred to, it seems very manifest that where the term "inhabitant" is used especially in describing the qualifications of voters, it does not mean the same thing as citizen. It must be conceded that while the two terms may to a certain extent mean the same thing, the term citizen has a more extensive signification than the term inhabitant, and it is therefore entirely fair to presume that when the framers of a law intend to express this larger meaning, they will use the larger term.

§ 46. The Constitution of Pennsylvania requires, among other qualifications of a voter, that he shall have resided one year in the State, "and in the election district where he offers to vote, ten days immediately preceding such election."

It was held in McDaniel's case [3 *Pa. Law Journal* 310, *Brightley's Election Cases* 238,] that an election district was any part of a city or county, having fixed boundaries within which the citizens residing therein must vote, as for example a ward in the city of Philadelphia. It was also held that a person who removed from one election district to another, within the ten days immediately preceding an election, lost his right to vote in the district removed from, and did not gain a right to vote at that election in the district removed to. The right to vote in the former does not continue until the same right is acquired in the latter, but is lost as soon as the removal is complete. There is therefore always a period following a change of residence, during which the citizen has no right to vote at any place. It is often laid down as a general proposition that in case of a removal by a person from one place to another, his first residence is not lost until the second is acquired. And this is true for some purposes, but not for the purpose of determining the right of such person to vote. That right ends in the place removed from, as soon as the voter completes his removal. It is acquired in the place removed to, only after such a residence therein as the law requires, and as no man can have two residences at the same time, it follows that he cannot *acquire* the right to vote in the new, by residing there, until he has ceased to have a residence in the old.

§ 47. A statute providing that "when two persons shall have an equal number of votes, the returning officer shall have the casting vote, but shall not vote in any other case whatsoever" is a constitutional and valid statute. (*State vs. Adams*, 2 *Stewart*, [*Ala.*] 231, *Brightley's Election Cases*, 286.) It is well settled that a citizen by accepting an office may waive a constitutional privilege. The constitution of each State grants the right of suffrage to all electors, and no elector can be deprived of this right otherwise than as prescribed by law. But the citizen can refuse to exercise this privilege, and he may also relinquish it for a time, in order to secure to himself a greater advantage, and therefore he may waive his right to vote, in common with other citizens, to secure the honors and emoluments of an office, and the power to give the casting vote in case of a tie.

§ 48. At common law voting by proxy is unknown, and every vote, whether given by a stockholder of a corporation, or by a freeman for his representative, must be personally given. A corporation may, however, by a provision in its charter, provide for voting by proxy, though it is to say the least, very doubtful whether a provision in the *by-laws* of a corporation, providing for voting by proxy, could be upheld. Upon this general subject see the following authorities: *State vs. Tudor*, 5 *Day*, 219. *Taylor vs. Griswold*, 2 *Green*, [*N. J.*] 223. *Angell & Ames on Corp. Chap.* 4, 57. *Brown vs. Commonwealth*, *Brightley's Election Cases* 282. *Phillips vs. Wickham*, 1 *Paige* 598.

§ 49. In most of the States electors are privileged from arrest, except for treason, felony or breach of the peace, during their attendance upon the election, and in going to and returning from the same. This privilege does not cease when the elector deposits his ballot, but it seems that he has a right to remain at the polls or near them until they are closed, and to plead his constitutional privilege if arrested while thus engaged. In *Swift vs. Chamberlain*, [3 *Connecticut*, 537,] it was held that an elector who, after depositing his vote, retired to a public house in the neighborhood, while the election officers were counting the votes, was "attending on the business of the election," and therefore privileged from arrest on civil process. As to what amounts to a breach of the peace, within the meaning of the Constitutional provisions referred to, see Mr. Brightley's note to the case of *Swift vs. Chamberlain*, *supra*, *Brightley's Election Cases*, *page* 280.

§ 50. The vote of an idiot, or person *non compos mentis*, ought not to be received, and if such a person has voted, his vote may be rejected upon a contest, without a finding in lunacy. *Thompson vs. Ewing*, (1 *Brewster*, 68-9.) But the vote of a man otherwise qualified, who is neither a lunatic nor an idiot, but whose faculties are merely greatly enfeebled by old age, is not to be rejected. (*Sinks vs. Reese*, 19 *Ohio*, *State R* 307.) When a vote is attacked on the ground that the voter who cast it was *non compos mentis*, it is necessary to establish satisfactorily, by competent evidence, the alleged want of intelligence, and the test would probably be about the same as in cases where the validity of a will is attacked on the ground that the testator was not of sound mind, when it was executed. If the voter knew enough to understand the nature of his act, if he understood what he was doing, that is probably sufficient.

§ 51. By the terms of the treaty of peace of 1848, between the United States and Mexico, it was provided that the inhabitants of the territories annexed to the United States, and detached from Mexico, might elect to remain citizens of Mexico, by making known such election within one year from the date of the treaty, but the manner of making such election was not prescribed either by the treaty or by any act of Congress. *Held*, that a declaration in writing, signed by persons so electing to remain Mexican citizens, and filed in one of the Courts of the territory of New Mexico, in pursuance of a proclamation from the Governor of the territory, was sufficient, and that the persons signing such declaration remained citizens of Mexico, and could, after making such declaration, become citizens of the United States, only by the ordinary process of naturalization, and that the votes of such persons for delegate in Congress were illegal, and should be rejected. *Oltero vs. Gallegos*, [1 *Bartlett*, 177.]

§ 52. Persons residing within the bounds of an Indian Reservation, in the Territory of Dakota, have no right to vote at an election for delegate in Congress. But it is otherwise with persons residing within the limits of a Military Reservation. It was so held by the House of Representatives, in the case of *Burleigh and Spink vs. Armstrong*, 42d Congress.

§ 53. The House of Representatives of the United States has frequently held that residents upon an Indian reservation have no right to vote. [*Daily vs. Estabrook*, 1 *Bartlett*, 299. *Morton vs. Daily*, *do* 402. *Bennett vs. Chapman*, *do* 204.] In the latter case the House sustained this doctrine against the report of the Committee. These cases, however, were all from the territory of Nebraska, and were decided upon the ground that the organic act of the territory provided that "territory occupied as an Indian reservation shall not be considered a part of Nebraska territory, but that all such territory shall be excepted out of the boundaries until, by arrangement between the United States and the Indians, the title of the latter shall be extinguished." A similar provision will be found in the organic acts of most, and probably of all the territories.

§ 54. Inasmuch as naturalization is in nearly all the States necessary to qualify an alien to vote, it is proper in this connection to state briefly the general requirements of the law upon that subject. Congress has power "to establish a uniform rule of naturalization." [*Const. Art.* 1, *Sec.* 8.] And the power of Congress under this clause of the Constitution is exclusive, so that no State can pass a naturalization law. [*Chirac* vs. *Chirac*, 2 *Wheat*, 269. *United States* vs. *Vallayo*, 2 *Dall.*, 372. *Thurlow* vs. *Mass.*, 5 *How.*, 585. *Smith* vs. *Turner*, 7 *ibid*, 556.]

The following is a summary of the naturalization laws:

1. The first step to be taken by an alien desiring naturalization is the declaration, under oath, of his intention, *bona fide*, to become a citizen of the United States, and to renounce forever all allegiance and fidelity to any foreign power, potentate, state or sovereignty whatever, and particularly by name, the prince, potentate, state or sovereignty whereof such alien may at the time be a citizen or subject. This declaration may be made before the Supreme, Superior, District or Circuit Court of some one of the States, or of the territorial districts of the United States, or a Circuit or District Court of the United States.

2. Such declaration of intention must be made two years at least prior to the time when such alien is admitted to citizenship, and may be made before the clerk of any of the courts above mentioned.

3. After having resided in the United States five years, and in the State or Territory where he applies for admission, one year at least, such alien may apply to any Court authorized to grant naturalization, and upon satisfying such Court that he has complied with the law in these respects—that he has made his declaration more than two years previously, and that he has behaved as a man of good moral character, attached to the principles of the Constitution of the United States and well disposed to the good order and happiness of the same—he may be admitted to citizenship by taking the oath of allegiance required by the statute. But the applicant can, in no case, prove his residence by his own oath alone.

4. In addition to the Federal Courts, "Every Court of record in any individual State having com-

mon law jurisdiction and a seal and clerk or prothonotary" may grant naturalization.

5. The naturalization of the parent also naturalizes all children of such parent under twenty one years of age, and dwelling in the United States.

6. Children of citizens of the United States, though born out of the limits and jurisdiction of the United States, are to be considered as citizens of the United States.

7. If an alien, who declares his intention to become a citizen, and continues to pursue the directions prescribed for perfecting his naturalization, shall die, before he is actually naturalized, the widow and the children of such alien shall be considered as citizens of the United States.

8. An alien minor who has resided in the United States three years next preceding his arriving at the age of twenty one years, and who has resided therein five years continuously, may apply for, and obtain naturalization without any previous declaration of intention.

9. Aliens honorably discharged from the military service of the United States, are allowed to be naturalized without any previous declaration, and on proof of only one year's residence. [*See naturalization laws, Revised Statutes U. S., page* 380.]

§ 55. A State law restricting the State Courts and their clerks from receiving applications, or entertaining jurisdiction, for the naturalization of aliens under the acts of Congress, is not contrary to the Constitution of the United States. Congress can confer jurisdiction upon State Courts to grant naturalization, but it cannot compel such Courts to exercise that jurisdiction in violation of a State law. The "powers given to the State Courts by the naturalization laws are naked powers, which impose no legal obligation on Courts to assume and exercise them, and such exercise is not within their official duty, or their oath, to support the Constitution of the United States." [*Case of Stephens*, 4 *Gray*, 550. *Morgan vs. Dudley*, 18 *B. Monroe*, 693. *Rump vs. Commonwealth*, 6 *Casey*, 475.]

§ 56. Application for naturalization must be made in open Court, and evidence of residence &c., must be taken by the oral examination of witnesses, and not by previously prepared affidavits. Certificates of naturalization issued by the clerk of a Court, without any hearing before the Judge, in open Court, are void, and confer no right of citizenship upon the holder. (*People vs. Sweetman*, 3 *Parker, C. R.* 358.)

§ 57. Under the acts of Congress, children born abroad, not only of citizens by birth, but also of naturalized citizens, are citizens of the United States. (*Sasportas vs. De La Motta*, 10 *Richardson Eq. Rep.* 38.)

§ 58. Soldiers in the United States army cannot acquire a residence by being long quartered in a particular place, and though upon being discharged from the service, they remain in the place where they have previously been quartered, if a year's residence in that place is required as a qualification for voting, they must remain there one year from the date of discharge before acquiring the right to vote. (*Biddle and Richard vs. Wing*, *Cl. & H.*, 512.)

§ 59. Under a provision in the Constitution of

Virginia, giving the right to vote to those who for twelve months have been housekeepers and heads of families, it was *held* that unmarried persons, who are living with their mothers or with younger brothers and sisters, having charge of the family, the father being absent or dead, are to be deemed "housekeepers and heads of families." Also, that in determining whether a person is a voter within the meaning of this provision of the Constitution it is not proper to inquire whether he is legally married to the woman with whom he lives and keeps house. [*Draper vs. Johnson, Cl. & H.*, 702.]

§ 60. The same Constitution required that in order to have the right to vote it was necessary to be "possessed of an estate of freehold in land," and under this provision it was held that a person possessed of a merely equitable interest in lands or holding a bond for a deed, was not entitled to vote. [*Ibid.*]

§ 61. And another provision of the same Constitution gave the right to vote to those who possessing certain other qualifications, "shall have been assessed with a part of the revenue of the commonwealth within the preceding year, and actually paid the same." Under this provision it was held by a majority of the committee, that where taxable property is owned and possessed by the son, and is assessed in the name of the father, but the tax is actually paid by the son, he having all the other qualifications required, is entitled to vote, but that if the property is both assessed to, and paid by the father, the vote is to be rejected.

Also, that where a revenue tax is duly assessed,

and the sheriff has paid the tax himself, and has not returned the party delinquent, that this is to be deemed a payment by the party so as to entitle him to vote. [*Ibid.*]

§ 62. In Pennsylvania the rule is that no person shall vote without having been assessed and paid a tax. Persons not assessed are, by the law of that State, required in order to vote, to answer certain questions under oath, as to tax, age, residence, &c., and in addition to prove their residence by the oath of a qualified voter of the division, and the statute made it the duty of the inspectors to require such proof, whether the voter be challenged or not. Under this law it has been held by the House of Representatives that persons who were not assessed, and who voted without answering any of the questions required to be answered, and without producing the testimony of a qualified voter as to their residence, are presumed to be illegal voters. And where the number of such votes was large enough to destroy the reliability of the return, there being no proof upon which the poll could be purged of such illegal votes, it was rejected. [*Myers vs. Moffatt*, 2 *Bartlett*, 564, *Covode vs. Foster*, 2 *Bartlett*, 600.] This decision is not in conflict with the general rule that a person who has voted is presumed, until the contrary is shown, to have been qualified. The contrary was presumptively shown by proof that these voters had failed to comply with the statute which required this evidence to be produced by them before voting. When it is thus shown that persons have voted without proving their qualifications as required by positive statute, it is incumbent upon the party claiming the benefit of the votes of such persons, to show affirmatively that they were qualified voters.

§ 63. It is not competent for a State Legislature in providing for a special election to determine the location of a county seat, or to determine any other matter, to require any other qualifications for voters at such election, than those prescribed by the Constitution. Constitutional provisions concerning the qualifications of voters apply to all elections, whether general or special. (*State vs. Williams*, 5 *Wis.*, 308, *State vs. Leon*, 9 *Wis.*, 279.)

§ 64. It is, however, competent for the legislature to prescribe questions to be propounded to voters calculated to draw from them the proof of their qualifications to vote at an election, and require the voter to answer thereto before he can vote. This does not add to the qualifications of voters; it only provides the means of testing the voters right. (*State vs. Leon, supra.*)

§ 65. In accordance with the principle that the legislature cannot add to the constitutional qualifications of voters, it has been held that where the Constitution requires that a person shall have a residence in the township where he offers to vote, without prescribing any period of residence, a statute which undertakes to require a residence in the township of twenty days, is unconstitutional and void. (*Quinn vs. The State*, 35 *Ind.* 486.) A residence *bona fide*, for a time however short, satisfies the constitutional requirement, and it is fair to presume that it was intended that a person having all the other qualifications, and removing from one township to another at any time prior to the day of election, should retain the right to vote. If twenty days residence in the township may be required under such a Constitution, a longer period may be, and thus the Constitution might be rendered meaningless or nugatory.

§ 66. The object of prescribing an oath to be taken by an elector who is challenged at the polls, or before registering officers, is to test the right of such person to vote or to register. It is doubtful whether a statute requiring a challenged person to take an oath, the nature of which is such as not in any degree to test his right, would be held valid. It would probably be held to be not a proper regulation of, but an unnecessary and unwarranted restriction upon the exercise of his right to vote. Thus in Nevada it was held that a statute requiring an oath to be taken by an applicant for registration, to the effect that he has not, since arriving at the age of eighteen years, voluntarily been engaged in rebellion against the government, is void, because the Nevada Constitution provides that persons who were engaged in the rebellion, and who were afterwards pardoned, may vote. (*Davies vs. McKerky*, 5 *Nevada*, 368.)

§ 67. An act purporting to authorize the Governor of a State to set aside the registration of the voters of a county, and thus deprive them of the right to vote, is unconstitutional and void. It is not doubted that the people of a State expressing their will in the form of a constitutional provision or otherwise, may prescribe the qualifications of voters, whereby the elective franchise may be bestowed upon persons not before entitled to it, and may be taken away from persons before entitled to it, subject to restrictions upon this power, contained in the Constitution of the United States. But the right of suffrage once conferred by a Constitution, the legislature has no power to divest it. It follows that where a person, entitled under the Constitution to vote has complied with such law, in regard to registration and the like, as the legislature may prescribe by way of regulating the exercise of the right, the legislature cannot authorize the Governor, or any other official, to take the right away from him. [*State vs. Staten* 6 *Caldw.* (*Tenn.*) 233. *Sheafe vs. Tillman* 2 *Bartlett* 907.]

§ 68. We have elsewhere seen that the act of Congress of March 3d, 1865, denying rights of citizenship to deserters from the army, must be held to apply to such persons only as have been duly convicted of the crime of desertion. It follows that to exclude a person from voting upon this ground evidence must be produced before the proper officers holding the election, that such person has been so convicted. It is the duty of such election officers to ascertain who are citizens, not to adjudge and enforce forfeitures of citizenship. In all cases where it appears that a person possesses the requisites as to birth or naturalization, age and residence of a voter, he must be presumed to be an elector until the contrary is shown by the best evidence, which in the case of a conviction for crime, must be the record, or a duly authenticated copy thereof. (*Gotchens vs. Matheson,* 58 *Barb,* [*N. Y.*] 152, 40 *Howard* [*N. Y.*] *Pr.* 97.)

§ 69. Where the Constitution confers upon the electors the right to choose an officer, it is as we have elsewhere seen, often a difficult question to determine how far the legislature may go in the way of providing the necessary regulations for the regular and orderly expression of that choice. Thus in Pennsylvania the Constitution provided that vacancies in judicial offices, happening by death, resignation or otherwise, should be filled "by appointment by the Governor, to continue until the first Monday of December *succeeding the next general election.*" Under this provision it was doubtless intended that an election by the people to fill any such vacancy, should be held at the next general election after its happening; but the General Assembly provided by law that all such vacancies should be filled at the first general election happening "*more than three calendar months after the vacancy shall occur.*" The question of the constitutionality of this act arose in *Commonwealth vs. Maxwell* (27 *Pa. State*, 44) and it was held to be constitutional. It was conceded by the Court in that case, as indeed it must be by all, that a law intended to take away or *unnecessarily and unreasonably postpone and embarass* the right of election, would be set aside, as unconstitutional. But it was held that a provision requiring three months for deliberation in the choice of a successor in case of a vacancy, fixes only a reasonable time, and is, therefore, a valid and proper regulation. This decision goes upon the sound principle that a Constitution cannot enforce itself; it lays down fundamental principles according to which the several departments it calls into existence are to govern the people; but all auxiliary rules which are necessary to give effect to these principles must, of necessity, come from the legislature.

§ 70. We have already seen that a residence within a place over which the United States has exclusive jurisdiction is not a residence within the State, County or township, for voting purposes. It has, however, been held in Ohio, that a constitutional requirement of residence, for a prescribed time, within the State, County or township, as a qualification for voters, is satisfied, if at the time of the election the voter has a residence within the proper political division, and has resided there for the prescribed length of time, although there may have been a change of jurisdiction, as where, during part of the time, the United States has had exclusive jurisdiction over the place, but has ceded it back to the State. [*Renner vs. Bennett*, 21 *Ohio St.*, 451.]

§ 71. The rule that every man is presumed to have a fixed domicile somewhere, applies as well to a single as to a married man, and though the domicile of the former may be more difficult to find and prove, yet the rules of evidence by which it is ascertained are the same as those applicable in determining the domicile of other persons. (*French vs. Lighty*, 9 *Ind.* 478.) And in the same case it was held that upon a question of domicile, evidence of the conduct or declarations of a party, afterwards, as well as before a given day, may be received to ascertain his intention, as to his place of abode on that day. This is upon the ground of course, that the question of domicile generally turns upon the question of *intent*, and thus can, in the nature of the case, be shown only by circumstances.

§ 72. The doctrine that the legislature cannot add to the constitutional qualifications of voters is founded upon the well settled rule of construction that when the Constitution specifies the circumstances under which a right may be exercised, or a penalty imposed, the specification is an implied prohibition against legislative interference, to add to the condition or to extend the penalty to other cases. (*Cooley's Constitutional Limitations*, 64. *Rison vs. Fair*, 24 *Ark.* 161.) And upon precisely the same ground it is held, that where the Constitution defines the qualifications of an officer it is not within the power of the legislature to change or superadd to them, unless the power to do so is expressly, or by necessary implication, conferred by the Constitution itself. (*Thomas vs. Owens*, 4 *Md.*, 189.)

§ 73. The better opinion seems to be that idiots and lunatics are by the common political law of England and this country disqualified from voting. (*Cooley's Const. Limitations*, 599.) But these unfortunate persons are expressly excluded from the right to vote, by the Constitutions of Delaware, Iowa, Kansas, Maryland, Minnesota, Nevada, New Jersey, Ohio, Oregon, Rhode Island, West Virginia, Wisconsin, and perhaps by other States. Paupers are excluded in New York, California, Louisiana, Maine, Massachusetts, New Hampshire, New Jersey, Rhode Island, South Carolina, and West Virginia. Persons under guardianship are excluded in Kansas, Maine, Massachusetts, Minnesota, and Wisconsin. Persons excused from paying taxes at their own request are excluded in New Hampshire. Capacity to read is required in Connecticut, and capacity to read and write in Massachusetts.

§ 74. A general and absolute pardon granted by

the Governor of a State by virtue of power conferred upon him to grant the same, relieves the person to whom it is granted, not only from the punishment provided by his sentence, but from all the consequential disabilities of the judgment of conviction, and restores such person to the full enjoyment of his civil rights including the right to vote. (*Wood vs. Fitzgerald*, 3 *Oregon*, 569, 4 *Blackstone's Comm.* 402, 8 *Bacon's Ab. Title Pardon. The People vs. Pease*, 3 *Johnson's Cases*, 333-4. *In re Deming*, 10 *Johnson* 233. *Perkins vs. Stevens*, 24 *Pick.* 277. *Ex parte Garland* 4 *Wall.*, 333.)

CHAPTER II.

OF THE QUALIFICATIONS, POWERS AND DUTIES OF ELECTION OFFICERS.

§ 75. In the House of Representatives of the United States there is a conflict of decisions touching the validity of the acts of a person acting as an officer of election, and who is such *defacto* only and not *de jure.* In some of the earlier cases in that body it was held that an election conducted by persons not duly qualified, was void. Thus in *Jackson vs. Wayne*, [*Cl. & H.* 47,] it was held that where the law required three magistrates to preside at an election, a return by three persons, two of whom were not magistrates, was defective. And in *McFarland vs.*

Culpepper, [*Cl. & H.* 221,] it was held, without much consideration or discussion, that a failure on the part of election officers to take the required oath vitiates the election, and this ruling was followed in *Easton vs. Scott*, [*Cl. & H.*, 272,] and in *Draper vs. Johnson*, *ibid.*, 702. In *Howard vs. Cooper* the vote of a precinct was thrown out because the election was presided over by but two inspectors, when the statute required three, (1 *Bartlett* p. 375,) and in *Delano vs. Morgan*, (2 *Bartlett*, *page* 168,) the vote of one township was thrown out, upon the ground that one of the three judges, was a deserter from the union army, and therefore not capable of taking or holding the office.

§ 76. On the contrary, however, the cases of *Mullikin* vs. *Fuller*, (1 *Bartlett*, 176,) *Clark* vs. *Hall*, (*ibid* 215,) *Flanders* vs. *Hahn*, (*ibid.* 443,) and *Blair* vs. *Barrett*, (*ibid* 313,) all seem to recognize the doctrine that, in the absence of fraud, the acts of an officer *defacto* of an election are valid as to third parties and the public. It is, however, undeniable that prior to the 41st Congress, the weight of authority in the House of Representatives was on the side of *Jackson* vs. *Wayne*, and the other cases above cited which followed that ruling down to, and including *Delano* vs. *Morgan*.

§ 77. But in the case of *Barnes* vs. *Adams*, which arose in the Forty-first Congress, (2 *Bartlett*, 760,) the question was reviewed at length, and most of the cases arising both in Congress and the Courts, were cited and examined, and the conclusion was reached both by the Committee and by the House, that in order to give validity to the official acts of an officer of elections, so far as they affect third parties and the public, and in the absence of fraud, it is only necessary that such officer shall have *color* of authority. It is sufficient if he be an officer *defacto*, and not a mere usurper. The report in this case, after quoting from numerous decisions, both in the House and in the Courts of this country, continues as follows:

"The question, therefore, regarded in the light of precedent or authority alone, would stand about as follows: The judicial decisions are all to the effect that the acts of officers *de facto*, so far as they affect third parties or the public, in the absence of fraud, are as valid as those of an officer *de jure*. The decisions of this House are to some extent conflicting; the point has seldom been presented upon its own merits, separated from questions of fraud; and in the few cases where this seems to have been the case the rulings are not harmonious. In one of the most recent and important cases, (*Blair* vs. *Barrett*,) in which there was an exceedingly able report, the doctrine of the courts, as above stated, is recognized and indorsed. The question is therefore a settled question in the courts of the country, and is, so far as this House is concerned, to say the least, an open one."

"Your committee feel constrained to adhere to the law as it exists and is administered in all the courts of the country, not only because of the very great authority by which it is supported, but for the further reason, as stated in the outset, that we believe the rule to be most wise and salutary. The officers of election are chosen of necessity from among all classes of the people; they are numbered in every State by thousands; they are often men unaccustomed to the formalities of legal proceedings. Omissions and mistakes in the discharge of their ministerial duties are almost inevitable. If this House shall establish the doctrine that an election is void because an officer thereof is not in all respects duly qualified, or because the same is not conducted strictly according to law, notwithstanding it may have been a fair and free election, the result will be, very many contests, and, what is worse, injustice will be done in many cases. It will enable those who are so disposed, to seize upon mere technicality in order to defeat the will of the majority."

§ 78. The report of the committee in this case was adopted by the House *nem. con.* after a full discussion, (*Cong. Globe, July* 1870, *pages* 5179 *to* 5193,) and the doctrine there asserted may now be regarded as the settled law of the House. The same point was decided in the same way, and by the same House, in the case of *Eggleston* vs. *Strader*, (2 *Bartlett*, 897,) and an admirable discussion of the question will be found in the report of the committee in that case made to the House by Mr. Hale of Maine. It is true that the writer of the report in the case of *Reid* vs. *Julian*, (2 *Bartlett*, 822,) asserted the contrary doctrine, but the case was decided independently of that question. It turned upon a question of fact, as to whether fraud was proven, so that this case cannot be regarded as an authority against *Barnes* vs. *Adams*, and *Eggleston* vs. *Strader*. The doctrine of the latter cases was reaffirmed in the case of *Gooding* vs. *Wilson*, 42*d Congress*.

§ 79. In the Courts of the country the ruling has been uniform, and the validity of the acts of officers of election who are such *de facto* only, so far as they affect third persons and the public, is nowhere questioned. The doctrine that whole communities of electors may be disfranchised for the time being, and a minority candidate forced into an office, because one or more of the judges of election have not been duly sworn, or were not duly chosen, or do not possess all the qualifications requisite for the office, finds no support in the decisions of our judicial tribunals. We here refer to some of the leading cases. In *People* vs. *Cook*, (4 *Selden*,) the Court says:

"The neglect of the officers of the election to take any oath would not have vitiated the election. It might have subjected those officers to an indictment if the neglect was willful. The acts of public officers being in by color of an election or appointment are valid, so far as the public is concerned."

Again:

"An officer *de facto* is one who comes into office by color of a legal appointment or election. His acts in that capacity are as valid, so far as the public is concerned, as the acts of an officer *de jure*. His acts in that capacity cannot be inquired into collaterally."

The same doctrine was laid down by the Supreme Court of Minnesota, in the recent case of *Taylor* vs. *Taylor*, *et. al.*, (10 *Minnesota*, 107,): One ground of contest in this case was that "in certain towns at said election the judges and clerks of said election did not take the prescribed oath or any oath." The Court say:

"If the votes of the citizens are freely and fairly deposited at the time and place designated by law, the intent and design of the election are accomplished. It is the will of the electors thus expressed that gives the right to the office, and the failure of the officers to perform a mere ministerial duty in relation to the election cannot invalidate it if the electors had actual notice and there was no fraud, mistake, or surprise."

Again the Court say:

"If the officers of election fail to perform their duty, the law provides a penalty; but the election is not necessarily rendered void."

Also, the Supreme Court of Pennsylvania, in the case of *Baird* vs. *Bank*, of Washington, (11 *S. & R.* 414.) We quote a sentence from the opinion in this case:

"The principle of colorable election holds not only in regard to the right of electing, but of being elected. A person *indisputably ineligible* may be an officer *de facto* by color of election."

Also, the Supreme Court of Illinois, in *Pritchett et. al.* vs. *The People*, (1 *Gilm.*, 529.) In the course of the opinion the Court say:

"It is a general principle of the law that ministerial acts of an officer *de facto* are valid and effectual when they concern the public and the rights of third persons; although it may appear that he has *no legal or constitutional* right to the office. The interests of the community imperatively require the adoption of such a rule."

The same Court, in *The People* vs. *Ammons*, (5 *Gilm.*, 107,) hold the same doctrine, and state it in this language:

"The proof offered would have shown that he was

an officer *de facto*, and as such his acts were as binding and valid when the interests of third persons or the public were concerned, as if he had been an officer *de jure*."

The Supreme Court of Missouri, in St. Louis County Court *vs.* Sparks, [10 *Mo.* 121,] says:

"When the appointing power has made an appointment, and a person is appointed who has not the qualifications required by law, the appointment is not therefore void. The person appointed is *de facto* an officer; his acts in the discharge of his duties are valid and binding. * * * A statute prescribing qualification to an office is merely directory, and although an appointee does not possess the requisite qualifications his appointment is not therefore void, unless it is so expressly enacted."

The supreme court of California, in the case of *Whipley vs. McKune*, (10 *Cal.*, 352,) hold the same doctrine. In this case the election of McKune to the office of district judge was contested upon the ground that "the officers conducting the election in a given district were not sworn as the election laws require." No fraud being shown the election was held valid, notwithstanding such failure of the officers to be sworn.

The supreme court of New York discusses this question in an elaborate opinion in the case of *The People vs. Cook*, (14 *Barbour*, 259,) from which we quote a few sentences:

"It becomes important in this case to determine whether the objections which are taken to the inspectors of elections in the several cases presented in the bill of exceptions, are of that character which should be held to invalidate the canvass in these several localities. These objections are of a two-fold character, extending to the regularity or legality of their appointment and to their omission to qualify by taking the proper oath of office. * * * It is sufficient that they were inspectors *de facto.* The rule is well settled by a long series of adjudications, both in England and this country, that acts done by those who are officers *de facto* are good and valid as regards the public and third persons who have an interest in their acts, and the rule has been applied to acts judicial, as well as to those ministerial in their character. This doctrine has been held and applied to almost every conceivable case. It cannot be profitable to enter into any extended discussion of the cases. The principle has become elementary, and the cases are almost endless in which the rule has been applied."

So, in the case of *Greenleaf* vs. *Low,* [4 *Denio* 168,] it was held that a person elected to the office of justice of the peace, who neglected to take the oath of office and to give the security required by law, is nevertheless in office by color of title, and his acts are valid as regards the public and third persons. The Court say:

"Sufficient facts appeared to show that Jones was a justice of the peace *de facto* at the time he rendered the judgment in question. He came into his office by color of title. It is a well settled principle that acts done by such an officer are as valid, so far as the public or the rights of third persons are concerned, as if he had been an officer *de jure,* and that the title of the office cannot be collaterally inquired into."

Exactly the same point was decided in the same way in the case of *Weeks* vs. *Ellis*, [2 *Barbour*, 324,] where a justice of the peace had entered upon the duties of his office without taking the oath prescribed by law.

And so, likewise, in the case of *Keyser* vs. *Mc Kisson*, [2 *Rawle*, 139,] it was held that the failure of county commissioners to take the oath prescribed by the constitution of Pennsylvania did not invalidate their acts as such, where the public or third persons were concerned.

So, in the case of *McGregor* vs. *Balch*, [14 *Vermont*, 428] it was held that, although a person could not legally hold the office of justice of the peace at all while holding the office of assistant postmaster under the United States, yet, having entered the former office under the forms of law, he was a justice of the peace *de facto*, and his acts as such were valid as to third persons and the public.

§ 80. A mere usurper in an office can have no authority, and can perform no valid official act. It is enough if he possess color of authority, but without this, his acts are void even as to third parties and the public. It was accordingly held that where certain persons were chosen county officers in an unorganized county in a territory, by a public meeting without the shadow of legal right or authority, and commissioned as such by the governor, who also acted without any color of right or authority, they were usurpers, and that an election held under their authority was void. [*Daily vs. Estabrook*, 1 *Purtlett*

299.] In the same case the rule was laid down that no valid election can be held in an unorganized county,—and that a county cannot be considered as organized until there has been an election of county officers.

§ 81. It is well settled that the duties of canvassing officers are purely ministerial, and extend only to the casting up of the votes and awarding the certificate to the person having the highest number; they have no judicial power. In *State vs. Steers*, (44 *Mo.*, 223,) which was a case in which the canvassing board had undertaken to throw out the returns from one voting precinct for an alleged informality, the court said: "When a ministerial officer leaves his proper sphere, and attempts to exercise judicial functions, he is exceeding the limits of the law, and guilty of usurpation." And again, "To permit a mere ministerial officer arbitrarily to reject returns, at his mere caprice or pleasure, is to infringe or destroy the rights of parties without notice or opportunity to be heard, a thing which the law abhors and prohibits."

§ 82. But of course it does not follow from this doctrine that canvassing and return judges must receive and count whatever purports to be a return, whether it bears upon its face sufficient proof that it is such or not. The true rule is this: they must receive and count the votes as shown by the returns, *and they cannot go behind the returns for any purpose*, and this necessarily implies that if a paper is presented, as a return, and there is a question as to whether it is a return or not, they must decide that question from what appears upon the face of the paper itself. Thus, in New York, it has been held that the duties of the canvassers were "to attend at the proper office and calculate and ascertain the whole number of votes given at any election and certify the same to be a true canvass; this is not a judicial act, but merely ministerial; they have no power to controvert the votes of electors. [*People vs. Van Slyck*, 4 *Conn.* 297, 323.) To the same safe effect is the ruling in *ex parte Heath*, (3 *Hill*, 47.)

§ 83. And in *Morgan vs. Quackenbush* (22 *Barb.* 77) we find this language: "they, (the canvassers) are not at liberty to receive evidence of any thing outside of the returns themselves; their duty consists in a simple matter of arithmetic." See also, *Thompson vs. Ewing*, (1 *Brewst.* 77,) where it is laid down that the return judges cannot enquire into a question of fraud. See also, *State vs. The Governor*, 1 *Dutch. N. J.* 348. *Brown vs. O'Brien*, 2 *Ind.* 483. *State vs. Jones*, 19 *Ind.* 365. *People vs. Kilduff*, 15 *Ill.*, 500. *People vs. Head.* 25 *Ill.*, 328. In the latter case the court say "they may probably judge whether the returns are in due form, but after that they can only compute the votes cast for the several candidates and declare the result." But in determining as to the form of the returns they must consider the substance, and not be too technical. If there is a substantial compliance with the law it is enough.

§. 84 The doctrine that canvassing boards and return judges are ministerial officers possessing no discretionary or judicial power, is settled in nearly or quite all the States:

Dishon vs. Smith, 10 *Iowa*, 212.
State vs. Cavers, 22 *Iowa*, 343.

Att'y General, vs. Barstow, 4 *Wisconsin*, 749.
People vs. Van Cleve, 1 *Michigan*, 362.
Thompson Circuit Judge, 9 *Alabama*, 338.
Mayo vs. Freeland, 10 *Missouri*, 629.
State vs. Harrison, 38 *Missouri*, 540.
State vs. Rodman, 43 *Missouri*, 266.
State vs. Steers, 44 *Missouri*, 228-9.
Bacon vs. York Co., 26 *Maine*, 491.
Taylor vs. Taylor, 10 *Minnesota*, 107.
O'Farrall vs. Colby, 2 *Minnesota*, 180.
Marshall vs. Kerns, 2 *Swan, Tennessee*, 66.

In *Att'y Genl. vs. Barstow, supra*, the Supreme Court of Wisconsin say that the canvassing officers "are to add up and certify by calculation the number of votes given for any office; they have no discretion to hear and take proof as to frauds, even if morally certain that monstrous frauds have been perpetrated."

§ 85. In *Morgan vs. Quackenbush*, [22 *Barb., N. Y.* 72,] this doctrine was again asserted. It was there held that it was the duty of the canvassing board to canvass the returns and declare the result, and that this was a purely ministerial act. They are judges of nothing, and not allowed to receive evidence of any thing outside of the returns themselves, and hence, they acted illegally in receiving affidavits of fraudulent practices at the polls and acting upon such evidence. It was, however, also held, that their determination, although based upon illegal evidence, must be received as *prima facie* evidence that the person declared elected was entitled to the office, and that in attempting afterwards to recanvass the vote and set aside their first certificate they transcended their authority, and assumed a power belonging only to a tribunal authorized to try cases of contested elections under the law.

§ 86. There are statutes in some of the States which expressly confer upon a board of canvassing officers the power to revise the returns of an election, to take proofs, and in their discretion, to reject such votes as they deem illegal. Such a statute exists in Texas, [*See Giddings vs. Clark*, 42*d Congress*,] and in Alabama. [See *Norris vs. Handley do.*,] and in Louisiana and Florida. Although this is an extraordinary, and a dangerous power, when placed in the hands of a board of this character, with such inadequate facilities for obtaining legal evidence and deciding upon questions of fraud; yet it seems that such statutes are not unconstitutional. And it has been held by the House of Representatives of the United States that the action of such a board, in pursuance of the power thus conferred, is *prima facie* correct and to be allowed to stand until shown by evidence to be illegal or unjust. [*See cases last above cited.*]

§ 87. The doctrine that the acts of an officer of election, within the scope of his authority, are presumed to be correct, is strongly stated and ably argued in *Littell vs. Robins*, (1 *Bartlett*, 138.) The rule is here placed upon two grounds, viz: *first*, that the presumption is always against the commission of a fraudulent or illegal act, and *secondly*, that the presumption is always in favor of the official acts of a sworn officer.

§ 88. In general, where a statute requires an official act to be done by a given day, for a public purpose, it must be construed as merely directory in regard to the time. Accordingly, it is uniformly held that a statute requiring an officer or board to certify the result of an election, or in any way to make known the result, or to issue a commission on or before a given day, or within a given number of days after the election, is directory and not mandatory. Such acts are valid though performed after the expiration of the time. (*Exparte Heath, et al.*, 3 *Hill*, 42.)

This doctrine has been uniformly maintained by the courts, and nothing is better settled. (*People vs Allen*, 6 *Wend.* 486, *and cases there cited. Colt vs. Eves*, 12 *Conn.*, 243-253 to 255, *and cases cited.*)

§ 89. If the officers conducting an election adopt and enforce an erroneous rule as to the qualification of voters, which prevents certain legal voters, who offer to vote, from giving in their votes, and being made known, prevents other legal voters similarly situated from offering to vote, the election may be set aside, especially if it appear that such votes if offered and received would have changed, or rendered doubtful, the result. [*Scranton Borough Election*, [*Brightley's Election Cases*, 455.] After a decision has been made by the election officers affecting the right of a class of persons to vote, and that decision becomes known, it is not necessary that every voter belonging to such class should offer his vote and have it formerly rejected. Nor is it necessary to prove in such a case how such person whose vote was excluded would have voted, if permission had been given; to require this, would be to take away the secrecy of the ballot.

§ 90. Where an election district is, by the enactment of a law, divided into two separate districts, with two separate places of holding an election, the functions of the election officers of the old district are destroyed, and they cannot act in either of the the new districts into which the old one is divided. It would be otherwise if part of an old district was formed into a new one, and if provision was only made for the new one. That would not annihilate the old district, but only change its boundaries. The forming of one old district into two complete new ones, does annihilate the old, and it is well settled, that the official functions of local officers fall with the political annihilation of the locality for which they were chosen or appointed. [*Penn. Dist. Election Case*, *Brightley's Election Cases*, 617. *North Whitehall vs. South Whitehall*, 3 *S. & R.* 121.]

§ 91. It is, as we have already seen, well settled that the acts of public officers within the sphere of their duties, must be presumed to be correct, until the contrary is shown. [*Goggin vs. Gilmer*, 1 *Bartlett*, 70. *Giddings vs. Clark*, 42d *Congress*.] If, therefore, the law allows the officers of the election, upon the happening of certain contingencies, to adjourn the election for one or more days,—if it be shown that they did in fact adjourn—it will be presumed that the adjournment was proper. And so, if the law empowers a board of returning officers to revise the returns, and it appears that they have exercised such authority, their action must stand until shown to have been wrong. Further illustrations of this rule are not necessary, as it is well settled and generally understood.

In *Goggin vs. Gilmer*, [*supra*] it was further held, and very properly, that where the officers of the election were authorized in case of inclement weather, the rise of water courses by rain, or the assembling of a body of voters too great to be accommodated in one day, to adjourn the election for not more than three days,—and where there was such an adjournment, even if the officers were mistaken as to the happening of any of these contingencies, the election should not be declared illegal and void in the absence of fraud. The officers of the election in such a case are the judges of the necessity for an adjournment, and their decision upon that point, in the absence of fraud is final. The power of adjournment in such cases is *discretionary* with the officers of election, and an honest error in its exercise is not fatal to the election.

And this is unquestionably the sound doctrine, notwithstanding a contrary decision in one of the earlier cases, from the same State. (*Basset vs. Bailey, Cl. & H.* 254.) In this latter case the committee went into inquiry as to whether in point of fact the contingency did or did not happen on which rested the authority of the sheriff to adjourn the election, and finding that in their opinion it did not happen, they ruled that the adjournment was illegal and rendered the subsequent proceedings illegal. The case, however, did not turn upon this question, and for this reason, perhaps, it was not more carefully considered. A similar question arose in the case of *Trigg vs. Poeston,* [*Cl. & H.*, 78,] and it was there held that an adjournment of an election by the sheriff under a statute giving him discretionary power to adjourn, in case of rain, was presumed to be a valid adjournment.

§ 93. A canvassing board having once counted the votes, and declared the result according to law, has no power or authority to make a recount. When this duty is once fully performed, it is performed once and forever, and cannot be repeated. [*Bowen* vs. *Hixon*, 45 *Mo.*, 350, *Gooding* vs. *Wilson* 42*d Congress.*] In the former case the Court say "To suppose that it could be renewed—that the canvass of one day could be repeated the next, and counter certificates be issued to different contestants as new light or influence was brought to bear upon the mind of the clerk would render the whole proceeding a farce." And in the latter case the report of the committee has this language:

"On examination of precedents, it does not appear that this House favors the setting aside of official and formal counts, made with all the safeguards required by law, on evidence only of subsequent informal and unofficial counts, without such safeguards. No instance was cited at the hearing where the person entitled by the official count was deprived of his seat by a subsequent unofficial count. On principle it would seem that if such a thing were, in the absence of fraud in the official count, in any case admissible, it should be permitted only when the ballot boxes had been so kept as to be conclusive of the identity of the ballots, and when the subsequent count was made with safeguards equivalent to those provided by law. In the absence of either of these conditions, the proof, as mere matter of fact, and without reference to statutory rules, would be less reliable, and therefore insufficient."

And see also *Hadley* vs. *City of Albany*, 33 *N.Y.*

603. *Hartt vs. Harvey*, 32 *Barb.*, 55. *Ramsay vs. Calaway*, 15 *La. An.* 464. *Chrisman vs. Anderson*, 1 *Bartlett*, 328.

§ 94. In Minnesota, it has been held, in accordance with the principle just stated, that if the board of canvassers, after canvassing the votes, adjourn without day, their power in the premises is at an end, and they cannot re-assemble, neither can a court, by mandamus, compel them to re-assemble or give them any power in case of their so doing. (*Clark vs. Buchanan*, 2 *Minn.*, 346.)

§ 95. If a voter, upon being challenged and questioned, admits that he has not been naturalized, or, that his naturalization certificate was issued by some court which the judges know had no jurisdiction of that subject, they may well decline to administer the oath, or to accept the vote. But the judges have no right, in California, to require the production of the certificate of naturalization. [*People* vs. *Gordon*, 5 *Cal.*, 235.] And a similar rule prevails in most of the States.

§ 96. In *Kline vs. Myers*, (1 *Bartlett*, 574,) the house refused to order a recount of ballots upon the request of the contestant. One reason was, that the contestant did not offer evidence sufficient to show even presumptively that the original count was erroneous or fraudulent. But another reason was the great danger of attempting to set aside the official count by a re-opening of the boxes, and a recount of the ballots, months after the election. And upon this latter point the committee, in their report, say: "To adopt a rule that the ballot boxes should be opened upon the mere request of the defeated candidate, would occasion more fraud than it could possibly expose. The number of ballot boxes in each congressional district is seldom less than fifty, and often more than two hundred. They are usually left in the care of a magistrate or some township officer, by whom they are deposited in no safer place than an upper shelf in a public office. The opportunities of tampering with the boxes thus scattered through the district, would be abundant, and if it was known in advance that a second count could be had without discrediting the first, the temptations to do so would be strong. It makes no difference in settling the rule that in this particular case the votes have been carefully guarded by the Mayor and Recorder, under a special law for the city of Philadelphia. The fact would only strengthen the confidence in the result of a recount in this case, but does not show the propriety of establishing a general rule, authorizing a recount whenever asked. It should be remembered that the fact sought is not what the ballot boxes contain six months or a year after the election, but what they did contain after the last vote was deposited on the day of the election. Certainly an impartial, accurate and public count then by the sworn officers would be better evidence of that fact than any subsequent count not more impartial, and not presuming to be more accurate than the first, and after boxes have long been exposed to the tampering of dishonest partisans."

§ 97. By a statute of Massachusetts "the Mayor and Aldermen and Clerk of each city" are required forthwith after an election to examine the returns from each ward, and if any error appears therein, "they shall forthwith notify" the ward officers, "who shall forthwith make a new and additional return under oath in conformity to truth." It is manifest however, that it was not intended by this statute to authorize an amended return, unless made "forthwith," and before the ballots, records, and election papers have passed out of the hands of the returning officers. These amended returns are required by the statute to be "received by the Mayor and Aldermen and city Clerk, at any time before the expiration of the day preceding that on which they are required by law to make their returns or declare the result of the election in said city." They cannot be made after the result is declared, and their value must depend upon their being made by the returning officers, without delay. (*Sleeper vs. Rice*, 1 *Bartlett*, 472.)

§ 98. A statute of Kentucky in force in 1833, required the certificate of election of Representatives in Congress, to be signed by all the sheriffs of the counties composing the district. In the case of *Letcher vs. Moore*, (*Cl. & H.*, 715,) the credentials presented were signed by the sheriff of four out of five of the counties in the district, and the question whether this was sufficient to give the holder of it the right to the seat *prima facie*, was debated in the house at great length, but was not decided, because, pending its discussion, both parties agreed to waive their claim to a seat until the case could be heard upon the merits. It would seem that the vote of one county was not canvassed at all by the sheriffs, it having been withheld by the sheriff having it in charge, without any sufficient cause, and it is evident that the house had good reason to believe that the vote of that county, if it had been canvassed by the board of sheriffs, would have changed the result and given the credentials to Letcher, instead of Moore. Under such circumstances the house hesitated, and very properly, to accept the certificate of a majority of the sheriffs, based upon a canvass of but four of the five counties of the district. The case did not come properly within the rule that the certificate of the majority of a board, is the certificate of the board, for while it is true, ordinarily, that less than the whole number may make a valid certificate in such a case, *it must be upon a canvass of the whole vote of the district.* If a part of the vote is omitted and the certificate does no more than to show that a canvass of *part* of the vote cast shows the election of a particular person, it is not even *prima facie* evidence, because *non constat* that a canvass of the *whole* vote would produce the same result.

§ 99. The act of Congress of May 31, 1870, (16 *Stat. at Large*, 145, *Sec.* 22,) provides for the punishment of "any officer of election" who shall "fraudulently make any false certificate of the result of any election in regard to a Representative" in Congress. In the case of *The United States vs. Clayton*, in the Circuit Court of the United States for District of Arkansas, the question arose whether the Governor of a State is liable to indictment and punishment under this act. By the statute of Arkansas it was the duty of the Governor to grant a certificate to the person duly elected Representative in Congress, and the indictment in this case charged the defendant, as Governor of Arkansas, with having falsely and fraudulently issued a certificate declaring John Edwards elected Representative in Congress in the forty-second Congress, from the third district of that State, when in truth and in fact the returns then on file in his office showed that one Thomas Boles was duly elected. (*See American Law Register, Vol.* 10, *p.* 739.) A demurrer was interposed which raised the question above suggested, and it was sustained, the Court (*Dillon J.*) being of the opinion that the Governor of a State is not an "officer of election" within the meaning of the said act of Congress. It was deemed by the Court highly improbable that Congress would (even if its power to do so be conceded,) provide for the trial and imprisonment of the Governor of a State for omitting or fraudulently performing, duties imposed upon him by State laws.

§ 100. The fact that the officers of an election caused the names on the registration list to be copied and arranged alphabetically, so that the names might be more readily found as the voters presented themselves to vote, and that they used this alphabetical copy in connection with the original, will not affect the validity of the poll. (*Hogan vs. Pile*, 2 *Bartlett*, 281.)

§ 101. In the case last cited one of the grounds of contest was, that the County Court being authorized to fix the places of voting, and arrange the voting precincts, had performed this duty so unfairly and improperly as to prevent a full vote for contestant. Upon this point the committee say:

"The legislature had the power to fix the voting districts or provide by law that the County Court should do so, and the law of Missouri having imposed upon the County Court the duty of establishing voting places, that Court had the right to fix tne number in its own discretion, and the exercise of that discretion cannot be reviewed. If, indeed, the Court should fraudulently refuse to establish voting places in such a manner as to disfranchise the citizens for partisan purposes, it might be necessary to set aside the entire election."

No doubt the true rule is here indicated, and it is this. If the board or officer having the power to fix the voting places, shall *fraudulently* so arrange them as to disfranchise a portion of the voters, and thus defeat the will of the electors, it would become necessary to set aside the election. If the fraudulent purpose must, in such a case, be proven, it may be established by circumstances.

§ 102. But the question may arise whether, even in the absence of proof of a fraudulent purpose, the fixing of the voting places in such a manner as to prevent a full and free election, must not render the election void? As for example, if all the voters of a county or city are required to vote at a single polling place, and if it should appear that the voters were so numerous that it was impossible for them all to vote, and that a part were in fact, for this reason, prevented from voting, in such a case, we think, the election should be held void without further proof. Perhaps, from these facts, a fraudulent purpose on the part of the board or officers, whose duty it was to fix suitable and convenient voting places, would be presumed, but if not, then the election should be held void, upon the ground, that whatever in point of fact prevents a fair and free election, whether so intended or not, must render the election null and void. (*b*.)

§ 103. Where the law requires that the polls shall be kept open until sunset, this is probably equivalent to declaring that they shall be closed at sunset, though upon this point the committee in *Hogan vs. Pile, supra,* refrained from expressing an opinion. It was, however, held in that case that the polls having been regularly closed at sunset, they could not be legally opened again during the evening, and there is no doubt but that if the polls are once regularly closed, the officers of the election cannot again open them. It is to be presumed that all voters who have not voted will have notice of the closing of the polls; that being a proceeding according to law they are bound to know it, and act upon it; but the re-opening is a proceeding of which no one will be bound to take notice, and if some do take notice of it, and deposit ballots, they are void as being both unlawful and a fraud upon the rights of other voters.

§ 104. The law is well settled that statute certifying officers can only make their certificates evidence of the facts which the statute requires them to certify, and when they undertake to go beyond this, and certify other facts, they are *unofficial,* and no more evidence than the statement of any unofficial person. (*Switzler vs. Anderson,* 2 *Bartlett,* 374.) This rule of course applies to election returns, and

(*b*.) Probably, there should be an exception to this rule, in cases where the legislature, by law, fixes the places of voting, and where no other authority has power to alter or change them. It would, probably, not be competent to show that the legislature had not fixed enough polling places, or had not established them in the right places.

to all certificates which are by law required to be made by officers of election, or of registration, or by returning officers. They can only certify to such facts as the law requires them to certify. The certificate of such an officer is not, however, vitiated by the fact that it contains the certification of facts outside of those which the officer has a right to certify. If it in fact certifies the proper facts it is good, and the remainder of the certificate is to be rejected as surplusage.

§ 105. The doctrine of *Gooding vs. Wison*, (*supra*,) was strongly asserted in *State vs. Dunniworth*, [21 *Ohio*, 216,] where it was held that the officers of an election board after its regular dissolution are *functus officio*, and their subsequent acts in that character unauthorized; and that where a municipal election board had regularly dissolved, and the box in which the canvassed ballots were placed had remained five days in an exposed place of easy access, a subsequent tally sheet made on the fifth day on re-count of ballots then found in the box, by four officers of the municipality, some of whom were members of the election board, will not be received to impeach the original canvass and tally sheet.

§ 106. The inspectors of an election having received the vote of a person, and deposited the same in the box, cannot afterwards enter into any inquiry as to the right of such person to vote. There are two sufficient reasons for this rule. In the first place, the voter is a necessary party to any such investigation, and in the second place, the inspectors cannot be presumed to know how any person voted, and, therefore, cannot know which ballot to exclude. The rule is, therefore, that the moment the ballot is deposited, all control over it, and all power to inquire as to its legality, by the officers of the election, is ended. (*Hartt* vs. *Harney*, 32 *Barbour*, 55.)

§ 107. A statute of New Hampshire required the town clerk to record the vote for representative in Congress, as counted and announced in his presence by the selectmen, and to send a copy thereof to the secretary of state. The statute further provided as follows: "If the clerk of any town shall make an incorrect or insufficient record or return of the votes given therein, at any meeting for any officer, the tribunal by whom said votes are opened and corrected may require said clerk, at his own expense, to come in and amend said record or return, according to the facts of the case."

It was held by the Supreme Court of that State that this statute only authorizes town clerks when required, to make their record to correspond with the declaration of the vote, as publicly made by the moderator, and does not authorize them to make by amendment a record which they could not have made in the first instance. (*Opinion of the Justices*, 53, *N. H.* 640.)

§ 108. When the law designates a place for holding an election for a given precinct, and provides a set of officers to conduct the same, and makes no provision for more than one voting place or ballot box within such precinct, it is not lawful for the officers of election to provide two or more ballot boxes at different places within such precincts. Especially is this true of an election for Representatives in Congress, at which, under the act of Congress of

February 28, 1871, a supervisor of election appointed under the authority of the United States, is entitled to be present. If the places of voting within a precinct may be multiplied, the local authorities may render it impossible for the supervisor to be present at the place for holding the election as required by law. Besides it is plain that for many other reasons the power to multiply voting places would be an exceedingly dangerous power and one which might be used for purposes of corruption and fraud. (*Sloan vs. Rawles*, 43*d Congress.*)

CHAPTER III.

OF THE TIME, PLACE AND MANNER OF HOLDING ELECTIONS, AND OF NOTICE.

§ 109. It is, of course, essential to the validity of an election, that it be held at the time, and in the place, provided by law. An interesting and important question arose, however, in many of the States of the Union, during the progress of the great rebellion, as to the validity of certain statutes, authorizing persons in the military service of the United States to vote while absent from their States, engaged in such service.

The constitutionality of these statutes generally turned upon the question whether it was competent for a State legislature to authorize a citizen to vote elsewhere than at the place of his residence. In the constitutions of most of the States there were provisions requiring that each elector should vote at the place of his residence, and not elsewhere. The Constitution of Michigan provided that the voter should have resided "in the township or ward *in which he offers to vote, ten days next preceding such election.*" The legislature of that State enacted that persons in the military service possessing the qualifications provided by the Constitution, should be allowed to vote wherever they might be, whether within the limits of the State or not. In the case of *Baldwin vs. Trowbridge,* 2 *Bartlett,* 46, the House of Representatives held this statute to be constitutional, in so far as it related to the election of Representatives in Congress. The decision was placed by the majority of the committee of elections, in their report, upon the ground that where there is a conflict between the State Constitution and a legislative act, in regard to fixing the place of an election for such Representatives, the power of the legislature is paramount. This was held as the necessary effect of Article one, Section four, of the Constitution of the United States, which provides as follows:

"The times, places, and manner of holding elections for Senators and Representatives shall be prescribed in each State by the *legislature* thereof; but the Congress may at any time, by law, make or alter such regulations, except as to the places of choosing Senators."

§ 110. It was held that, by this provision, the power is conferred upon the legislature of the State, and that in fixing the place of the election for representatives in Congress, it acted under, and derived its authority, from the Constitution of the United States, and not from the Constitution of Michigan. This view of the subject was ably presented in the report made to the House by Mr. Scofield, of Pennsylvania. The reasoning of the report may be thus stated: The place of the election, for representative in Congress, is to be fixed by the legislature of the State. So declares the National Constitution. But in Michigan, the Convention which framed the State Constitution, undertook to determine the place where all such elections should be held. This was an attempt to take from the legislature the power plainly conferred by the Federal Constitution. In so far, therefore, as the Constitutional convention undertook to fix the "place" for "holding elections for representatives" it went beyond its authority, because it was not "the legislature of the State."

§ 111. A very similar question arose in *Shiel vs. Thayer*, (2 *Bartlett*, 349.) In that case, the constitution of Oregon had fixed the time of holding the election for representative in Congress, and the legislature had not acted upon the subject. The case is, therefore, to be distinguished from *Baldwin vs. Trowbridge*, in this, that the former was not like the latter, a case of conflict between the State Constitution and any act of the State legislature. It is true, that the committee, in their report, express the opinion that the Constitution of the State had fixed "beyond the control of the legislature" the time for holding the election for representative in Congress; but this point was not necessarily involved in the case, and it is evident, from the debate in the House, that there was a wide difference of opinion upon it.

The case does decide, that where a State is admitted into the Union with a Constitution which fixes a time for holding the election for representatives in Congress, the time thus fixed will be regarded as the proper and legal time, but it does not decide, because it does not involve the question, whether that time can be subsequently changed by the legislature of the State.

§ 112. But the reasoning in *Baldwin vs. Trowbridge,* whether sound or not, applies, of course, only to elections for representatives in Congress, since it was within the province of the constitutional convention to fix the times and places for holding all other elections; and it would seem quite clear that under the Constitution of Michigan the act in question, in so far as it applied to State elections, was unconstitutional. Where a constitutional provision clearly requires the citizen to vote at the place of his residence, it is certainly not within the power of the legislature to provide that he may vote elsewhere, and that a soldier has no residence in the field or camp, is also a clear proposition. (*Chase vs. Miller*, 41 *Pa., State R.*, 403. *Bourland vs. Hildreth*, 26 *Cal.*, 161. *Opinion of Judges*, 30 *Conn.*, 591. *Opinion of Justices*, 44 *N. H.*, 633.) In Iowa a statute of this character was held constitutional, upon the ground that a district residence was not required by the Constitution of that State. (*Morrison vs. Springer*, 15 *Iowa*, 304.) See also *Lehman vs. McBride*, 15 *Ohio, State R.*, 573, *and Chandler vs. Main*, 16 *Wis.*, 343.

§ 113. In the Constitutions of some of the States we find provisions not only fixing the qualifications of voters, but also fixing the place of voting. Where the Constitution stops with an enumeration of the qualifications of an elector, and does not expressly declare that the elector must vote at the place of his residence, it is competent for the legislature to provide for the reception of votes out of the precinct or county of his residence. [*Morrison vs. Springer, supra.*] So that the question must turn upon the language employed in the particular constitution to be construed.

§ 114. Those provisions of law which fix the time or place of holding elections, are to be construed as mandatory, and not as merely directory. The reason for this is obvious. Every voter is presumed to know the law, and to be thereby informed as to the time when, and the place where he may deposite his ballot; but, if that time or place be changed without proper authority and due notice, no voter can be held as legally bound to take notice of the change, and it can never be known how many voters have been deceived thereby, unless, indeed, all the persons entitled to vote should actually attend and vote at the illegal place, which might, perhaps, be held as a waiver of all objection thereto, provided the place was within the voting precinct. As to the time of the election, of course the day cannot be changed even by the consent of all the voters, and the general rule is, that if the polls are not kept open for as many hours as the law directs, and if legal voters in numbers sufficient to change the result, or to render it doubtful, are thereby deprived of the privilege of voting, the election must be set aside. A few minutes delay in opening the polls will make no difference, but several hours delay, may render the election void, and certainly will have that effect if the party complaining of it can show that he has been injured thereby. (*Chadwick vs. Melvin, Brightley's Election Cases*, 251, 68 *Pa. State*, 333. *Juker vs. Commonwealth*, 20 *Pa., State R.*, 484. *Dickey vs. Hurlburt*, 5 *Cal.* 343. *People vs. Murray*, 15 *Cal.*, 321. *Knowles* vs. *Yeates*, 31 *Cal.*, 82.)

§ 115. In *Chadwick* vs. *Melvin, supra*, the Supreme Court of Pennsylvania held that, to remove the place of election three miles from that designated by law, or from a village to a place a half mile therefrom, and across a considerable stream, or from a designated school house to a vacant house more than half a mile distant therefrom, without authority or any absolutely controlling circumstances, must render the election therein void, and in the course of the opinion Thompson, C. J. says: "A fixed place, it seems to me, is as absolutely requisite according to the election laws, as is the time of voting. The holding of elections at the places fixed by law, is not directory; it is mandatory and cannot be omitted without error. I will not say that in case of the destruction of a designated building on the eve of an election, the election might not be held on the same or contiguous ground as a matter of necessity—*necessitas non habet legem*. But then the necessity must be absolute; discarding all mere ideas of convenience." [See also *Journal of House of Representatives of Pa.*, 1856, *page* 204, *case of Beck* vs. *McGhee*. *Miller* vs. *English*, 1 *Zab.*, (*N. J.*,) 317. *Commonwealth* vs. *Commissioners*, 5 *Rawle*, 75. *Marshall* vs. *Kerns*, 2 *Swan*, 68. *Foster* vs. *Scarff*, 15 *Ohio State R.*, 535.]

The same rule prevails where the place of holding the election is fixed by a court, or by a board or officer, thereunto duly authorized by law. When once legally fixed by proper authority, it can only be changed by proper authority, and in the manner provided by law.

§ 116. While it is true, that notice is essential to the validity of an election, it is not always essential that the particular form or manner of giving notice, which may be prescribed, shall be followed. It is essential that the electors should have notice of the time, place and objects of the election. That is, they should have knowledge of them, but an omission to follow the particular mode provided by statute for publishing such notice, may not render the election void, and will not, if the electors have actual notice, and do, in fact, take part in the election. This doctrine was laid down very broadly by the Supreme Court of Iowa, in *Dishon* vs. *Smith* (10 *Iowa*, 212.) The Court in that case say: "The Courts have held that the voice of the people is not to be rejected for a defect or even a want of notice, if they have, in truth, been called upon and have spoken. In the present case, whether there were notices or not, there was an election, and the people of the county voted, and it is not alleged that any portion of them failed in knowledge of the pendency of the question, or to exercise their franchise."

§ 117. It is, doubtless, perfectly true, that where the election has been held at the proper time, and the proper place, and the electors have had notice and participated in it, the want of such notice as the law provides, will not render it void. But if it appear that due notice has not been given, and that a portion of the electors have been thereby deprived of their right to vote, and particularly, if the number thus deprived, is sufficient to have changed the result if they had voted on one side or the other,—in such a case the election is clearly void.

§ 118. The general rule upon this subject is given by Judge Cooley as follows: "Where, by the express provision of the statute, the election is to be held after proclamation, or notice, announcing the time or the place, or both, and where no such proclamation has been made, or notice given, the election is void. But where both the time and the place of an election are prescribed by law, every voter has a right to take notice of the law, and to deposit his ballot at the time and place appointed, notwithstanding the officer, whose duty it is to give notice of the election, has failed in that duty. The right to hold the election in such a case, is derived from the law, and not from the notice. And this rule will apply to an election to fill a vacancy, if the same occurs long enough before the election, to have become generally notorious, and if it was in fact generally known." (*Cooley, Constitutional Limitations*, 603.)

§ 119. The doctrine, that want of formal notice of an election will not render the election void, unless it appear that the failure to give such notice has, in fact, either changed or rendered doubtful the result was recognized as early as 1796, by the House of Representatives of the United States in *Lyon* vs. *Smith* (*Cl. & H.*, 101.) In that case it appeared that no notice had been given of the time and place of holding the election in two towns of the district, but as it did not appear that the votes of all the freemen of those towns could have changed the result, if duly given, the House refused to set aside the election.

§ 120. In the case of *McKune vs. Weller*, (11 *Cal.*, 49,) the question whether a proclamation, giving notice of the holding of a special election, held to fill a vacancy caused by the death of the incumbent, was necessary to the validity of such election, is discussed at length. The authorities upon the subject are there reviewed with care, and the conclusion is reached that there is an important distinction to be observed between general and special elections. The time, place and manner of holding the former being fixed by law, the electors may, and indeed must, take notice of them, and as to such electors the statutory requirement of public notice by proclamation or otherwise, may be regarded as directory only. But it was held that the statute requiring the Governor to issue his proclamation of election *to fill vacancies*, which occur not in the ordinary way, by the expiration of the term, but by death or resignation, before the term expires, is mandatory, and an essential prerequisite to all such elections.

§ 121. In the same case it was further laid down that an election cannot take place without statutory regulation. All the efficacy given to the act of casting a ballot is derived from the law making power and through legislative enactment, and the legislature must provide for and regulate the conduct of an election, or there can be none.

The case, *supra*, was followed in *People vs. Martin*, (12 *Cal.*, 409.)

§ 122. A statute of the State of New York provided that the citizens of the several towns qualified to vote are required annually to assemble and hold town meetings in their respective towns, *at such place in each town, as the electors thereof in their town meeting shall from time to time appoint;* and if at any annual town meeting no place is fixed by the electors for the next annual town meeting, such town meeting shall be held at the place of the last annual town meeting. The electors of the town of Northfield at their annual town meeting in 1847, omitted to fix the place for the annual town meeting in 1848, and by reason of this omission the law fixed the place at the Bull's Head tavern, where the previous annual meeting was held. On the proper day, in 1848, the electors assembled at that place and organized, when a motion was made, in the presence of the electors assembled, "that the annual town meeting for the year 1848 be held at the place aforesaid, until twelve o'clock at noon of that day, and then be adjourned to the house of W. C. Martin, within the town where it shall be held for the remainder of the day." This motion was carried, and the election was accordingly held at the one place until twelve o'clock, and then adjourned to the other, and there held the remainder of the day. The Court of appeals of New York held, not without some hesitancy, that this action was legal. (*The People vs. Martin*, 5 *N. Y.*, 1 *Selden*, 22.) Paige J., in delivering the opinion in this case, says: "I confess that I have had some difficulty in coming to this conclusion, and I think that the power of adjourning a town meeting to another time and place, may, under peculiar circumstances, be oppressively exercised, and lead to a defeat of the popular will. This power ought not to be exercised except in a case of extreme necessity." Under the same statute above referred to, the Supreme Court of N. Y. held that the electors on the town meeting being opened, had a right to adjourn the meeting to the next day, to be held at another place, and that the electors were the exclusive judges of the necessity of the adjournment. (*Goodell vs. Baker*, 8 *Cow.*, 286.) In both these cases, however, the question was upon the construction of a statute, and it is very clear that neither the time nor place of holding an election can be changed after being once legally fixed, unless such change is authorized by statute, and it may also be observed that statutes which authorize an adjournment to another place after the election has been opened, are very objectionable and inexpedient. Some of the electors may not attend in the early part of the day, and may, therefore, have no notice of the change. Statutes ought to be, and generally are provided, to allow a change of the place of opening the polls, or holding an election, in case of necessity, such as might arise from the destruction of the building designated for that purpose, but aside from cases of this kind, adjournments, or changes, are not as a general rule permitted.

§ 123. In a contested election case, very little attention should, ordinarily, be paid to mere irregularities in the proceedings of the election officers, which do not affect the real merits of the case. Thus it was held by the Court of Appeals of New York, in *People* vs. *Cook*, (8, *N. Y.*, 67,) that where the evidence goes only to show an irregularity without fraudulent intent, and by which nobody is injured, the Court is not bound even to submit it to the jury as an open question. The question, in that case, was, whether ballots cast for Benjamin C. Welch jr. and Benjamin Welch, should be counted for Benjamin Welch jr. Evidence was admitted to show the voters' intention, and it was such as to leave no room for doubt, that all these ballots were intended for the latter, and the court, below, instructed the jury to find accordingly. This rule was affirmed in the Appellate Court.

§ 124. And in *Borleau's Case*, tried before the Court of Common Pleas of Philadelphia, it appeared that in the afternoon of the day of election, one of the clerks of the election became so much intoxicated as to be unfit for his duties, and, at the request of the inspectors, one Samuel C. Coxe, acted as clerk for the balance of the day, and until about three o'clock in the morning of the succeeding day, when the clerk, having recovered from his debauch, appeared and signed the returns. Mr. Coxe was not sworn and was a candidate for assessor at this election. *Held*, that these facts were not such as should induce the court to set the election aside, and the ground of the decision was, that the evidence did not disclose any bad faith on the part of the officers, nor any fraud. (2 *Parsons*, 503; *Brightley's Election Cases*, 268.)

§ 125. In the same case, it further appeared, that one John Haines, a candidate for Judge, was occasionally in the room where the election was held, during its progress, and after the polls closed; that he opened a few of the tickets, but being admonished, desisted. Several witnesses testified to his handling tickets and to his intermeddling, and it is clear that his conduct was improper in the extreme. But the Court say that "it has not been pretended that this election is in any particular tainted with actual fraud; no evidence has been adduced either showing legal votes to have been rejected, or illegal votes received; the election seems to have been honestly conducted," and for these reasons the court declined to set it aside.

§ 126. While it is well settled, that mere irregularity on the part of election officers, or their omission to observe some merely directory provisions of the law, will not vitiate the poll, there has been some confusion and conflict as to what we are to understand by irregularities, and as to what provisions of statute are to be regarded as directory and what mandatory. A few remarks upon this subject will be proper in this connection. The language of the statute to be construed must be consulted and followed. If the statute expressly declares any particular act to be essential to the validity of the election, or that its omission shall render the election void, all courts whose duty it is to enforce such statute, must so hold, whether the particular act in question goes to the merits, or affects the result of the election, or not. Such a statute is imperative, and all considerations touching its policy or impolicy, must be addressed to the legislature. But if, as in most cases, the statute simply provides that certain acts or things shall be done, within a particular time, or in a particular manner, and does not declare that their performance is essential to the validity of the election, then they will be regarded as mandatory if they do, and directory if they do not, affect the actual merits of the election.

§ 127. Those provisions which affect the time and place of the election, and the legal qualifications of the electors are generally of the substance of the election, while those touching the recording and return of the legal votes received, and the mode and manner of conducting the mere details of the election, are directory. (*People vs. Schermerhorn*, 19 *Barb.*, 540.) The principle is that irregularities which do not tend to affect results, are not to defeat the will of the majority; the will of the majority is to be respected even when irregularly expressed. (*Juker vs. Commonwealth*, 20 *Penn. St. R.*, 493. *Carpenter's Case*, 2 *Pars.* 540.)

§ 128. The officers of election may be liable to punishment for a violation of the directory provisions of a statute, yet the people are not to suffer on account of the default of their agents. And see, upon this general subject, the following authorities: *Piatt vs. People*, 29 *Ill.*, 72. *Hardenburgh vs. Farmers & Merchants Bank*, 2 *Green*, (*N. J.*,) 68. *Day vs. Kent*, 1 *Oregon*, 123. *Taylor vs. Taylor*, 20 *Minn.*, 107. *People vs. Bates*, 11 *Mich.*, 362. *McKinney vs. O'Connor*, 26 *Texas*, 5. *Jones vs. State*, 1 *Kansas*, 279. *Gorham vs. Campbell*, 2 *Cal.*, 135. *Sprague vs. Norway*, 31 *Cal.*, 173. *Keller vs. Chapman*, 34 *Cal.*, 635. *Brightley's Election Cases*, 448, 449, 450.

§ 129. This doctrine was again recognized, and enforced in the case of *Arnold vs. Lea*, (*Cl. & H.*, 601,)—a case which affords an apt illustration of the rule. In this case it appeared that at one of the voting places, the inspectors who were required by law "to take charge of the ballot box" between the adjournment on the first and the opening of the polls on the second day of the election, delivered it to the sheriff, and directed him to lock it up in some place where it would be safe. The sheriff locked the box up in a trunk, and left the trunk in a storehouse which was also locked. It was clear from the proof that the box was not tampered with, and that no person had been injured by the irregularity, and the House, therefore, refused to reject the vote.

It also appeared that, at one of the precincts, "a large *gourd* was made use of by the inspectors for the reception of the tickets, and upon the closing of the polls on the evening of the first day, the gourd was carefully stopped and tied up in a handkerchief, and delivered to one of the inspectors for safe keeping; that the same was taken by him, to his home, and locked up until next morning, and then returned and used the second day." There was no evidence of fraud or mismanagement in any other way. This was in clear violation of the statute which required that the ballots be "placed in a box which shall be locked or otherwise well secured." It also appeared that some of the officers of the election were not sworn as the law required. But the committee were of the opinion that "notwithstanding some irregularities in conducting the election in a number of precincts," it was "managed by the officers appointed to hold the same, honestly and fairly and impartially, and according to the spirit and meaning of the law of the State of Tennessee, if not strictly within the letter of the statute, and that a fair expression of public opinion has been obtained at the several places referred to," and for these reasons the committee reported against excluding the vote of these precincts, and the house adopted the report.

§ 130. Under the laws of some of the States it is necessary to keep separate boxes for the reception of ballots for State officers, and for members of Congress. In cases where by mistake ballots have been dropped into the wrong box, as, for instance, ballots for a member of Congress placed in the box for State officers, some question has been made as to the right of the judges of the election to correct such mistake by removing such ballots from the wrong box to the right one. In the lower house of Congress it has been held that ballots once deposited in the wrong box were lost, and could not be changed to the right one either by the voter or the officers of the election. (*Washburn vs. Ripley, Clark and Hall*, 679.) But the same question arose again in the House in the more recent case of *Newland vs. Graham*, (1 *Bartlett*, 5.) In that case one of the judges of the election testified that he and the other judges finding that a few ballots had been by mistake placed in the wrong box, had them changed. There was no doubt as to the mistake, nor that the judges acted fairly, and in good faith. The committee submitted to the house the question whether these ballots should be counted,—at the same time, however, intimating very clearly their opinion that they should be. In this case the recommendation of the committee was not adopted by the house—or at least was adopted only in part, the seat being declared vacant while the committee recommended the seating of the contestant.

§ 131. The question, therefore, being unsettled by the decisions of the house, let us inquire what is the safe and sound rule upon the subject. A little reflection will satisfy any one that the doctrine of the report in *Washburn vs. Ripley*, is open to grave objections. In the first place it puts it within the power of a corrupt election officer, to deprive the voter of his ballot, by *designedly* placing it in the wrong box; and, in the second place, it accomplishes the same result, in case the ballot is placed in the wrong box by accident or mistake. It is a rule, well grounded in justice and reason, and well established by authority and precedent, that the voter shall not be deprived of his rights as an elector, either by the fraud or the mistake of the election officer, if it is possible to prevent it. It does not appear from the report in *Washburn vs. Ripley*, that any proof was offered to establish the mistake, beyond the simple fact that the ballots were found in the wrong box. It is evident that the proof should go farther than this. It should be shown that the ballots were handed in by legal voters, and deposited in the wrong box by the mistake, accident, or fraud of the officer, and any facts and circumstances tending to establish, or to disprove this proposition should be brought out in evidence.

§ 132. It is safe to say, that a mistake will always be corrected, if it can be corrected, and therefore, the purpose of the party seeking to get the benefit of ballots cast into the wrong box, should be to prove that they were good and honest ballots and were placed there by mistake, or without his fault. Wherever this is clearly shown, the mistake may be corrected, if not by the officers of the election, at least by the tribunal trying the contest; but, if it is not a clear case of mistake, or if there is any appearance of fraud on the part of the voter, the ballot should be rejected. In other words, the party who, in case of a contest, claims that ballots found in the wrong box should be counted, should be put to the proof that such ballots were fairly and honestly cast by legal voters. It is unjust that the voter should be disfranchised, because the officer receiving his ballot, deposited it in the wrong box. In determining this and similar questions, in cases of contested elections, it should be kept constantly in mind, that the ultimate purpose of the proceeding is to ascertain, and give expression to, the will of the majority, as expressed through the ballot box, and according to law. Rules should be adopted and construed to this end, and to this end only.

§ 133. The view here expressed is fully confirmed by the decision of the Supreme Court of Michigan in *People vs. Bates*, (11 *Mich.*, 362.) In that case it was held that an elector is not to be deprived of his vote either by the mistake or fraud of an inspector, in depositing it in the wrong box, if the intention of the voter can be ascertained with reasonable certainty. Nor should ballots be rejected because of being put in the wrong box by the honest mistake of the voters themselves. In that case a State and city election were both held at the same time and place, under the charge of the same officers, and seven ballots for city officers were found at the closing of the poll in the State box. The circumstances of the case made it, in the opinion of the Court, reasonably certain that these ballots were in good faith put in by electors, and they were accordingly counted.

§ 134. It sometimes happens that the officers of election, though acting in good faith commit errors which will vitiate the election. Thus, if they have adopted an erroneous rule in regard to the qualifications of voters, by which legal voters were excluded, or illegal voters admitted, in numbers sufficient to change, or to render doubtful the result, the election is void, unless there is proof upon which the poll can be purged of illegal votes, and the true result shown. And in such a case, if the erroneous rule affects a class of voters, and it has become generally known to the persons who are excluded by it, they may submit to it, without waiving any rights although they do not present themselves at the polls, and offer their ballots. They have the right to take notice of the decision of the board in other cases precisely like their own. To require each voter belonging to a class of excluded voters to go through the form of presenting his ballot, and having a separate ruling in each case, would be an idle and useless formality. We are to look at the substance, and not the formality.

§ 135. It must be conceded by all, that time and place are of the substance of every election, while many provisions which appertain to the manner of conducting an election, may be directory only. (*Dickey vs. Hulburt*, 5 *Cal.*, 343.) It does not, however, follow that due notice of the time and place of holding an election, is always essential to its validity. Whether it is so or not depends upon the question whether the want of due notice has resulted in depriving any portion of the electors of their rights. In Indiana it was held, that an election for County Auditor was not void by reason of an omission to give public notice that it would take place. (*State vs. Jones*, 19 *Ind.*, 356.) See also *People vs. Cowles*, 13 *N. Y.*, 350. *People vs. Brenham*, 3 *Cal.*, 477. *People vs. Hartwell*, 12 *Mich.*, 508.

§ 136. In the case of *Foster vs. Scarff*, (15 *Ohio, State R.*, 532,) it was held, that where notice was not given, according to law, of an election to fill a vacancy in the office of probate judge, and where it was also apparent that the great body of the voters had in fact no notice, and were not aware that the office was to be filled, and where a small number cast their votes for a single candidate, and no votes were cast for any other, the election was void. But the court (*Brinkerhoff, J*) says: "In deciding this case, however, we do not intend to go beyond the case before us as presented by its own peculiar facts. We do not intend to hold, nor are we of opinion, that the notice by proclamation, as prescribed by law, is *per se*, and in all supposable cases, necessary to the validity of an election; if such were the law, it would always be in the power of a ministerial officer by his malfeasance to prevent a legal election. We have no doubt that where an election is held in other respects, as prescribed by law, and *notice in fact* is brought home to the great body of the electors, though derived through means other than the proclamation which the law prescribes, such election would be valid. But where, as in this case, there was no notice, either by proclamation or in fact, and it is obvious that the great body of electors were misled for want of the official proclamation, its absence becomes such an irregularity as prevents an actual choice by the electors; prevents an actual election in the primary sense of that word, and renders invalid any semblance of an election which may have been attempted by a few, and which must operate, if it operate at all, as a surprise and fraud upon the rights of the many."

§137. It is, of course, more important and essential, that due and regular notice be given of an election to fill a vacancy, than that such notice be given of the regular election provided by law, for the obvious reason, that there is less probability that the electors will be informed of the former without such notification. Accordingly, we find in the decisions of the Courts some conflict as to the validity of a special election to fill a vacancy which is held without the notice provided by law. *In people vs. Cowles* (13 *N. Y.*, 359,) it was held, that in case of the death of a judge of the supreme court after it was too late to give the notice required for filling the vacancy at the next ensuing election, it was competent for the electors to take notice of the vacancy, and to fill it at that election.

§ 138. This case, however, was decided upon the ground that the Constitution of New York required that, in the event of a vacancy in the office of Judge of the Supreme Court, it should be filled "at the next general election of Judges * * * by election for the residue of the unexpired term." And, under this provision, the majority of the Court seemed to be of the opinion that all electors were bound to take notice of a vacancy in that office, without any formal notice, and that such voters as did so, had the right to fill such vacancy, although it occurred but a very short time prior to the election. Such may be the true construction of the Constitution of New York, but ordinarily, and in most, if not in all the other States, there must be either formal notice of the vacancy, and of the time of filling it, or such general notoriety as will amount to notice to the great body of the electors.

§ 139. In Michigan it was held that the default of a clerk in publishing notice of an election to make mention of an existing vacancy, will not invalidate the election, but the decision was put upon the ground that there was in fact such publicity as to amount to notice. (*People* vs. *Hartwell*, 12 *Mich.*, 508.) And see *State* vs. *Orris*, 20 *Wis.*, 235. *State* vs. *Goetz*, (22 *Ibid*, 363.) *State* vs. *Jones*, 19 *Ind.*, 218.

But in Indiana it has been held that an election to fill a vacancy, cannot be held where such vacancy did not occur long enough before the election to enable the proper notice to be given. *Beal* vs. *Ray*, (17 *Ind.*, 554.) And the same point has been repeatedly ruled in California. (*People* vs. *Porter*, 6 *Cal.*, 26. *People* vs. *Weller*, 11 *Ibid*, 49. *People* vs. *Martin*, 12 *Ibid*, 409. *People* vs. *Roseborough*, 14 *Ibid*, 180.)

§ 140. It appears that a statute requiring that the polls shall be opened at sunrise, and kept open until the setting of the sun, is so far directory that before an election can be set aside, because of a deviation from the statute in this respect, it must be shown that legal votes were excluded, or illegal votes received in consequence thereof. [*People vs. Cook*, 8 *N. Y.* 67.] Whether the fact of closing the polls before the hour fixed by statute, or keeping them open after such hour, will of itself vitiate the election, must depend upon the terms of the statute. A slight deviation from the direction of the statute in this respect, will not render void the election, unless it is fraudulent, and operates to deprive legal voters of their rights, or unless the statute in express terms, makes the hour of opening and closing the polls of the essence of the election.

The better opinion seems to be, however, that a *considerable* deviation from the hours fixed by law for keeping open the polls, must render the election void. Thus, in Pennsylvania, it has been determined that where the law required the polls to be kept open until ten o'clock, and they were closed at eight, the election must be set aside. (*Penn. Dist. Election*, 2 *Parsons*, 526.) So also if they be opened at a much later hour than the time prescribed by law, (*Chadwick* vs. *Melvin*, *Brightley's Election Cases*, 251.) And it was at one time held in Ohio that if the polls were closed for any purpose within the hours fixed by law for holding the election, it would render it illegal and void. (*State* vs. *Ritt*, 16 *Am. Law Reg.*, 88.) But this doctrine was overruled in *Fry* vs. *Booth*, (19 *Ohio St. Rep.* 25,) where it was held that the Statute requiring the polls to be kept open between the hours specified during the entire day, was so far directory that to close the polls during the dinner hour does not vitiate the election.

§ 141. Where the polls were kept open after the proper hour for closing, and it appeared that enough votes had been cast after the legal hour for closing the polls to have changed the result, the election was set aside, (*Locust Ward Election*, 4 *Penn. Law Journal*, 341.) In Illinois it has been held, under similar circumstances, that it must be shown affirmatively that votes were received after the proper hour, which *did* change the result, (*Piatt* vs. *People* 29 *Ill.*, 54.)

§ 142. From all the somewhat conflicting authorities upon the subject, the following may be gathered as the governing rules:

1. If the Statute fixing the hours during which the polls shall remain open expressly declares that a failure in this respect shall render the election void, it must be strictly enforced.

2. But in the absence of such a provision in the Statute, it will be regarded as so far directory only, as that, unless the deviation from the legal hours has affected the result, it will be disregarded.

3. If the deviation from the legal hours is great, or even considerable, the presumption will be that it has affected the result, and the burthen will be upon him who seeks to uphold the election, to show affirmatively that it has not. But if the deviation from the legal hours is but slight, the presumption will be that it has not affected the result, and the burthen will be upon him who attacks the validity of the election, to show affirmatively the contrary.

4. If the number of votes illegally cast after the legal hours, and the persons for whom cast can be shown, they may be rejected from the count.

§ 143. A question of great importance arose in the Twenty-Eighth Congress, as to the constitutionality of the second section of "an act for the apportionment of Representatives among the several States, according to the sixth census," approved June 25th, 1842. That section provided as follows:

"That in each case where a State is entitled to more than one Representative, the number to which such State shall be entitled under this apportionment shall be elected *by districts composed of contiguous territory*," &c. The laws in force in many of the States, prior to the passage of this act, provided for the election of Representatives upon a general ticket, to be voted for by the people of the State at large, and the States of New Hampshire, Georgia, Mississippi and Missouri, refused to change their system in obedience to the act of Congress, and elected their Representatives to the Twenty-Eighth Congress in the old way, by a general ticket. The question was as to the power of Congress to abrogate a State law, providing for an election of Representative upon a general ticket, and to require the State to divide its territory into districts, and to choose Representatives by districts. And the decision of this question depended upon the construction of the fourth section of the first article of the Constitution of the United States, which is in these words:

"The times, places and manner of holding elections for Senators and Representatives, shall be prescribed in each State by the legislature thereof, but the Congress may, at any time, by law, make or alter such regulations, except as to the places of choosing Senators."

The majority of the committee of Elections held the second section of the apportionment act, above quoted, to be unconstitutional and void, and this view was ably supported in an elaborate report submitted by Hon. Stephen A. Douglass, of Illinois. (1 *Bartlett*, 47 to 55.) But the contrary view was maintained with scarcely less ability, and in the opinion of the writer of this treatise, with better logic, by the minority of the committee, whose views were presented by Hon. Garrett Davis of Kentucky. (*Ibid*, 55 to 69.) The house did not pass upon the resolutions submitted by the committee, but the members who had been elected in disregard of the act of Congress, upon a general ticket, were allowed to serve out their time. It seems quite clear that the Constitution confers upon Congress power:

1. To *make* regulations concerning the time, place and manner of holding elections for Representatives. This power can be exercised, and was doubtless intended to be exercised, in the absence of any regulations by the State legislature, but the language of the Constitution does not permit us to say that it can only be exercised in the absence of State regulations.

2. To *alter* such regulations as may have been prescribed by the States concerning the true place and manner of holding such elections. This power is legitimately exercised when a regulation requiring representatives to be chosen by the people of a State at large, is so *altered* as to require that such representatives be chosen by districts.

§ 144. The House of Representatives, however, in the more recent case of *Phelps and Cavanaugh of Minnesota*, (1 *Bartlett* 148,) followed the ruling of the majority of the committee in the case last cited, and held that the election of the members by the State at large in disregard of the Act of Congress was valid. The weight of authority, so far as the action of the House is concerned, is therefore in favor of this view, and yet it is manifest that these rulings have been influenced largely by the consideration that to have decided the other way would have left States for the time being unrepresented.

§ 145. In the case of *Brockenbrough* vs. *Cabell*, (1 *Bartlett*, 79,) it was held that where the State law required votes given for a Representative in Congress to be returned to the Secretary of State within thirty days from the day of the election, the Statute was directory only, and that legal votes returned by the proper officers after that day should be counted. The substance of this ruling has since been followed in many cases presenting kindred questions, and the point is well settled. (*Case of John Richards, Cl.& H.* 96. *Spaulding* vs. *Mead, Cl & H.* 157.) And in the case last cited it was distinctly held that, inasmuch as the house is made, by the Constitution, the exclusive judge of the elections and returns, as well as of the qualifications of its own members, the returns from the State authorities must be regarded as *prima facie* evidence only of what they contain, and are not conclusive on the house.

And in *Mallery vs. Merrill*, (*Ibid* 328,) it was held that votes fairly given to a party may be counted in his favor, *though they have never been returned to the proper State authorities,* the failure to make such return not being chargeable upon such party.

§ 146. A statute of New York provided that it should not be lawful for any person "*to contribute money for any purpose intended to promote the election of any particular person or ticket,* except for defraying the expenses of printing, and the circulation of votes, hand bills and other papers, previous to any such election." Under this statute it was held in *Jackson vs. Walker,* (5 *Hill,* 27,) that a contract to pay the plaintiff $1000, for erecting and keeping open a building known as a log cabin for the use of the Whig party during the campaign of 1840, and for the use and benefit of the candidates of that party, was void. The court held that it was not necessary to show fraud, as the statute clearly forbade the contract, by declaring that with two specified exceptions money intended to promote an election shall not be contributed.

§ 147. In *Hurley vs. Van Wagner,* however, (28 *Barbour,* 109,) it was held, under same statute, that an action will lie to recover compensation for services rendered to another, under a contract, in putting up and taking down a tent, used by the employer as a place for holding public meetings of the friends of a particular candidate for the presidency, during a canvass preceding a presidential election. And in this latter case the Court expressed the opinion that the ruling in *Jackson vs. Walker,* went too far and could not be reconciled with the spirit or the letter of the statute, of which it is an exposition. The true rule, independent of any statute, doubtless, is, that all contracts entered into for the purpose of improperly or corruptly influencing the voters at an election are void, because against public policy.

§ 148. The giving, or offering to give facilities for the public convenience of the whole county, as an inducement to remove a county seat, or the offering of a public advantage to an entire community as an inducement for the members of such community to vote for such removal, does not constitute bribery, and will not avoid an election held to decide the question of such removal. (*Dishon vs. Smith*, 10 *Iowa*, 212.)

§ 149. It is now well settled that a wager upon the result of an election is wholly void as being contrary to public policy, and that no action can be maintained for its recovery. [*Loyal vs. Myers*, 1 *Bailey*, 486.] In a few of the older English cases actions upon wagers were allowed to be maintained. [*Andrews vs. Herne*, 1 *Lev.* 33. *DeCosta vs. Jones*, *Cowp.* 729, *Lord March vs. Pegot*, 5 *Burr.*, 2802.] In none of these early cases, however, was the question of the immoral tendency of such transactions raised or considered. [16 *East* 158, *do* 162.] The more recent decisions in Great Britain, show a great desire and tendency, on the part of the judges, to get rid of the rule thus inadvertently adopted by their predecessors, and they show how much the more enlightened jurists of a later period, have been trammeled by it. They have endeavored to make a distinction between those wagers the subject matter of which is perfectly innocent, and those in which it is not; and they seek to apply the early decisions sustaining the validity of a wager to those cases, where the subject matter is of the former kind. But they forget that it is the *wager* itself which is immoral, and can never be innocent, and that therefore the subject matter of the bet can make no difference, in its moral quality.

§ 150. But in this country the decisions are uniform, and all adverse to the validity of any bet or wager of any kind or character whatever. [*Bunn vs. Riker*, 4 *Johns*, 426. *Lansing vs. Lansing*, 8 *do*, 454. *Vischer vs. Yates*, 11 *do*, 28. *Smyth vs. Mc Masters*, 2 *P. A. Browne*, 182.] And in *Lansing* vs. *Lansing*, the Court held that if the loser had given his negotiable note for the amount of the wager the invalidity of the contract was a good defense against the indorsee of the note. But in that case the indorser of the note took it with notice, and the question as to the rights of an innocent purchaser of such paper is not considered. Where the amount of the wager has been deposited with a third party as stakeholder, an action will lie against him by the loser to recover back the amount of the deposit. [*Vischer* vs. *Yates*, *supra*.] And see also *Johnson* vs. *Russell*, [37 *Cal.*, 670.] *Reynolds* vs. *McKinney*, [4 *Kansas*, 94.] *Jennings* vs. *Reynolds*, [*Ibid.*, 101.]

In Illinois it is held that if a negotiable note be given for an illegal wager, the illegality of the consideration is no defense to a suit by an indorsee for value. [*Adams* vs. *Woodbridge*, 4 *Ill.*, 255. *Sherlty* vs. *Howard*, 3 *Chicago Legal News*, 230. *Gregory* vs. *King*, *Ibid.*, 349.] And there seems to be no reason to doubt the correctness of these decisions.

§ 151. In case a foreign state is acquired or annexed to the United States, it does not come to us with its political organization *intact*, but upon the acquisition, it is incumbent upon the United States to establish a government for such state. Hence, it was held upon this ground, that the territory of New Mexico, which had been a duly organized territory of the Mexican Republic, could not, upon being acquired by the United States, proceed to elect a delegate to Congress in advance of the establishment of a territorial government therein. [Case of *Hugh N. Smith*, 1 *Bartlett*, 107.] The same rule would doubtless apply to any territory of the United States, and an act of Congress organizing the territory, and authorizing the inhabitants to choose a delegate, will, in all cases, be held indispensable to the validity of an election for delegate in Congress. See also case of *A. W. Babbitt, of Deseret*, [1 *Bart.*, 116.] *Case of W. S, Messervy*, [*ibid.* 148].

§ 152. There has been of late years much earnest discussion in the courts of this country as to what questions may be submitted to a popular vote. It is a well settled principle that legislative power cannot be delegated or transferred from the legislature to the people at large. Our governments are republican and not democratic. Laws must be enacted by the representatives of the people, and not by the people themselves. Nor can any State change this. Every State must have a "republican form of government,"—this is the requirement of the National Constitution, and it is complied with only by that form of State Government which vests the law-making power in the representatives of the people.—[*Rice vs. Foster*, 4 *Harrington* (*Del.*) 479. *Brightley's Election Cases* 3. *Parker vs. Commonwealth*, 6

Pa. State R. 507. *Barto vs. Himrod,* 8 *N. Y.* 483. *Cincinnati, Wilmington & Zanesville R. R. Co. vs. Commissioners,* 1 *Ohio State R.,* 84. *Geebrick vs. State,* 5 *Iowa,* 491.] See also authorities cited in note to case of *Rice vs. Foster, Brightley's Election Cases,* 24.

§ 153. While the correctness of the general rule above stated is not questioned by any of the authorities, there is a conflict among them as to its application to a species of legislation now becoming very common in this country. In several of the States acts have been passed to confer upon the voters of cities or municipalities the power to decide, by ballot, whether the sale of intoxicating liquors shall be licensed or not. In several of the cases above cited, acts of this character are held to be unconstitutional and void. Such is the ruling in Delaware, Pennsylvania and Iowa. In the latter State, however, the decision is put, partly, upon the ground that all laws are required, by the Constitution to "have a uniform operation," and, inasmuch as some towns or cities might adopt license, and others vote it down, the operation of the law was held not to be uniform. (*c*) But on the other hand, there are decisions holding laws of this character to be valid. Of this class is *Hammond vs. Haines,* 25 *Maryland,* 541. *State vs. Noyes* 10 *Fost.* (*N. H.*) 279. *State vs. O'Neall,* 24 *Wis.* 149.

(*c.*) The act of the legislature of Iowa held to be unconstitutional, was peculiar. It was not only a "local option" law, but it declared that a previous act prohibiting the sale of intoxicating liquors, should not be "repealed in any county of the State, unless the people of such county shall by vote" adopt license. So that the act not only authorized the people of a county to grant license by a popular vote, but also undertook to authorize them to repeal, as to such county, a previous act which the legislature did not in terms repeal.

These cases proceed upon the theory that the legislation referred to, does not vest the law-making power in the people at large, but only confers upon cities or municipalities such powers as may properly be conferred by legislative act. It is enough to say here, that in every case the real question is, does the act in question attempt to confer upon the people at large, the power to make laws, or the power to say whether or not an act of the legislature shall have the force of law? If it does plainly attempt to do this, it is null and void. Upon this general subject the reader is referred to the following authorities, in addition to those already cited: *State vs. Morris, Common Pleas, Am. Law Reg. Vol.* 12, *page* 32, (*new series.*) *State vs. Parker*, 26 *Vt.*, 356. And see, also, an able discussion of the subject in *American Law Register, vol.* 11, *page* 129, (*new series.*)

§ 155. We have seen in another connection that a certificate of election which shows that it is based upon a partial canvass, is fatally defective, because a full canvass might show a different result. A similar rule is sometimes applied to the return from a county which embraces a number of precincts or voting places. Thus in *Niblack vs. Walls*, 42*d Congress*, a county return was rejected, because the county canvassers rejected the vote of three precincts, and counted that of two only. Each party was required to prove his vote by evidence other than the return.

§ 156. In the same case it was held that a return which showed one hundred and fifty two votes for Niblack, and none for Walls, might be impeached by parol proof that forty-two votes were in fact cast and counted out for the latter. And the committee refused to allow Mr. Niblack the votes shown by the return, and to Mr. Walls the forty-two votes shown by evidence *aliunde* to have been cast for him. On this point the committee said:

"It is suggested by counsel that we might allow the one hundred and fifty-two votes which, according to this return, were cast for contestant, and also allow the sitting member the forty-two votes which are shown to have been cast for him and not returned. But the committee hold, that it having been shown that the return is fraudulent and false, in a matter so material as the suppression altogether of the whole of the sitting member's vote, it cannot be received for any purpose."

§ 157. And in the same case the returns from Manitee county were objected to, for the following reason:

"Because the returns made by the county board, which, by the statute, are required to be duplicates, are not such. One return states that the board met and canvassed the votes "on the 29th day of November, 1870," while the other states that the board met and canvassed the vote "on the 1st day of December, 1870," and the former is dated November 29, and the latter December 1."

But this objection was overruled, the committee being of the opinion that the difference of one day between the dates of the two papers was not material.

§ 158. We have stated in another connection the rule, that where a certificate is by law required to be made by a board of officers composed of three or more persons, it is sufficient if a majority of such board join in such certificate. But it was held in *Niblack vs. Walls*, *supra*, that if less than the majority sign, the certificate is not good. Upon this point the committee say:

"The statute of Florida requires that the returns shall be signed by the judge of the county court, the clerk of the circuit court, and one justice of the peace.

The return from this county, relied upon as proof of the vote of the county, is signed by but one of these three officers, the county judge.

The committee are of opinion that where the law requires the certificate to be made by three officers, a majority at least must sign, to make the certificate evidence.

This is not a merely technical rule; it is substantial, because the refusal or failure of a majority of the board to sign the return raises a presumption that it is not correct.

It is fair to infer that if it had been free from objection, a majority of the board at least would have signed it.

It is enough, however, to say that the law requires the certificate of the three officers, and all the authorities agree that at least two must certify or the certificate is inadmissible."

§ 159. A statute providing that two ballot boxes be kept at each poll, one for the reception of ballots for representative in Congress, and the other for the reception of ballots for state officers, was held to be directory only, in the case of *Boyden vs. Shober*, [2

Bartlett, 904,] in which case the report of the committee has this language:

"It is said that the law of North Carolina, rightly construed, required that two ballot boxes should have been kept at each poll, and that all ballots for members of Congress should have been deposited in one, and all ballots for electors for President and Vice President in the other.

"There seems to be some doubt as to the true construction of the statute of North Carolina, but assuming that the construction contended for by contestant is correct, we are of opinion that the statute is directory only, and that the failure to provide two ballot boxes, and the deposit of all the ballots in one box, did not render the election void, in the absence of fraud. If the ballots were freely cast, if they were honestly and fairly counted, and correctly returned, we should be unwilling to hold that a mere mistake of the election officers, as to whether the ballots should go into one box or two, should be allowed to defeat the will of the majority."

§ 160. In most of the States the law requires that county returns shall be forwarded to the secretary of State, by mail. The question has been raised whether under such a statute a return can be received and counted if sent by private conveyance. In *Niblack vs. Walls*, 42*d Congress*, the return from one of the counties which should have been sent by mail, was not only forwarded by private conveyance, but was addressed to, and received by, one of the candidates, and by him handed to the secretary of State. Under these circumstances the house ordered further evidence to be produced to show the true state of the poll. And in *Chavis vs. Clever*, (2 *Bartlett*, 469,) it appeared that the statute required returns to be sent to the secretary of State "by special messenger." This provision of the statute was violated, and the return delivered to one Moore, an army sutler, and by him sent, *by express*, to the Governor of the territory, who delivered it to the secretary. These facts, together with some evidence, tending to show that the return was tampered with on the way, were deemed sufficient to exclude it. If, however, it be made to appear on the trial of a contested election case, that a return which has been sent in, in an irregular and unlawful way, has not been tampered with but is in fact the genuine return without alteration or amendment, duly signed and certified, it will not be rejected, because of its irregular transmission. It is the policy of the law to discountenance everything which affords an opportunity for evil-disposed persons to tamper with ballot boxes or returns, and for this reason the sound rule would probably be to require proof of the genuineness of all such returns as are transmitted through private, and unauthorized channels.

§ 161. The legislature of a State having once elected a Senator in Congress, cannot reconsider its action and elect another person afterwards. The moment the result is declared and the certificate of election signed, jurisdiction passes from the State legislature to the Senate of the United States, which latter body is to judge of all questions touching the election returns and qualifications of its members. On the 19th of January, 1833, Mr. Robbins was elected a senator from Rhode Island, for the term of six years from March 4, 1834. His credentials were in due form. In October, 1833, the General Assembly of Rhode Island undertook to set aside this election, and to elect Mr. Potter, Senator, alleging that the body which had elected Mr. Robbins was not the legislature of Rhode Island. It was held, after much debate, that Mr. Robbins held the proper *prima facie* evidence of title to the seat, his credentials being in due form and of prior date to those of Mr. Potter, and he was accordingly sworn in pending the investigation. Mr. Robbins was ultimately confirmed in his seat. *Potter* vs. *Robbins*, (*Cl. & H.*, 877.) Where, however, two bodies, each claiming to be the legislature of a State, have each chosen a Senator in Congress to represent such State, it is the duty of the Senate, in deciding between such claimants, to consider and determine which body was, in fact and in law, the legislature. (*Spencer's case*, 43*d Congress*.)

§ 162. A statute of Virginia in force in 1832, authorized the sheriff, in case the electors were so numerous that all could not be polled before sunsetting, or in case by rain, or the rising of water courses, many of the electors are hindered from attending, to adjourn the election "*until the next day*, and *so from day to day*, *for three days*, Sundays excluded, giving public notice thereof, by proclamation," &c. Under this provision it was contended that the polls might be adjourned from day to day, for three days, and that the first day is to be excluded in computing the three days. But it was held otherwise, the committee being of the opinion that the election could not be kept open for any purpose more than three days. Votes cast on the *fourth* day after an adjournment from the third, were accordingly excluded. [*Draper* vs. *Johnston*, *Cl. & H.*, 702.] It was also held in the same case that as to the regularity of the appointment of election officers, it is sufficient that they acted under color of authority, and that no other persons claimed the right.

§ 163. Under a statute requiring that separate boxes shall be kept for the deposit of ballots for State officers and for members of Congress, the voter must hand in both his tickets at one and the same time, and having once voted for State officers, and been recorded as voting, he cannot afterwards come forward and claim the right to vote for representative in Congress. [*Draper* vs. *Johnson*, *Cl. & H.*, 711.]

In the same case, it was held that the presumption is that the officers of election have taken the oath required by law, until the contrary is shown. We have elsewhere endeavored to show that the ruling in this case, and in some others, that a failure to take the oath required by law to be taken by officers of the election, of itself, vitiates the election, is erroneous.

§ 164. The manner of electing United States Senators is, in the absence of congressional action, to be prescribed in each State by the legislature thereof. A rule adopted by such a legislature, providing that "a majority of all the members elect composing the two houses of the general assembly, shall be necessary to determine all elections devolving upon that body" is a legitimate exercise of its power to regulate the manner of such elections. And under this rule, where there were twenty-nine votes cast in the joint convention for David L. Yulee, and twenty-nine blank, it was held that there was no election. [*Yulee* vs. *Mallory*, 1 *Bartlett*, 608.]

§ 165. Under that clause of the constitution providing that senators may be "chosen by the legislature" of each State, an election of senator, to be valid, must be participated in by both houses of the legislature in their organized capacity. It is not enough that a majority of the members of each should participate. [*Case of Harlan*, 1 *Bartlett*, 621. *Case of Bright and Fitch*, *do*. 629.]

§ 166. In accordance with the rule, that the errors of a returning officer shall not prejudice the rights of innocent parties, it has been held that where it was the duty of the presiding officer to return the votes, *sealed up*, a return of them, *unsealed*, in the absence of any proof or suspicion of fraud is good. Also, that where the statute prescribes the form of a certificate of the votes given to be executed by an officer of the election, it is sufficient if the certificate is substantially according to such form, and a literal following of the form is not required. Also, that if the presiding officer, by mistake, insert the wrong name in his return of persons voted for, the error may be corrected. (*Mallory vs. Merrill*, *Cl. & H.*, 329.) And in same case it was held that votes fairly given and not returned at all, may be proven and allowed. And see also *Colden vs. Sharpe*, (*Cl. & H.*, 369.)

§ 167. The same principle was recognized and enforced by the house of Representatives of the United States in *Root* vs. *Adams*, (*Cl. & H.*, 271,) where it was held that the error of a clerk in incorrectly spelling the name of one of the candidates in making the return of the election, should be corrected by the house as soon as ascertained. And when, by such correction, it was made apparent that the contestant had a majority of the legal votes, he was admitted to the seat.

§ 168. And in *Guyon* vs. *Sage*, (*Cl. & H.*, 348) the house corrected a mistake in the inspectors, return, by which the word "junior" was omitted when it ought to have been inserted. There are, of course, two kinds of errors and mistakes, which may occur in making up the returns of an election, viz; such as may be corrected from what appears upon the face of the record, without a resort to extrinsic evidence, and such as cannot be so amended. In the case of a mistake of the former kind, it may be corrected by the court or tribunal trying the contest, as soon as discovered; but if a mistake occur which cannot be corrected by the record,—that is to say—one which is not apparent upon the face of the record, evidence *aliunde* is admissible, and should always be resorted to to correct it, and to establish the very truth of the matter.

§ 169. In the case of *Sundry Citizens vs. John Sargeant*, (*Cl. & H.*, 516,) it appeared that at the election in the second congressional district of Pennsylvania, in October, 1826, John Sargeant and Henry Horn had the highest and an equal number of votes. The Governor of Pennsylvania seems to have considered the result as leaving the office vacant, but did not issue writs for a new election until Messrs. Sargeant and Horn had each informed him in writing that they released all claim to the seat. Thereupon a new election was ordered, and at that election Mr. Sargeant was duly chosen. Subsequently certain citizens petitioned the house to give the seat to Mr. Horn, on the ground that he was in fact chosen at the first election. But it was held that he had waived his claims, and voluntarily relinquished his rights, whatever they may have been, under the first election. (*d.*)

§ 170. The case of *Reed vs. Corden*, (*Cl. & H.*, 353,) presented the important question whether a State has the constitutional power to provide, that in case of a tie between two candidates for Representative in Congress, the question which of the two shall be the Representative, may be determined by lot. It was held that the statute of Maryland, authorizing the Governor and Council, in such a case, to proceed to decide by lot, which of the two shall receive the certificate, and be entitled to the seat, was unwarranted by the constitution, and that the record of such a decision was not admissible in evidence. This decision was put upon two grounds,

1. That the house of Representative is composed of members chosen every second year, by the *people* of the United States, and that the law of Maryland in effect gave the choice to the Governor and Council of that State, in case of a tie, and

2. That the house being by the Constitution "the judge of the election returns, and qualifications of its own members," it can never sanction the doctrine

(*d.*) But it is very doubtful whether the relinquishment of claim to the seat here referred to should have been regarded as either legal or binding. The *constituency* were chiefly interested, and they were not consulted.

that any State can confer upon any officer or tribunal, power to decide a question of this kind. The committee seemed to be of opinion that in case of a tie, there is no election by the people, and no certificate of election should be given by the State authorities to any one, and this is doubtless the correct rule. The Representative must be chosen by the people. If an equal number of votes are given to each candidate, there is no choice, and the only remedy is in a new election.

§ 171. The failure or refusal of the proper officer to issue a certificate of election to a person duly elected to an office, cannot operate to deprive such person of his rights. The certificate or commission is the best, but not the only evidence of an election, and if that be refused, secondary evidence is admissible. (*Richard's case, Cl. & H.*, 95.) Where, therefore, the Governor of Tennessee claiming that the State had seceded from the Union, refused to certify the result of an election for Representatives in the Congress of the United States, it was held that other proof of such election was admissible, and that the house being satisfied from such proof that claimant was elected, he should be admitted. (*Clement's Case*, 1 *Bartlett*, 266.)

§ 172. When the people of an organized territory have been empowered by Congress to form a Constitution preparatory to admission into the Union, they may, in anticipation of such admission, elect representatives in Congress, who, in the event of the admission of such territory as a State, will be entitled to their seats. The act of admission relates back to, and legalizes every act of the territorial authorities exercised in pursuance of the enabling act. (*Case of Phelps and Cavanaugh of Minnesota*, 1 *Bartlett*, 248.) But if the territory is not organized at the time of the holding of an election for delegate, the same is void. (*Case of J. S. Casement*, 2 *Bartlett* 516.)

§ 173. Whether, when a State government is formed of a part of an organized territory, the remainder of such territory continues to enjoy the benefits of the original territorial organization, and among them the right to be represented in Congress by a delegate, seems to be an unsettled question. In *Fuller vs. Kingsbury*, (1 *Bartlett* 251,) the house held against the report of the majority of the committee, that upon the admission of the State of Minnesota, the territory of Minnesota ceased to be, and that so much of the territory as lay outside the limits of the State, was left without any legally organized government, and that the people thereof were not entitled to elect a delegate in Congress until that right was conferred upon them by Statute. And this ruling would seem to accord with reason, and yet it appears that the opposite rule was adopted in the case of *Paul Fearing* of Ohio Territory in 1802, and in the case of *Henry H. Sibley* of Wisconsin Territory in 1848. (See report of majority of committee in *Fuller vs. Kingsbury*, 2 *Bartlett*, 253.) There may be a distinction between a case where the territory is very large and a State is formed out of it, leaving yet a large territory and considerable population within the original territorial limits, and one where the State when formed embraces the principal part of the territory and its population, and this may explain the apparent conflict.

§ 174. In *Chrisman vs. Anderson*, (1 *Bartlett*, 328,) it was held to be the duty of the house of Representatives in the investigation of an election contest to go behind all certificates for the purpose of correcting mistakes brought to its notice. In the same case however it was held that a return not signed or certified by any of the officers of the election, was not admissible, and the same point was held in *Barnes* vs. *Adams*. (2 *Bartlett*, 760.) It is the duty of the party seeking to avail himself of a vote which is not legally certified or returned, to make the necessary proof to supply the place of the usual formal certificate and return, and if he fails to do so, such vote cannot of course be received.

§ 175. Where the Statute directed the returns of an election for representatives in Congress to be filed with the County Judge, and an abstract forwarded to the Secretary of State, and the County officers mistaking their duty forwarded the original returns to the Secretary of State, it was held that this did not vitiate the election, or furnish proper ground for throwing out the vote of the entire county. In the absence of fraud, an irregularity of this character, not affecting the result in any way, cannot be regarded as sufficient cause for rejecting the vote of a county, or even of a voting precinct. (*Bennett* vs. *Chapman*, 1 *Bartlett*, 204,) and see also *Clark* vs. *Hall*, (*Ibid.* 215.) The Statute in question clearly belonged to that class of statutory provisions concerning the conduct of elections, which are directory merely.

§ 176. It was held by the House of Representatives of the United States, after a long and able discussion, that where the legislature of a State has failed to provide the time, place and manner of holding an election to fill a vacancy occurring in the house; that the Governor of such State, upon being informed of the vacancy, may issue a writ of election, and therein fix the time and places of holding such election. [*Case of John Hoge, of Penn. Cl. & H.*, 135.] The power given to the Governor, by the second section of the first article of the Constitution, to issue writs of election to fill vacancies, carries with it the power to fix the times and places of holding such election in cases where such times and places are not fixed by law.

It is of course desirable and indeed necessary, that proclamation be made of such election, or that it appear that it was generally known for a reasonable length of time, though in the case just referred to it was held, that a very short notice (only two or three days) was sufficient, when it appeared that the election was fixed for the same day as the election for President and Vice President of the United States, and where it was evident that the great mass of the electors were in fact apprised of it, and participated in it.

§ 177. If a case should arise where no authority, either State or federal, has fixed either the time or place of electing a Representative in Congress, no election could be legally held. And yet, if, in such an event, the electors, by common consent should come together and choose a Representative, the house might validate their action, and admit their chosen Representative. Such action would be within the power, and therefore, within the discretion of the house.

§ 178. But whether a *military* Governor may, under any circumstances, order or fix the time of an election for Representatives in Congress, has been much discussed. The better opinion seems to be that if the government of a State has been disorganized by insurrection and rebellion, or otherwise, so that there are no State officials, and can be none until an election occurs, the United States may take military control of the territory of such State, and appoint a military Governor, who may perform such acts as may be required of the executive of such State, as a prerequisite to the holding of an election. The reason for this doctrine was thus stated by the report of the committee of elections in the *Louisiana case*, in the 37th Congress, (1 *Bartlett*, 446,) and again repeated in case of *M. F. Bonzano*, (2 *Bartlett*, 1,) as follows:

"Representation is one of the very essentials of a republican form of government, and no one doubts that the United States cannot fulfill this obligation without guaranteeing that representation here. It was in fulfillment of this obligation that the army of the Union entered New Orleans, drove out the rebel usurpation, and restored to the discharge of its appropriate functions, the civil authority there. Its work is not ended till there is representation here. It cannot secure that representation through the aid of a rebel Governor. Hence the necessity for a military Governor to discharge such functions, both military and civil, which necessity imposes in the interim between the absolute reign of rebellion and the complete restoration of law. Suppose Governor Moore to be the only traitor in Louisiana;

one of two things must take place: the people must remain unrepresented, or some one must *assume* to fix a time to hold these elections. Which alternative approaches nearest to republicanism, nearest to the fulfillment of our obligations to guarantee a republican form of government to that people—closing the door of representation, or recognizing as valid the time fixed by the military Governor? Are this people to wait for representation here till their rebel Governor returns to his loyalty and appoints a day for an election, or is the government to guarantee that representation as best it may? The committee cannot distinguish between this act of the military Governor, and the many civil functions he is performing every day, acquiesced in by everybody. To pronounce this illegal, and refuse to recognize it, is to pronounce his whole administration void and a usurpation. But necessity put him there and keeps him there."

§ 179. In the case of Jared Perkins of New Hampshire, (1 *Bartlett*, 142,) the following facts appeared: On the second day of July, 1846, the State of New Hampshire was divided by an act of her legislature into four Congressional districts, and in March, 1849, a representative in Congress was chosen from each of said districts, and the gentlemen so chosen took their seats as members of the 31st Congress. In July, 1850, by another act of the legislature, said State was re-districted, and the boundaries of the several districts changed. In September, 1850, Hon. James Wilson, who was the representative from the *old* third district, resigned. A vacancy having been thus created, the Governor ordered an election to be held by the *new* third district to fill it. At this election Mr. Perkins was chosen. There was a majority report from the committee of Elections in his favor, and after debate in the house he was admitted to the seat by the very close vote of 98 to 90. There are grave reasons for questioning the soundness of this decision. Let us suppose, for example, that after an election by a district, it is divided into two equal parts, and one-half placed in one new district and the other half in another. If under these circumstances a vacancy occurs, by which of the new districts shall it be filled? Or we may suppose that the territory composing a district may be distributed among three, four, or half-a-dozen new ones. In such cases there is no sound principle upon which to determine which, if any, of the new districts shall fill a vacancy which may occur from the old. The true rule, therefore, must be that a district once created, and having elected a representative in Congress, should be allowed to continue *intact* for the purpose of filling any vacancy which may occur, until the end of the Congress in which it is represented. And if a State legislature shall abolish such district after it has elected its representative, and shall make no provision for filling a vacancy, it may, in the event of a vacancy, be obliged to go unrepresented for the time being.

§ 180. The case of Jared Perkins, *supra*, was expressly overruled in the more recent case of *Hunt* vs. *Menard*, (2 *Bartlett*, 477.) In this latter case the committee said:

"The act of the legislature of Louisiana of August 22, 1868, making a new division of the State into its five congressional districts, by its terms, purports to repeal all laws and parts of laws in conflict with said act, but is silent on the subject of vacancies that might occur in the districts as then existing.

"The language of the minority report in the case of Perkins on the New Hampshire statute, is appropriate on this point as well as on this case generally, and we quote from it as follows:

"It does not purport to provide for any method of filling vacancies that might occur in the future, and, beyond all question, it was understood as providing only for the election of members of future Congresses. Such are the terms of the act, and such must also be its spirit. A vacancy in the house of Representatives is the occurrence of an event by which a portion of the people are left unrepresented, and the filling of that vacancy is directed by the Constitution in such explicit language as requires no aid from State enactments to perfect the right. The second section of the first article in the Constitution contains the following provision: "When vacancies occur in the representation from any State, the executive authority thereof shall issue writs of election to fill such vacancies." This is the only provision of law on the subject of vacancies, and it is ample and sufficient. No act of the legislature of New Hampshire purports to interfere in the matter, and the act of July ought not, in our belief, to be understood as requiring the vacancy occasioned by General Wilson's resignation to be filled by any other people than those whose representative he was. Had such been the purpose of the act, we believe it was incompetent for the law-making power of that State to accomplish the object while this House hold the right to judge of the election of its members.

"It would not be preservation of the purity of the elective franchise, nor would it be a just guardianship of the republican principle that all shall have a right to be represented, to admit the power of a State legislature to provide that a portion of the people should have two representatives in Congress, while another portion should have none, or not be represented by the man of their choice. * * * It is, besides, in disregard of the law of Congress of June, 1842, which declares that no one district shall be entitled to two representatives. If the people who choose a representative are not entitled to fill the vacancy happening by his resignation, it is impossible to tell what portion of the population may most properly exercise this privilege. It seems to be assumed in this case that the new district made by the act of July 11, 1850, and numbered three, has the right to send a representative in place of General Wilson because the number corresponds with that which General Wilson represented. But the order of numbering is an unimportant circumstance, and the first or the fourth district might have been as properly called the third as any other; yet it would be a strange assertion that, on this account, such district would be authorized to have two representatives during the remainder of the thirty-first Congress."

"This reasoning, which your committee consider as sound and pertinent, applied to the case under consideration seems to be conclusive against this election; and it may also be added that whatever power a State legislature may have in the matter, it is absurd to say that a district when once established and a representative chosen therein, is not to continue for the whole Congress, for which the election has once been operative. No election to fill the vacancy caused by the death of Mr. Mann, appears to have been notified or held in the whole of said district as represented by him."

§ 181. A statute of Kentucky required all votes to be given in the *presence* of the high sheriff of the county or his deputy. In *Letcher vs. Moore*, (*Cl. & H.*, 843,) it appeared that at one of the polls both the high sheriff and his deputy were absent for several hours. The sheriff had been called away by sickness in his family, and after he left, and before the arrival of his deputy, a number of votes were cast by legal voters. The only objection to these votes was that they were not given in the presence of the sheriff or his deputy. A majority of the committee reported in favor of rejecting these votes, but the House, upon principles perfectly sound, reversed this decision, and ordered the votes to be counted. The House in the same case overruled the decision of the committee rejecting certain votes otherwise legal, for the reason that they were cast while one of the judges of the election was not present, and while one Moses Grant was acting under an illegal appointment by the sheriff.

§ 182. In *Marshall vs. Kews*, (2 *Swan*, 68,) it appeared that two men were candidates for the office of Circuit Court Clerk, that the majority for one of them as shown by the returns, was three votes only; and that at one precinct some twenty voters were deprived of their right to vote, by a failure to open the polls. Under this state of facts the election was declared void, because it was impossible to know whether the successful candidate would have been elected upon a full expression of choice by all who desired and were entitled to vote.

But in a subsequent case in the same State (1 *Sneed*, 693,) it was held that an election should not be set aside upon a showing that in "one precinct no election whatever was opened and held," without a further showing that the result of the election was affected thereby.

§ 183. Where a statute requires a question to be decided, or an officer to be chosen, by the votes of "a majority of the voters of a county," this does not require that a majority of all persons in the county entitled to vote shall actually vote affirmatively, but only that the result shall be decided by the majority of the votes cast, provided always that there is a fair election, and an equal opportunity for all to participate. In such a case the only proper test of the number of persons entitled to vote is the result of the election as determined by the ballot box, and the Courts will not go outside of that to inquire whether there were other persons entitled to vote who did not do so. The "voters of the county" referred to by all such statutes are necessarily the voters who vote at the election, since the result in each case must be determined by a count of the ballots cast, and not by an inquiry as to the number not cast. This doctrine is well settled by the authorities. (*People vs. Warfield*, 20 *Illinois*, 163. *People vs. Gamer*, 47 *Ill.*, 246. *People vs. Wiant*, 48 *Ill.*, 263. *Railroad Co. vs. Davidson Co.*, 1 *Sneed* 692. *Augell*

& Ames on Corp., *9th Ed.*, *Secs.* 499–500. *Bridgeport vs. Railroad*, 15 *Conn.*, 475. *Talbot vs. Dent.*, 9 *B. Monroe*, 526. *State vs. The Mayor*, 37 *Mo.*, 272. *St. Joseph Township vs. Rogers*, 16 *Wallace*, 644.)

§ 184. Where the managers of an election are clearly shown to have committed a fraud in the conduct of the election, or the counting or returning of the votes, and where the effect of the fraud discovered, does not affect or change the result, it is a grave question whether the result should not be the rejection of the return *in toto*. In *Judkins vs. Hill*, [50 *N. H.*, 140,] it appeared that there were declared as cast at one of the precincts, twenty seven more votes for county Commissioner than were marked on the check list. The Court said "if from the fact of this discrepancy, the Court ought to find that it was the result of fraud in the managers of the election, the Court would hesitate long to count any of the votes cast at an election so tainted, on the ground that with such proof of fraudulent, and corrupt purposes, no confidence could be entertained in coming to any reliable conclusion, as to what votes were actually given." And the safe rule probably is that where an election board are found to have wilfully and deliberately committed a fraud, even though it affect a number of votes too small to change the result, it is sufficient to destroy all confidence in their official acts, and to put the party claiming anything under the election conducted by them, to the proof of his votes, by evidence, other than the return.

§ 185. It was, however, decided in the case last cited, that no inference of fraud can fairly be drawn from the single fact that the votes declared, exceeded by twenty-seven, the number of persons marked on the check list as having voted. This discrepancy, the Court say, might have resulted from a failure to check all the names of persons voting; or from double voting without the knowledge of the board; or from a mistake in counting, and in either case the board may have acted in good faith. The presumption is that an election is honestly conducted, and the burthen of proof to show it otherwise, is on the party assailing the return. What we mean here to assert, is only this, that where a return is clearly shown to be wilfully and corruptly false, in any material part, the whole of it becomes worthless as proof. For if false and corrupt in one part, it may be in others, and all faith in its reliability is destroyed. In such a case, however, it must not be assumed that the *election* is necessarily void. If satisfactory proof of the actual vote can be made, and the result thus ascertained, the election may stand, although the return falls to the ground.

§ 186. A statute providing for a special election to be called on ten days notice, will be construed as not coming within the provisions of a previously enacted registry law, for the reason that it would be impossible to make the registry, give the statutory notice, and revise the lists within ten days. Such at least, was the ruling in Illinois in the case of *People vs. Ohio Grove,* [51 *Ill.*, 191,] and it is probable that under the provisions of none of the registry acts in this country, could a registration be legally perfected within so short a period. Of course, where a registry act is by its terms to be applied to all elections by the people, it must be applied to an election subsequently authorized, unless the act authorizing such subsequent election contains provisions which make it impracticable so to apply it, in which case the subsequent act must stand and be held as modifying the registration act.

§ 187. It sometimes happens that a statute is passed providing that a particular officer named shall be chosen each year, "at the general election," without further provision as to the time. In most, and it is presumed in all the States, the time for holding the general election, is fixed by a constitutional provision, and there can be no room for doubt but that a statute fixing the election of an officer "at the general election," should be construed to mean on whatever day the proper authority may fix as the day for that election. And hence, if, after the passage of such an act, the time for holding the general election is changed, the time for holding the election of the particular officer named would be changed with it. The purpose of selecting the day of the general election in such cases, is not to select a *particular* day of the month or year, but to provide for the convenience of the people, by holding one, instead of several elections. See *West Virginia Cases*, 43*d Congress.*

§ 188. A different rule prevails, however, where a statute provides that an election shall occur on a given day of the month, every year, or in given years, even though the day is also described as the day of the general election. Thus, for example, a statute of Illinois provided that certain commissioners should be elected "at the next general election,

on the first Monday in August, 1874, and every year thereafter," and it was held that the change of the time for holding the general election did not change the time for the annual election of said commissioners. In the former case the statute should be construed as fixing the day of the general election, and not a particular day of the month, but in the latter the particular day of the month and week in each year being specified, it must be presumed that the term "general election" was used as descriptive of the election, the time of holding which was fixed "on the first Monday in August" in each year. [*People vs. Sloan*, 14 *Ill.*, 476.]

§ 189. A statute of Michigan authorized the election of two commissioners, but the election was conducted in all respects as if but one was to be chosen. Two persons were opposing candidates, and each voter voted for one of the two, but in no instance did a ballot contain more than one name for the office. Evidently the electors acted under the belief that only one commissioner was to be elected. It was held that only the one receiving the highest number of votes was elected, and that as to the other, there was a failure to elect, and the office remained vacant. [*People vs. Canvassers*, 11 *Mich.* 111.]

§ 190. An election will not be held void and set aside, on the ground that the mere police regulations of the election law, under which it was held were unconstitutional. The citizens possess the prerogative of voting, and the legislature cannot take that right away by encompassing an election law with unconstitutional provisions. If the voters think proper to go forward and vote under a defective law, those who were candidates ought to be the last to complain when the result has been affected by neither the unconstitutionality of the law, fraud, error nor collusion. [*Andrews vs. Lancier*, 13 *La. An.*, 301.] But, of course, where, by reason of the enforcement of unconstitutional and void regulations, even of a police character, the result is affected, the rule is different, and in such a case, the election cannot stand.

§ 191. The right to vote for, and be represented by county and state officers, being a constitutional right, it cannot be impaired or taken away by legislation. Hence, it has been held upon constitutional ground, that if an act for the organization of a new county was so framed that the inhabitants of such new county could not participate in the election of Judges and State Senators, the same was unconstitutional and void. And the fact that a future legislature was expected to remedy this difficulty by incorporating such new county in a senatorial and judicial district, does not cure the defect in such an act. [*Lenning vs. Carpenter*, 20 *N. Y.*, 447. *People vs. Maynard*, 15 *Mich.*, 471. *Cooley's Const. Limitations*, 616.]

§ 192. The principles of public policy, which forbid and make void, all contracts tending to the corrupting of elections held under authority of law, apply equally to what are called primary or nominating elections, or conventions, although these are mere voluntary proceedings of the voters of certain political parties. It is quite as much against public policy, to permit contracts to be made for the purpose of corrupting a convention or primary election, as to permit the same thing to be done to corrupt voters at a regular election. The buying and selling of votes, or of influence at a nominating convention or election, is quite as injurious to the public, and quite as abhorrent to the law, as the same corrupt practices when employed to influence an election provided for by statute. The too common practice of providing liquors to be used to influence voters in a convention, primary election, or regular legal election, is a practice which the law will not tolerate. A contract made for such a purpose is utterly void. [*Strasberger vs. Burk*, 13 *Am. Law Reg.* (*N. S.*) 607. *Nichols vs. Mudgett*, 22 *Vt.*, 546. *Duke vs. Ashbee*, 11 *Iredell*, 112. And upon the general question of the invalidity of contracts made in violation of the established policy of the law, see *Spaulding vs. Preston*, (21*st Vermont Reports*, 9.)

§ 193. In *Nichols vs. Mudgett, supra*, the following were the facts: The defendant being opposed to plaintiff, who was a candidate for town representative, the parties agreed that the former should use his influence for the plaintiff's election, and do what he could for that purpose, and that, if the plaintiff was elected, that should be a satisfaction of his claim. Nothing was specifically said about the defendants voting for the plaintiff, but he did vote for him, and would not have done so, nor favored his election, but for this agreement. The plaintiff was elected. *Held*, that the agreement was void, and constituted no bar to a recovery upon the demand. And in *Meachem vs. Dow*, 32 *Vt.*, 721, it was held, that a note given in consideration of the payee's agreement to resign a public office in favor of the maker, and to use influence in favor of the latter's appointment as his successor, was void, in the hands of the payee. An agreement between two voters to "pair off" and both abstain from voting is void, and the officers of the election cannot refuse to receive the vote of one of the two, on account of such an agreement.

§ 194. The chief reason for the general adoption of the ballot in this country is, that it affords the voter the means of preserving the secrecy of his vote. And this enables him to vote independently and freely, without being subject to be overawed, intimidated, or in any manner controlled by others, or to any ill will or persecution, on account of his vote. The secret ballot is justly regarded as an important and valuable safeguard for the protection of the voter, and particularly the humble citizen against the influence which wealth and station may be supposed to exercise. And it is for this reason that the privacy is held not to be limited to the moment of depositing the ballot, but is sacredly guarded by the law for all time unless the voter himself shall voluntarily divulge it. (*People vs. Pease*, 27 *N. Y.*, 81.)

§ 195. All devices by which the secrecy of the ballot is destroyed by means of colored paper used for ballots, or by other similar means, are exceedingly reprehensible, and whether expressly prohibited by statute or not, should be discountenanced by all good citizens. Judge Cooley, in his admirable work on Constitutional Limitations, expresses the opinion that in as much as the voter himself cannot be compelled to disclose for whom he voted, it is but reasonable to conclude that "others who may accidentily, or by trick or artifice, have acquired knowledge on the subject, should not be allowed to testify to such knowledge, or to give any information in the courts upon the subject. "Public policy," he declares, "requires that the veil of secrecy should be impenetrable, unless the voter himself voluntarily determines to lift it. His ballot is absolutely privileged, and to allow evidence of its contents, when he has not waived the privilege, is to encourage trickery and fraud, and would in effect establish this remarkable anomaly, that while the law, from motives of public policy, establishes the secret ballot with a view to conceal the electors action, it at the same time encourages a system of espionage, by means of which the veil of secrecy may be penetrated, and the voters action disclosed to the public." (*p.* 506 *and* 507.)

§ 196. The case of *People vs. Cicote*, (16 *Mich.*, 283,) is cited to sustain the views just expressed. At the same time the author concedes that in lgislative bodies it has been held that when a voter refuses to disclose for whom he voted, evidence is admissible of the general reputation of the political character of the voter, and as to the party to which he belonged at the time of the election, but the hope is expressed that this rule of evidence will not be adopted by the courts. In practice it will be found that it can in general only be important to prove the contents of a ballot deposited in the box by a person claiming the right to vote, for one or the other of the following purposes.

1. When it is alleged that the person casting such ballot was not a legal voter, and for the pupose of excluding it.

2. When it is deemed important to show how many good votes were cast for a particular candidate at a given poll, for the purpose of impeaching the return and showing that such candidate has not been allowed all the votes cast for him.

When the object is to exclude the ballot as cast by a person not qualified to vote, as we have elsewhere seen, it is necessary to show *first* that the ballot was illegal. This being done, the person who cast it may be compelled to answer as to its contents, or if he cannot be found or fails to remember the contents of such illegal ballot may be shown by circumstances. If the object is to show how many good votes a particular candidate has received, for the purpose of impeaching the return, it is to be presumed that the voters who cast such votes will as a general rule not object to giving testimony, because the evidence is sought as a means of protecting their rights and defeating an alleged fraud by reason of which their votes have not been honestly counted and returned. But if any voter under these circumstances should refuse to waive his privilege and testify as to the contents of his ballot, and should object to his secret being divulged by any other witness, his refusal and objection must prevail, unless he has himself at the time of voting, voluntarily made public his ballot, and its contents, in which case such contents may be proven by the testimony of those persons to whom they were voluntarily communicated.

§ 197. In the absence of any statutory provision expressly requiring more, a plurality of the votes cast will elect. It is only in cases where the statute so provides, that a majority of all the votes cast, is necessary to the choice of an officer. In this country where candidates may be numerous, and the votes of the electors divided among a number of different persons, to require a majority to elect, would be to prevent a choice in very many cases; hence it is that a majority is seldom required in a popular election. (*Augustin vs. Eggleston*, 12 *La., An.* 366. *Cooley's Const. Lim.*, 619–620.) In those States, where a majority is required to elect, (and such is the requirement in Vermont, and perhaps in a few other States,) provision is made by statute for a second election, in case there is no choice at the first.

§ 198. A statute of Pennsylvania provides that upon the petition of at least five citizens of the county, stating under oath, that frauds are apprehended in any election district of such county, the Court of Common Pleas may appoint two judicious, sober, and intelligent citizens of the county to act as overseers of said election; said overseers to have the right to be present with the officers of the election, during the whole time the same is held, the votes counted and the returns made out, and signed by the election officers. They are to keep a list of voters if they see proper, to challenge voters, and generally to aid in preventing or detecting frauds. The statute further provides, that if the officers of the election "shall refuse to permit said overseers to be present and perform their duties as aforesaid, or if they shall be driven away from the polls by violence or intimidation, all the votes polled at such election district may be rejected by any tribunal trying a contest under said election." *In re Duffy*,

(4 *Brewster*, 531,) it was held that where overseers duly appointed under this statute, were not permitted to serve, but were driven away by threats and intimidation, there is necessarily such a violent presumption of fraud, that in the absence of a perfect showing of legality, fairness, and regularity, the whole poll should be invalidated. "In the absence of any improper conduct on the part of overseers appointed by the Court in conformity with plain statutory requirement," says the Court in that case, "we can hardly conceive of an excuse for not permitting them to serve, or for driving them away, which ought to find favor or apology."

§ 199. In the case of Duffy, *supra*, the Court laid down the rule that incompetency, inefficiency, and a reckless disregard of essential requirements of the law, on the part of officers conducting an election, to such an extent as that, their acts become unreliable, must of necessity work the same result as actual fraud. No doubt this is so, for it may be regarded as a fundamental principle of the law of elections, that whatever renders the returns or certificates of election officers unreliable, or which, in other words, destroys their value as evidence, is sufficient to set them aside, and to make it necessary to prove the fairness and legality of the election by other evidence. Speaking of this rule, however, the Court, in the case just cited, well says: "While this is the only safe and true doctrine, still, a construction might be given to the statutes relating to elections so strict as to foster and encourage fraud, rather than to crush it and stamp it out."

§ 200. It is often a perplexing question whether

a statutory provision concerning the manner of conducting elections is mandatory or only directory. We have already stated pretty fully the general rules upon this subject and cited numerous authorities. These statutes are numerous and various in this country and it would be an endless task to point them all out and discuss the effect of each. The rule of construction to be gathered from all the authorities was thus stated in *Jones vs. The State*, (1 *Kansas* 279,) and approved in *Gilleland vs. Schuyler*, (9 *do* 569,) "unless a fair consideration of the statute shows that the legislature intended compliance with the provisions in relation to the manner to be essential to the validity of the proceedings, it is to be regarded as directory merely." And in the latter case the court said, "Questions affecting the purity of elections are in this country of vital importance. Upon them hangs the experiment of self government. The problem is to secure, first, to the voter a free untrammelled vote: and secondly a correct record and return of the vote. It is mainly with reference to these two results that the rules for conducting elections are prescribed by the legislative power. But these rules are only means. The end is the freedom and purity of the election. To hold these rules all mandatory and essential to a valid election is to subordinate substance to form, the end to the means. Yet on the other hand, to permit a total neglect of all the requirements of the statute, and still sustain the proceedings, is to forego the lessons of experience and invite a disregard of all those provisions which the wisdom of years have found conducive to the purity of the ballot box.

Ignorance, inadvertence, mistake or even intentional wrong on the part of local officials should not be permitted to disfranchise a district. Yet rules, uniformity of procedure, are as essential to procure truth and exactness in elections, as in anything else. Irregularities invite and conceal fraud."

If we keep in view these general principles, and bear in mind that irregularities are generally to be disregarded, unless the statute expressly declares that they shall be fatal to the election, or unless they are such in themselves as to change or render doubtful the result, we shall find no great difficulty in determining each case as it arises under the various statutes of the several States.

§ 201. By an act of Congress, approved July 25, 1866, [14 *State at large*, 243,] it is provided that "the legislature of each State which shall be chosen next preceding the expiration of the time for which any Senator was elected to represent said State in Congress shall, on the second Tuesday after the meeting and organization thereof, proceed to elect a Senator in Congress in place of such Senator so going out of office:"

The power to pass this act is derived from Sec. 4, Art. 1, of the Constitution which authorizes Congress to make or alter regulations concerning the time and manner of holding elections for Senators. Senators must be chosen by the legislature which shall have been "chosen next preceding the expiration of the term" of the Senator elected to represent the State in Congress, and a person chosen as Senator by any other legislature, can have no right to the seat. (*Norwood's Case Senate Report, No.* 10, 42*d Congress.*

§ 202. Where a State government is organized and senators and representatives chosen, either in a territory or within the limits of a state, which has been disorganized by reason of participation in rebellion, the subsequent recognition by Congress of the State thus organized, relates back to, and makes valid, the election of such senators and representatives. [*Case of Abijah Gilbert, Senator from Florida,* 41*st Congress, and of Morgan C. Hamilton, Senator from Texas,* 42*d Congress.*]

§ 203. It is not necessary under the act of Congress, of July 28, 1866, to regulate the time and manner of holding elections for senators in Congress, that the election by the legislature should actually take place on the "second Tuesday after its organization." It is enough if on that day the legislature takes action on the subject, and actually votes, though unsuccessfully, for a person to fill the office of senator. [*Case of Abijah Gilbert, supra.*] The legislature must, however, continue to meet in joint convention until a choice is reached. The principal purpose of the act of Congress was, to deprive one house of the legislature of the power to prevent an election by refusing to go into a joint convention for that purpose.

CHAPTER IV.

OF THE PRIMA FACIE RIGHT TO AN OFFICE.

§ 204. Where two or more persons claim the same office, and where a judicial investigation is required to settle the contest upon the merits, it is often necessary to determine which of the claimants shall be permitted to qualify and to exercise the functions of the office, pending such investigation. If the office were to remain vacant pending the contest it might frequently happen that the greater part of the term would expire before it could be filled; and thus the interests of the people might suffer for the want of the services of a public officer. Besides, if the mere institution of a contest was to be deemed sufficient to prevent the swearing in of the person holding the usual credentials, it is easy to see that very great and serious injustice might be done. If this were the rule, it would only be necessary for an evil disposed person, to contest the right of his successful rival, and to protract the contest as long as possible, in order to deprive the latter of his office for at least a part of the term. And this might be done, by a contest having little or no merit on his side, for it would be impossible to discover, in advance of an investigation, the absence of merit. And again, if the party holding the ordinary credentials to an office, could be kept out of the office by the mere institution of a contest, the organization of a legislative body, such for example as the House of Representatives, of the United States, might be altogether prevented, by instituting contests against a majority of the members, or what is more to be apprehended, the relative strength of political parties in such a body might be changed, by instituting contests against members of one or the other of such parties. These considerations have made it necessary to adopt, and to adhere to, the rule, that the person holding the ordinary credentials shall be qualified, and allowed to act pending a contest and until a decision can be had on the merit.

§ 205. No particular form of credentials is required. It is sufficient if the claimant to an office presents a certificate signed by the officer or officers authorized by law to issue credentials, and stating generally the fact that the election was duly held and that the claimant is duly elected to the office in question. If several officers or persons, are by law required to join in such a certificate, it is generally sufficient if a majority have signed it.

§ 206. Where the statute requires the votes of several counties composing a congressional district to be canvassed by one judge from each county, and that the result shall be certified by a board composed of one judge from each county, the certificate of four out of five of such judges based upon a full canvass of the vote is, *prima facie*, sufficient. The refusal of the fifth judge to join in the certificate will not invalidate it, (*Coffroth vs. Kountz*, 2 *Bartlett* 25.)

§ 207. In the absence of any express provision of the State law authorizing any officer to certify to the due election of members of Congress, it is presumed that under the usages of the House a certificate under the great seal of the State, signed by its chief executive officer, would constitute sufficient credentials, within the meaning of the statute of 1867. (*W. T. Clark's Case 42d Congress.*)

§ 208. It is enough for a *prima facie* case, if the certificate comes from the proper officer of the State, and clearly shows that the person claiming under it has been adjudged to be duly elected by the officer or board on whom the law of the State has imposed the duty of ascertaining and declaring the result. *Ibid.* And see *Kerr vs. Trego,* (47 *Pa. State R.* 292,) where it is held that the certificate of election sanctioned by law or usage, is *prima facie* evidence of title to the office, and can only be set aside by a contest in the form prescribed by law. In this latter case will be found also an elaborate and able discussion of the general subject of the organization of legislative bodies, to which the reader who may desire to investigate that subject is referred.

§ 209. Where the statute gives the Governor of a State the power, and makes it his duty, to commission the person elected to an office, the issuing of a commission by him confers a vested right upon the person commissioned, which nothing but a judicial decision can take away or authorize the Govenor to recall. It was accordingly held in *Ewing vs. Thompson,* (43 *Pa. State R.,* 372,) that where the Governor in 1861 commissioned Ewing as sheriff of the city and county of Philadelphia, and afterwards undertook to commission Thompson as duly elected at the same election, to the same office, the latter commission was void, and the former valid, until set aside by a contest. "The power of the Governor" says Strong, J., in that case, "to revoke a commission once issued to an officer, not removable at the pleasure of the Governor, may well be denied; even where he has the power of appointment of such an officer; an appointment once made is irrevocable; much more, it would seem is a commission issued by him, incapable of being recalled or invalidated by himself, when the appointing power is located elsewhere, and where his act in issuing the commission, is not discretionary with him, but is only the performance of a ministerial duty." And see the important case of *Marbury vs. Madison*, (1 *Cranch*, 137.)

§ 210. But, of course, a commission given by the Governor, or other competent authority, does not oust the jurisdiction of the proper tribunal, in a contested election case. It is simply evidence of the right to hold the office; gives *color* to the acts of the incumbent, and constitutes him an officer *de facto.* The election being set aside, or the person holding the commission being held not elected, by a tribunal of competent jurisdiction, the commission falls to the ground. The person duly commissioned must exercise the functions of the office until, upon an investigation *upon the merits*, it is judicially determined otherwise. Upon the subject of the effect of a commission, see *Ewing vs. Filley*, (43 *Pa. St. R.*, 384.) *State vs. Johnson*, (17 *Ark.*, 407.) *Hunter vs. Chandler*, (45 *Mo.*, 453.)

§ 211. In the case of *Morton vs. Daily*, (1 *Bartlett*, 402,) there were two certificates of election issued by the same Governor; first, a certificate declaring Mr. Morton duly elected, and at a later date a certificate declaring Mr. Daily duly elected. The second certificate was issued upon the alleged discovery by the Governor, of fraud, in the vote counted for Mr. Morton, and by the second certificate the Governor revoked, as far as he was able, the first. The house allowed the holder of the last certificate to be sworn in, and to occupy the seat, pending the contest. By so doing, however, the house assumed that the Governor might go behind the returns, investigate questions of fraud, and assuming a judicial character, determine such questions, and it also assumed that the Governor possessed the power to revoke a certificate once issued by him. But there seems to be no doubt but that, in the absence of a statute authorizing the Governor to institute a judicial inquiry into the manner of conducting an election, he is bound by the returns, and has no power beyond the certification of the result, as shown thereby. The duty of investigating charges of fraud, and deciding upon them can never be justly assumed by an executive officer, but belong exclusively to such judicial or *quasi* judicial tribunal, as the law may designate for that purpose. (*Switzler vs. Dyer*, 2 *Bartlett*, 777. *State ex. rel. Bland vs. Rodman, Sec'y of State*, 43 *Mo.*, 256, *State vs. Steers*, 44 *Mo.*, 224–228. *Switzler vs. Anderson*, 2 *Bartlett*, 374.)

§ 212. The case of *Morton vs. Daily* was followed by the House in *Hoge vs. Reed*, (2 *Bartlett* 540.) But it must have been without due consideration, for the same House held the contrary doctrine in

Wallace vs. Simpson, (2 *Bartlett* 552.) In that case the board of State canvassers being by law required to certify the result of the election, gave their certificate declaring that W. D. Simpson "was duly elected by a majority of votes, representative in the forty-first congress," and upon that certificate, the Governor issued to Mr. Simpson the usual commission or certificate of election. By another certificate, the board of canvassers declared that Alexander Wallace had "received a majority of the *legal* votes" cast for representative, and as explanatory of this contradiction on their part, they made and signed a "statement" addressed to the House of Representatives, detailing certain alleged irregularities and frauds committed in the conduct of this election, and declaring that, although they had felt themselves in duty bound to issue the certificate of election to Mr. Simpson, yet, they were convinced that he was not duly elected. Upon these papers the majority of the committee of elections reported that Mr. Wallace was entitled, *prima facie*, to the seat, and they submitted a resolution that he be sworn in, pending the contest, upon the merits. But the house, after debate, adopted minority report, which decided the *prima facie* case against Mr. Wallace. This decision of the House appears to have been based upon the following grounds:

1. That the certificate of election signed by the Governor was in due form and declared the election of Simpson, and that the House should not look beyond it in deciding the *prima facie* case.

2. That the subsequent statement was an unauthorized and unofficial paper of no value as evidence,

and could not be properly considered; but, if considered, it showed upon its face that the board of canvassers had gone outside of their province, in order to investigate charges of fraud and violence in the conduct of the election.

3. That the board having made a certificate of the result, and transmitted the same to the Secretary of State, had no power thereafter to make another and different certificate. The correctness of these propositions is, as we have had occasion to show elsewhere, well established by judicial decisions, as well as by frequent decisions of the House of Representatives itself.

§ 213. In the case of *Sheafe vs. Tillman*, (2 *Bartlett*, 907,) a like question was again considered, and the sound rule that a ministerial or executive officer can exercise no judicial functions, was adhered to. In the report in that case the doctrine is laid down as follows: (p. 910.)

"There is no law of the State of Tennessee that gives authority to the Governor to reject the vote of any county or part of a county; his duty is only to compare the returns received by him with those returned to the office of the Secretary of State, and upon such comparison being made, to "deliver to the candidate receiving the highest number of votes in his district the certificate of his election as Representative to Congress." (*Code of Tennessee, Sec.* 935, *page* 239.) If illegal votes have been cast, if irregularities have existed in the elections in any of the counties or precincts, if intimidation or violence has been used to deter legal or peaceable citizens from exercising their rights as voters, to this

House must the party deeming himself aggrieved, look for redress. This great power of determining the question of the right of a person to a seat in Congress, is not vested in the executive of any State, but belongs solely to the House of Representatives. (Constitution United States, Art. 1, Sec. 5.)

The action of the Governor, so far as he has thrown out the votes of counties or parts of counties, is to be disregarded, and the matters in dispute are to be settled upon the actual returns and the evidence introduced, independent of the doings of the executive."

And this ruling is according to the weight of authority in the House, while it has the support not only of reason and sound policy, but of an almost unbroken line of judicial decisions, extending far back through our history as a nation.

§ 214. There is still another class of cases which have arisen in the lower house of Congress, in which neither party holds credentials, the Governor or other returning officer having refused to declare either party elected. In some of these cases the house has undertaken upon such documentary evidence as it has been able to bring before it, without delay, to decide the *prima facie* claim, and order one or the other to be sworn in, pending the contest. (*Kountz vs. Coffroth*, 2 *Bartlett*, 25. *Foster vs. Covode*, *do* 519.)

§ 215. Of course the House must, in each case of this character, judge whether there is before it, sufficient *prima facie* evidence of the election of either one of the claimants, but, as a general rule, it is believed that in the absence of credentials, no one should be admitted to the seat in aavance of an investigation upon the merits. And if this general rule is to be departed from in any case, it should be only after a special investigation, by a committee, into the *prima facie* case, and after a report thereon. And such special inquiry and report can scarcely be possible, unless there is something in the nature of credentials or of written evidence of the election of one or the other claimant. If the returns are duly certified the House may act upon these, or if there is an informal certificate the House may order an inquiry into its effect. But if there is no record or other documentary evidence to show what the result of the election was, it is believed that a full investigation upon the merits should precede the swearing in of either applicant. If the House finds itself obliged to take testimony generally, to decide the *prima facie* case, it will generally find that it cannot stop short of hearing all the evidence and deciding upon the merits.

§ 216. It is to be observed in this connection that while in determining the *prima facie* right to a seat, the House of Representatives will not look behind the certificate, if it be signed by the proper officers, and if it contains a statement in unequivocal terms of the result of the election; yet something may appear upon the face of the certificate itself to destroy or impair its value as *prima facie* evidence.

§ 217. If, for instance, the certificate states that the vote of one county out of five, has not been canvassed, it seems that this would make it necessary even to the determination of the *prima facie* case to inquire what the vote was in the county omitted. And if it appear that the vote of the county omitted would have changed the result, the value of such a certificate is destroyed. But if it appear that the vote of the omitted county was not material to the result, then, according to the ruling of the House in *Kountz vs. Coffroth*, (2 *Bartlett* 25,) the certificate is good, although based only up on the four counties canvassed. Whenever, therefore, it appears upon the face of a certificate of election, that one or more of the counties composing the district, have been omitted from the canvass, it is the duty of the house, before determining the *prima facie* case, to inquire into the effect of such omission upon the result of the canvass, and to treat the certificate as *prima facie* good only in case it appears that the omitted vote would not change the result, or contradict the certificate, if admitted.

§ 218. The principal, and almost the only case in which the lower House of Congress has ever denied to a person holding regular credentials, the right to be sworn and to take his seat, pending the contest, is the celebrated *New Jersey Case*, (1 *Bartlett*, 19.) In that case one set of claimants held the regular certificate of election signed by the Governor, and another set held the certificate of the Secretary of State, that they had received a majority of the votes cast in their respective districts. After a long and angry debate the house, (being yet unorganized,) refused to admit either set of claimants to their seats. Subsequently, and after a partial investigation, the holders of the Secretary's certificate were admitted to seats pending the contest, and at the end of the contest these persons were confirmed in their seats. This precedent has never since been followed in a single instance. It is so clearly wrong and as a precedent, so exceedingly dangerous, that the House has not hesitated to disregard it entirely, on every occasion, when the question has arisen.

§ 219. The effect of the returns of an election is not open for consideration in a proceeding in which the title to the office comes up collaterally. Hence it was held in New York that the law having committed to the common council of a city, the duty of canvassing the returns and determining from them the result of the election for mayor, and the council having performed that duty, and made a determination, the question as to the effect of the returns could not be considered, in an action where the person declared elected was not a party, and in which the question of his right to the office arose collaterally. "If," says *Denio, J.*, "the question had arisen upon an action in the nature of a *quo warranto* information, the evidence would have been competent," and the evidence referred to was that offered to impeach the canvass made by the common council. "But," he continues, "it would be intolerable to allow a party affected by the acts of a person claiming to be an officer, to go behind the official determination to prove that such official determination arose out of mistake or fraud. (*Hadley vs. City of Albany*, 33 *New York*, 603.) And see also *Peyton vs. Brent*, (3 *Cr. CC.*, 434,) and *Hunter vs. Chandler*, (45 *Mo.*, 453.) The true rule is, that the certificate of the board of canvassers declaring the result of the election, is, in a controversy arising between the party holding it and a stranger, conclusive, but in a proper action, properly entitled, to impeach it, and try the title to the office, it is only *prima facie* evidence of the right. See *People vs. Cook*, 8 *N. Y.*, 67. *People vs. Vail*, 20 *Wend.*, 12. *People vs. Jones*, 20 *Cal.*, 50. *Commonwealth vs. Co. Commissioners*, 5 *Rawl*, 75.

§ 220. The merits of a contested election cannot be taken from the proper tribunal authorized by law to try it, and brought for adjudication into a court of equity, upon a bill to enjoin the party holding the certificate of election from using it, upon the ground that it was procured by fraud. This doctrine is strikingly illustrated by the decision of the Supreme Court of Pennsylvania in *Hulseman vs. Rems*, (41 *Pa. State R* 396,) which was a petition for an injunction upon this ground. The court, although satisfied that the officer in question held a certificate based upon the grossest of frauds, amounting even to the actual forgery of some of the returns; yet refused to interfere by injunction, and for the following among other reasons: "If" says the court "in this way we suffer a gross fraud to pass through our hands without remedy, it is not because we have any mercy on the fraud, but because we cannot frustrate it by any decree of ours without an act of usurpation. Another tribunal is appointed to administer the remedy and we believe that on proper application, it will administer it rightly according to the evidence it may have; and if we had any doubts of this we should still not be justified in interfering."

§ 221. There can be no doubt, but that a certificate of election regular in form, and signed by the proper authority, constitutes *prima facie* evidence of title to the office, which can only be set aside by such proceedings for contesting the election as the law provides. (*Commonwealth vs. Baxter*, 35 *Penn. St. R.* 263. *Kerr vs. Trego*, 47 *Pa. State R.* 292. *The State vs. The Governor*, 1 *Dutch* [*N. J.*] 331. The certificate whether rightfully or wrongfully given, confers upon the person holding it, the *prima facie* right to the office. (*People vs. Miller*, 16 *Mich.* 56. *Crowell vs. Lambert*, 10 *Minn.* 369. *State vs. Sherwood*, 15 *Minn.* 221. *State vs. Churchill*, *ibid*, 455.] If, however, the certificate contains upon its face a recital of facts, and these facts show affirmatively that the party holding it was not duly elected, it may be disregarded. (*Hartt vs. Harvey*, 32 *Barbour*, 61.

§ 222. The regular certificate of election properly signed, is, as we have seen, to be taken as sufficient to authorize the person holding it to be sworn in. It is *prima facie* evidence of his election and the only evidence thereof which can be considered in the first instance, and in the course of the organization of a legislative body. But there are questions which may be raised, touching the *qualifications* of a person elected, which may be investigated and decided as a part of the *prima facie* case, and as preliminary to the swearing in of the claimant. Thus, if a specific and apparently well grounded allegation be presented to the House of Representatives of the United States, that a person holding a certificate of election, is not a citizen of the United States, or is not of the requisite age, or is for any other cause ineligible, the House will defer action upon the question of swearing in such person, until there can be an investigation into the truth of such allegation. It is necessary, however, that such allegation should be made by a responsible party; it is usually made or vouched for at least, by some member or member elect of the House. It is to be presented at the earliest possible moment after the meeting of the House for organization, and generally at the time that the person objected to, presents himself to be sworn in. The person objected to upon grounds such as these, is not sworn in with the other members, but stands aside for the time being, and the House through its committee with all possible speed proceeds to inquire into the facts.

§ 223. The certificate of election does not ordinarily, if ever, cover the ground of the due qualification of the person holding it. It may be said that by declaring the person "duly elected," the certificate, by implication, avers that he was qualified to be elected, and to hold the office. But it is well known that canvassing officers do not in fact inquire as to the qualifications of persons voted for; they certify what appears upon the face of the returns, and nothing more. The certificate, therefore, must be regarded as evidence of the *election* of the person named therein, so far conclusive, that it cannot be attacked except in the ordinary mode provided for contesting, but it is not evidence of the *qualifications* of the person named. The presumption always is, that a person chosen to an office is qualified to fill it, and it is never incumbent upon him to prove his eligibility. The certificate of election does not add to this presumption, but simply leaves it where the law places it, and he who denies the eligibility of a person who is certified to be elected, must take the burthen of proving that he is not eligible. During the rebellion the House of Representatives repeatedly decided that a disloyal person should not be sworn in as a member of that body, and it was also decided that a charge of disloyalty against a member elect should be investigated and decided, previous to his being allowed to take his seat. In the case of the *Kentucky election*, (2 *Bartlett*, 329,) this was the ruling of the House. The doctrine was thus stated in the committee's report:

"The committee are of opinion that no person who has been engaged in armed hostility to the government of the United States, or who has given aid and comfort to its enemies during the late rebellion, ought to be permitted to be sworn as a member of this House, and that any specific and well-grounded charge of personal disloyalty made against a person claiming a seat as a member of this House ought to be investigated and reported upon before such person is permitted to take the seat; but all charges touching the disloyalty of a constituency in a State in which loyal civil government was not overthrown during the late rebellion, or the illegality of an election, are matters which pertain to a contest in the ordinary way, and should not prevent a person holding a regular certificate from taking his seat."

§ 224. The case of *Hunt vs. Chilcott*, (2 *Bartlett* 164,) is one of the very few cases in which a certificate of election signed by the proper authority, has been held insufficient to entitle the holder to be sworn in a member of the House of Representatives of the United States, and to occupy the seat, pending a contest. The reason for this action, however, was that the party holding the certificate had voluntarily offerred evidence which impeached it. The committee said in their report:

"But Mr. Hunt did not rest his case upon that paper alone. He introduced Governor Cummings in its support. The governor informed the committee, that on the said 5th of September a canvass of the votes cast for delegate was had in his presence, by the board of canvassers; that two of said board found that a majority of all the votes had been cast for George M. Chilcott, and that one of said board dissented from this conclusion, and that he, the governor, considering himself one of the board, agreed with the dissenting member, making a tie, whereupon he determined the election himself, and made a certificate in opposition to the conclusion of two members of the board. In addition to the governor's statement, among the papers submitted by the House, is a report of the board of canvassers, signed by Frank Hall, Secretary of the Territory, and Richard E. Whitsitt, Auditor of the Territory, and addressed to the governor, in which they state that at the canvass held in his presence, according to law, they find that Mr. Chilcott had 3,529 votes, and A. C. Hunt had 3,421 votes, by which it would appear that Mr. Chilcott was elected delegate by 108 majority. The certificate of the Governor thus appears to have been issued in violation of the laws of the Territory, in order to reverse the facts of the canvass. Under this state of facts the committee do not feel authorized to report that Mr. Hunt is entitled, *prima facie*, to a seat as delegate."

While, therefore, it was conceded that the House should not insist upon looking beyond the certificate in determining a *prima facie* case, it was held that if the party holding the certificate saw fit to offer evidence in addition to the certificate, the House might take notice of it.

§ 225. While it is, as we have seen, true that where a certificate of election is confined to a statement that the person to whom it is given is duly elected, or words to that effect, it is *prima facie* evidence that such person is entitled to the office, it is also true that where it recites the facts, upon which the certifying officer relies as his justification for issuing it, and where, from those facts, it clearly appears that the person named was not elected, the certificate destroys itself. [*Hartt vs. Harvey*, 32 *Barb*. 55.]

CHAPTER V.

OF ELIGIBILITY TO OFFICE, AND OF TENURE.

§ 226. The qualifications for federal offices are fixed by the federal constitution or federal law, and the qualifications for state offices, are fixed by state constitutions or state laws. It is not competent for any state to add to or in any manner change the qualifications for a federal office, as prescribed by the constitution or laws of the United States. Nor can the United States add to, or alter the qualifications for a state office, as fixed by State regulations.

§ 227. The constitution of the United States fixes the qualifications of representatives in congress, in the following words:

"No person shall be a representative who shall not have attained the age of twenty-five years and have been seven years a citizen of the United States and who shall not when elected be an inhabitant of that State in which he shall be chosen." (*Constitution Art.* 1, *Sec.* 2.) A State law requiring that a representative in Congress shall reside in a particular town or county within the district from which he is chosen, is unconstitutional and void. (*Barney vs. McCreery. Cl. & H.*, 169.)

§ 228. The constitution of Illinois, of 1848, provided as follows:

"The judges of the Supreme and Circuit Courts shall not be eligible to any other office or public trust of profit in this State, *or the United States*, during the term for which they are elected nor for one year thereafter. All votes for either of them for any elective office, (except that of judge of the Supreme or Circuit Courts) given by the General Assembly or the people, shall be void."

The House of Representatives held that this clause of the constitution of Illinois, so far as it related to the election of member of Congress, was void, because in conflict with the federal constitution, and, also because it was an unauthorized attempt on the part of the State of Illinois to fix or to change the qualifications of Representatives in Congress. Mr. Marshall and Mr. Trumbull, of Illinois, were elected Representatives in the thirty-fourth Congress. They had previously been elected, respectively, judge of the Supreme and Circuit Court of that State, for terms which had not expired. This was held to be no objection to their holding the office of Representative in Congress. (*Taney vs. Marshall*, 1 *Bartlett* 167. *Fouke vs. Trumbull*, 1 *Bartlett* 167. The United States Senate adopted the same rule in *Trumbull's case*, (*ibid* p. 619.)

§ 229. The Supreme Court of Pennsylvania has held that the trial and conviction of a sheriff of the offence of bribing a voter, previously to his election, does not constitutionally disqualify him from exercising the duties of his office, because it is not a conviction of "any *infamous* crime," within the meaning of the constitution of that State. (*Commonwealth vs. Shover*, 3 *Watts and Sergeant*, 338, *Brightley's Election Cases*, 134.) In the opinion in this case will be found an elaborate discussion of the meaning of the terms "infamous crime," and a reference to many authorities upon that subject. It seems that infamous crimes are treason, felony, and every species of the *crimen falsi*, such as forgery, perjury, subornation of perjury, &c.

§ 230. The acceptance for a term of years of an office, the duties of which require the incumbent to reside outside of the limits of a given place, does not necessarily render him ineligible to another office, one of the qualifications of which is residence within such place. If the office accepted is for life, the law presumes that upon its acceptance the incumbent elects to make his residence permanently where its duties are to be discharged, but if it be an office only for a term of years, or for an indefinite period, the presumption is that no change of residence is intended, and none of the rights or privileges of his residence are lost by the acceptance of it. (*Commonwealth vs. Jones*, 12 *Penn. State R.*, 67.)

§ 231. We come now to a question which has been much discussed, and upon which the authorities are somewhat conflicting; it is this: suppose the candidate who has received the highest number of votes for an office is ineligible, and that his ineligibility was known to those who voted for him before they cast their votes, are the votes thus cast for him to be thrown out of the count, and treated as never cast, and should the minority candidate, if eligible, be declared elected in such a case? No doubt the English rule is, that where the majority candidate is ineligible, and sufficient notice of his ineligibility has been given, the person receiving the next highest number of votes being eligible, must be declared elected. Great stress is laid upon the fact of notice having been given, and the reason of the English rule is said to be "that it is wilful obstinacy and misconduct in a voter to give his vote for a person laboring under a *known* incompetency." (*Southwark on Elections, p.* 259.) An examination of the English cases will show that in some of them the election was declared void, and sent back to the people, on the ground that there was not sufficient notice of the incapacity of the successful candidate, while in others the minority candidate was declared elected, on the ground that due notice of the ineligibility of the person receiving the majority was given. The following are some of the principal English authorities upon the subject. *Rex vs. Monday, Cowp.*, 537. *Rex vs. Coe, Heywood* 361. *Rex vs. Bissell, ibid* 360. *Rex. vs. Parry,* 14 *East,* 549. *Regina vs. Coaks,* 28 *Eg. L. and Eq.*, 304, 7 *Q. B.*, 406. *Heywood on County Elections,* 535. *Male on Elections,* 336. *King vs. Hawkins,* 10 *East,* 210. *Claridge vs. Evelyn,* 5 *B. and A.*, 8. *Clarke on Election Committees, page* 156. *Southwark on Elections, page* 259.

§ 232. Although the law of the British parliament, as well as that administered in the courts of that country, recognizes the rule as laid down in the cases just cited, the House of Representatives of the United States has refused to adopt it. See the case of *Smith vs. Brown,* (2 *Bartlett,* 395,) in which, in an able report, submitted by Mr. Dawes, chairman of the Committee of Election, the authorities are reviewed, and the conclusion is reached, "that the law of the British parliament, in this particular, has never been adopted in this country, and is wholly inapplicable to the system of government under which we live." And the courts of this country generally take the same view.

§ 233. Thus, in *Commonwealth vs. Cluley,* 56 *Pa. St. R.* 270, the Supreme Court of Pennsylvania held that where at an election for Sheriff, a majority of the votes are cast for a disqualified person, the next in vote is not to be returned as elected; and the Supreme Court of California in *Saunders vs. Haynes,* (13 *Cal.* 145,) holds the same doctrine and enforces it, by cogent reasoning. And in Wisconsin we have the same ruling in *State vs. Giles,* (1 *Chand.* 112,) and in *State vs. Smith,* (14*th Wis.* 497. And see opinion of judges, 32 *Maine,* 597. *State vs. Boal,* 46 *Mo.* 528. *Cushing Election Cas.* 496, 576, and see,

State vs. Anderson, (1 *Cox N. J.* 318. *People vs. Clute*, 50 *N. Y.*) But in Indiana the doctrine of the English authorities has been followed. (*Gulich vs. New*, 14 *Ind.* 93. *Carson vs. Phetridge*, 15 *Ind.* 327,) and see *Stewart vs. Hoges* in Circuit Court of Stephenson County, Illinois. [3 *Chicago Legal News* 117.]

§ 234. Thus, it will be seen that the weight of authority in this country is decidedly against the adoption here of the English doctrine. And we think that sound policy, as well as reason and authority, forbids the adoption of that doctrine in this country. It is a fundamental idea with us that the majority shall rule, and that a majority or at least a plurality shall be required to elect a person to office by popular vote. An election with us, is the deliberate choice of a majority or plurality of the electors. Any doctrine, which opens the way for minority rule in any case, is anti-republican and anti-American. The English rule, if adhered to, would in many cases result in compelling very large majorities to submit to very small minorities, as an ineligible person may receive, and in many cases has received, a great majority of the votes. It is enough, in such a case, to hold the election void.

§ 235. This question was elaborately discussed and settled, so far as the Senate of the United States is concerned, in the case of *Joseph C. Abbott of North Carolina*. The decision in that case was against the adoption of the English rule in this country, and Abbott, who, notwithstanding he received only a minority of the votes cast, claimed a seat, upon the ground that he was the only eligible person voted for, was declared not elected. And it was distinctly asserted, in the report of the committee, that the fact that the voters have notice of the ineligibility of the candidate at the time they cast their votes for him, makes no difference. The remark of Judge Strong, in *Commonwealth vs. Cluley*, [*supra*,] that "the disqualified person *is a person still*, and every vote thrown for him is formal," is quoted with approbation. The broad doctrine was asserted that in this country an election, by a minority of the persons voting, is not to be tolerated under any circumstances. Mr. Carpenter, from the minority of the committee, submitted an elaborate report maintaining the right of Mr. Abbott to the seat, and the debate was exhaustive, but the Senate sustained the majority of the committee. (*Senate Rep. No.* 58, 42*d Congress, Second Session.*)

§ 236. If the official term of a public officer is limited to a given number of years, of course, at the end of such term, unless a successor has been chosen and qualified, the office becomes vacant. Hence it is that in most of the States there are constitutional or statutory provisions, to the effect that all public officers shall hold for a given period, and until their successors are duly qualified. Such a clause is to be found in the constitution of Pennsylvania, and under it the Supreme Court of that State held that where the person elected to an office dies before being qualified, the previous incumbent holds over. (*Commonwealth vs. Hauley*, 9 *Pa. St. R.* 513.) In such a case the death of the person elected creates no vacancy. Never having occupied the office, his death made no change in it. Therefore, though the Governor be authorized to fill all vacancies by appointment, he had no power in such a case to appoint.

§ 237. To the same effect is *State vs. Jenkins*, (43 *Mo.*, 261.) *State vs. Robinson*, (1 *Kansas*, 17.) *State vs. Benedict*, (15 *Minn.*, 199.) It is very clear that no appointment can be made to fill a vacancy until the office has once been full. And, accordingly, it has been held by the Senate of the United States that the words "all vacancies that may happen during the recess of the Senate," mean such vacancies as occur from death, resignation, promotion or removal. [*Sargeant Const. Law*, 373.] See also the decision of Caldwell, J., in the Circuit Court of the United States, eastern district of Arkansas, April term, 1868, in *Schenck vs. Peay*. *Story on the Constitution*, *Sec.* 1559. *Ex parte Dodd.*, 6 *Eng.*, 152.

§ 238. It is well settled that the acceptance by a member of Congress of a disqualifying office after he has taken his seat, operates as a forfeiture of it, and creates a vacancy in the house to which such member belongs. (*Case of Van Ness, Clark and Hall*, 122. *Cases of Baker and Yell*, 1 *Bartlett*, 92. *Byington vs. Vandever*, *do* 395. *Stanton vs. Lane*, *do* 637.)

Whether the incumbent of one office becomes disqualified by accepting another, depends upon the question whether the law forbids the holding of the two offices by the same person, and if not, then upon the further question whether the functions and duties of the two offices are incompatible.

§ 239. If there is a statutory or constitutional provision prohibiting the same person from holding both the offices at the same time, then of course the question of their incompatibility does not necessarily arise, for in such a case the acceptance of the second is *ipso facto*, the abandonment and resignation of the first, though the duties of the two may be entirely compatible. But if the statute and constitution are silent upon the subject, then the question whether the two offices can be held at the same time by the same person, depends upon their compatibility.

§ 240. The sixth section of the first article of the constitution of the United States provides that, "no person holding any office under the United States, shall be a member of either House during his continuance in office." Under this provision it has been frequently held, that the acceptance of a commission as an officer of volunteers in the U. S. Army, is the acceptance of an office under the United States, and that the acceptance of such commission by a member of Congress, vacates his seat. [*See cases last above cited.*] While it is true that the commissions of officers of volunteers are ordinarily issued by the State authorities, it does not follow that they are State officers. They serve the United States, they are paid by the United States, and subject to the orders of the President. They are responsible only to federal authority for the faithful performance of their duties. These tests show them to be officers of the United States.

§ 241. But an important question has arisen, as to whether a member of Congress *elect*, who has not yet been qualified as such, may be an officer of volunteers. In the case of Robert C. Schenck, of Ohio, this identical question arose in the House of

Representatives of the thirty-eighth Congress. In that case it was held that if a "member of Congress, *after he has qualified or entered upon the discharge of his duties as such member*, accepts or enters upon the discharge of any office under the United States, he, *ipso facto*, vacates or forfeits his seat as a member of Congress." Gen. Schenck was elected to the thirty-eighth Congress in October 1862. That Congress did not organize until December 1863. On the 16th of March 1863, he was commissioned a Major General of volunteers, and entered upon the discharge of his duties as such, but resigned prior to the meeting of Congress in December 1863, and did no act as a Representative in Congress and indicated no acceptance of it, until after his resignation as Major General, nor until the meeting of Congress at the time above named.

§ 242. The case of Gen. Blair of Missouri decided at the same time, was precisely similar to that of Gen. Schenck in all respects except one. Gen. Blair continued to exercise the functions of the office of Major General *after Congress met and organized*, having resigned his commission January 1, 1864, in order to take his seat in the House. The two cases were alike in this; each held another office under the United States after his *election* to the thirty-eighth Congress, and after the legal existence or constitutional term of that Congress commenced, to-wit, March 4th, 1863; they were unlike in this; General Schenck resigned his commission in the army, before Congress met, and consequently before he had an opportunity to *elect* between the two offices, whilst Gen. Blair continued to hold his commission in the army and to exercise his functions, under it, after Congress met and *after* he had such option or election. Because of this important difference between the two cases, the seat of Gen. Blair was declared vacant, while that of Gen. Schenck was declared not vacant. So far as Gen. Schenck's case was concerned the question presented had been previously decided by the House, it having been held that a person may continue to exercise the functions of an office under the United States, after he is elected a member of Congress, and after the constitutional term of Congress commences, and prior to his taking his seat. (*Hammond vs. Herreck, Cl. & H.*, 28. *Case of Elias Earle, Ibid*, 314.) But Gen. Blair's case presented a new question. An able and interesting report upon these two cases was made from the committee of elections by its chairman, the Hon. Henry L. Dawes of Mass. (*Report No.* 110, 1*st. Sess. thirty-eighth Congress.*) From this report, which contains an elaborate discussion of the whole subject, it is deemed proper here to quote as follows:

"The authorities are equally clear that the mere appointment or election to an office, the duties of which are incompatible with those of one already held, will not vacate such office. This is true even in England, where the appointment to office cannot always be avoided, and where once assumed it cannot, as we have seen, be always voluntarily resigned by the incumbent. [*Willcock on Mun. Corp.*, 243, 248.] And in this country, where the acceptance of office is purely voluntary, and its resignation equally so, the reason of the thing as well as authority clearly leads to the same conclusion. The incumbent is free to choose in which of the two offices he will serve. He cannot be compelled to serve in the one or forced to vacate the other, except in some manner provided in its tenure. The mere appointment or election to one office, unaccompanied with consent or acceptance, cannot force a man out of an office he already holds. Anciently it was tried in England. A man who was town clerk was elected alderman without his consent, in order to turn him out of his former office, they being incompatible, and thereupon he prayed a writ of restitution to the office of town clerk, which was granted. (*Dyer* 332, 6, *in the notes.*) So that consent and acceptance create the vacancy. And Willcock, in his Treatise upon Municipal Corporations, before cited, states that the election of an officer to an incompatible office does not vacate the former before acceptance by the officer, [*p.* 243.] In this country, *Angel and Ames on Corporations* (*Sec.* 434,) adopt this same language, and incorporate it into the text of their treatise. In *Whitney vs. Canique*, before cited, [2 *Hill*, 93,] the same doctrine is clearly stated in the following words: "The appointment of a person to a second office incompatible with the first is not absolutely void, but on his subsequently *accepting* the appointment and *qualifying*, the first office is *ipso facto* vacated." And Mr. Cushing, in his Law and Practice of Legislative Assemblies, [Sec. 479,] lays down the same rule, in stating a case which is the converse of the one involved in this reference. He says: "It may be considered as a rule founded in the reason of the thing, and corresponding with the practice, as far as it is known, of all our legislative assemblies, that in order to vacate the seat of a member by the acceptance of the disqualifying or incompatible office, the election or appointment thereto alone is not sufficient, but the member must either have signified his acceptance of the office in a formal manner, or have done what is incumbent on him to qualify him to discharge its duties, or have actually entered upon its discharge."

"The common law has been shown to be clear that the election alone to an incompatible office will not vacate one already held. The language of the Constitution is, that "no person holding any office under the United States, shall be a member of either House during his continuance in office." The words are, "shall be a *member*," not "shall be elected." No one can be made a "member" against his will. He may be *elected* without his consent or knowledge, for he may be in a foreign land; but to "become a member" he must not only be elected, but he must take the oath of office. The Constitution says: "Each house shall be the judge of the elections, returns, and qualifications of its own *members*;" that is, of those who have qualified and taken seats. Again: "A majority of each shall constitute a quorum, but a smaller number may adjourn from day to day, and may be authorized to compel the attendance of absent *members*." But the attendance of a representative elect was never yet compelled. And, again: "Each house may determine the rules of its proceedings, punish its *members* for disorderly behavior, and, with the concurrence of two-thirds, expel a *member*." The committee are not aware of any attempt to punish a representative elect, and of but one instance of an attempt to expel one. A resolution was adopted by the last House, under the previous question, to expel a person who was a representative elect, but had never signified his acceptance of the office, or qualified, or even appeared in Washington for the purpose of taking his seat. But when the Constitution uses the word "*representative*," it is in this connexion: "The times, places, and manner of holding elections of Senators and *Representatives*, shall be," &c. "No person shall be a *Representative* who shall not have attained to the age of twenty-five years." In the clause now under consideration, the language is: "No person holding any office under the United States shall be a *member* of either House during his continuance in office." No one doubts that the object of the constitutional inhibition was to guard the *House* against Executive influence. This object is attained, so far as it can be by this provision, if the inhibition attaches the moment the member enters upon the discharge of his duties as such, and nothing is gained by an earlier application of it.

The committee are, therefore, of opinion that the reasons in which this constitutional provision originated, as well as its express language and the practice of the House under it, are in harmony with the rule of law which existed before the formation of the Constitution, that the acceptance and entering upon the discharge of the duties of an office, which, from the nature of its duties, or from express legal or constitutional prohibition, is incompatible with another previously held, vacated the former office from the time of such acceptance and entering upon the duties assigned to the latter office.

And, consequently, when a person elected to Congress accepts that office, or qualifies and enters upon the discharge of its duties, he vacates or forfeits any office he may then hold under the United States. And when any member of Congress, after he has qualified or entered upon the discharge of his duties as such member, accepts or enters upon the discharge of the duties of "any office under the United States," he, *ipso facto*, vacates or forfeits his seat as a member of Congress.

But this record raises another question which, so far as the committee can learn, has not before arisen, and which it becomes necessary to examine. Mr. Blair was appointed a Brigadier General, August 7, 1862, and a Major General, November 29, 1862, the duties of which latter office he discharged till January 1, 1864, when he tendered his resignation, which was accepted January 12, 1864. On this latter day he was qualified, and took his seat in the House of Representatives. The first regular session of the thirty-eighth Congress, fixed by law, commenced on the first Monday of December, 1863. It therefore appears that Mr. Blair held and discharged the duties of the office of Major General for more than a month after the commencement of the session fixed by law of the Congress in which, after resigning that office, he subsequently took his seat. Now, if the reasoning already submitted, and the conclusions which the committee have drawn therefrom, be correct, viz., that the acceptance of an office incompatible with one already held must be deemed and treated as a resignation of the former, then does it not follow that the continuance in the discharge of the duties of the former office, after the time at which the law requires the entering upon and discharge of the incompatible duties of the latter, must be deemed and treated as a declination of this office? If two offices are tendered at the same time to the same person, and he is at liberty to choose between the two, but either the nature of the offices, or the requirements of the law or Constitution, forbid the acceptance of both, no one will doubt but that, after an election between them is made and the duties of one have been entered upon, it is too late then to take the other. As both cannot be taken, the one is declined in the acceptance of the other. Does the fact that these two offices are tendered at the same time, make any difference in the principle? A man in the discharge of the duties of one office is tendered another, whose duties he is required to enter upon at a certain time, but the functions of both he cannot perform. When the time arrives at which the duties of the latter office commence, he is at liberty to choose. If he takes the latter, the functions of the former, *ipso facto*, cease as the result of his choice. If he determines to continue to hold the former, does he not of necessity decline the latter, as a like result of that choice? When he accepts one office, the law interprets the act as a surrender of any incompatible office. Shall it not put a like interpretation upon a continuance to discharge the duties of the other? If he may be permitted to keep vacant the one office one month by continuing in the incompatible one during that time, he may two or twelve, or during its whole term. If those *acts* are not to be taken as an election on his part, then that election is yet to be made; and what interposes to require it to be made till the day before the term expires, or then? And thus may the people of any district, or any number of districts, be deprived altogether of representation. The committee cannot arrive at any conclusion fraught with such results, but are of opinion that, when the time arrives at which the duties of two incompatible offices are by law to be discharged, a man at liberty to choose between the two, as effectually declines one not entered upon, by continuing in the one already held, as he would vacate the former if he did enter upon the latter.

It therefore follows that Mr. Blair, by voluntarily continuing to hold and discharge the duties of the office of Major General till January, 1864, declined and disqualified himself for the office of representative, the duties of which, by law, commenced on the first Monday of the December preceding."

§ 243. A person who held a federal office after being elected to Congress, but who had ceased to discharge its duties before taking his seat as a member of Congress, is qualified for the latter office without having formally resigned the former.—(*Case of George Mumford, Cl. & H.* 316.) And there can be no doubt, but that the accepting of the office of Representative in Congress and entering upon the discharge of its duties, amounts to a resignation and abandonment of any incompatible office previously held, and hence a formal resignation is not necessary in any such case.

§ 244. As early as the year 1791, it was decided in the lower House of Congress that a member of that body may tender his resignation to the Governor of his State, and that such Governor may issue a writ for a new election, without any notice to, or action by the House of Representatives. (*Case of John J. Mercer, Clark & Hall*, 44. *Case of Benj. Edwards, Ibid*, 92.) The constitution provides that, "when vacancies happen in the representation from any State, the executive authority thereof shall issue writs of election to fill such vacancies." (*Const. Art.* 1. *Sec.* 2.) It is now well settled that the consent of the House is not necessary to the resignation of a member. The right to resign is absolute, and may be exercised even by a member when under charges, or pending a resolution for his expulsion. (*Case of Matteson,* 38*th Congress, and of Whittemore, forty-first Congress.*) Such being the law, it is of course not essential to the validity of a resignation that it be addressed to the House, or to its Speaker. If addressed to the Executive of the State, it is sufficient, and creates a vacancy for the filling of which he may issue a writ in accordance with the law of the State. It is however highly proper, that the House be informed of the resignation of one of its members, at the earliest moment practicable, and if the House be in session at the time of such resignation, it is the uniform custom, for the member resigning to address a letter to the Speaker, informing him and the House of the fact, that he has sent his resignation to the Executive of the State.

§ 245. Where the qualifications required for office are "a residence in the State of one year" and that one shall be "a citizen of the United States," if a person elected has resided in the State for the time required it is not essential that he shall have been a *citizen* during the whole of that time; it is sufficient if he were naturalized at the time of the election. "It is not the citizen who is required to have resided in that quality for one year next preceding the election. It is the person, the individual, the man, who is spoken of, and who is to possess the qualifications of residence, age, freedom, &c., at the time he offers to vote, or is to be voted for." (*Biddle vs. Richard, Cl. & H.*, 407.)

§ 246. The constitution, Art. 1, Sec. 3, provides, "no person shall be a Senator who shall not have attained the age of thirty years and been nine years a citizen of the United States, and who shall not when elected be an inhabitant of the State for which he shall be chosen." Mr. Shields of Illinois, who was an alien by birth, and who was elected Senator before he had been a citizen of the United States the term of years required, was held not entitled to a seat under said election. Such an election is entirely void. (*Case of James Shields*, 1 *Bartlett*, 606.)

§ 247. A member of the Senate of the United States holding the office under executive appointment, has a right to occupy his seat until the vacancy is filled by the State legislature and the credentials of the person so elected are presented to the Senate. (*Case of Winthrop*, 1 *Bartlett*, 607.)

§ 248. Art. 1, Sec. 3, of the constitution provides, that if vacancies happen in the Senate of the United States, "by resignation or otherwise during the recess of the legislature of any State, the executive thereof may make temporary appointments until the next meeting of the legislature, which shall then fill such vacancies." In the case of *Phelps of Vermont*, (1 *Bartlett*, 613,) it was held that an executive appointment made to fill a vacancy expires with the adjournment of the next session of the legislature of the State, after such appointment is made, so that if the legislature meets after such appointment is made and adjourns without electing a Senator, the seat becomes vacant. The appointee of the executive cannot hold over after the failure of the legislature to elect. The language of the constitution "until the next *meeting* of the legislature" was construed to be equivalent to the words, "until the next *session*" &c., and the appointee was held entitled to hold the seat until the adjournment of the legislature without action, when his term of service was held to have expired. The case of Senator Phelps, in which these propositions may be said to have been finally settled, was decided by the Senate after full discussion, and against the majority of the judiciary committee and sustaining the views of the minority. This minority report has become the law of the Senate upon the subject. It is an able and exhaustive discussion of the whole subject, and contains a citation of all the precedents. It will be found in 1 *Bartlett*, pages 613 to 618 inclusive.

§ 249. It will be seen by reference to the constitution of the United States, Art. 1, Secs. 2 and 3, that no person can be a Representative " who shall not, when elected, be an *inhabitant* of the State in which he shall be chosen," and that no person shall be a Senator who shall not, "when elected, be an *inhabitant* of that State, for which he shall be chosen." The meaning of the term inhabitant, as employed in these provisions, has been somewhat discussed. That it was intended to express something different from the word resident, is apparent from the fact that the latter word was in the original draft of the constitution, and was stricken out by the convention, and "inhabitant" inserted. It would seem that the framers of the constitution were impressed with a deep sense of the importance of an actual *bona fide* residence of the representative among the constituency—a residence in the sense of actual living among them and commingling with them,—and therefore employed the term inhabitant in the sense of living or abiding, and not in the sense of technical residence. This view of the subject was sustained in an elaborate report made to the House of Representatives, in 1824, in case of *John Bailey* of Massachusetts, who was elected a Representative from that State while he was a clerk in the Department of State, at Washington, D. C., and temporarily residing in that city while in the discharge of his official duties. He was held not entitled to the seat. (*Clark & Hall*, 411.) The conclusion reached in that case was that an inhabitant of a State, within the meaning of these clauses of the constitution, is one who is *bona fide* a member of the State, subject to all the requisitions of its laws, and entitled to all the privileges and advantages which they confer.

§ 250. The case of one who is abroad, representing the government at a foreign Court, was held to be different from that of a person employed in the *domestic* service of the government, out of the limits of his own State. The foreign representative carries with him the sovereignty of the government to which he belongs; his rights as a citizen are not impaired by his absence; children born in the house he occupies, are considered as born within the territory and jurisdiction of the government in whose service he is; he does not possess the capacity by residence in the foreign country, to become one of its citizens, or to lose his allegiance to the country from which he comes. None of these things attach to those persons who are employed in the home service of the government. It was accordingly held by the Committee of Elections, in the case of *John Forsyth of Georgia*, (*Cl. & H.*, 497,) that a person can be chosen a Representative in Congress while absent from the country, as a minister to a foreign Court, and that this case did not conflict with the case of John Bailey, *supra*.

§ 251. Where the constitution of a State authorizes the Governor to fill vacancies that may happen in certain offices during the recess of the Senate, by granting commissions, &c., such Governor has no power to create a vacancy by a declaration that one exists, and granting a commission to fill it. The decision of the Governor in such a case that a vacancy exists, is not conclusive as to the rights of others, and if, upon a judicial investigation, by a Court of competent jurisdiction, it is determined that no vacancy existed, the appointment by the Governor is void, and must be set aside. (*Page vs. Hardin*, 8 *B. Mon.*, 648.) The judiciary must, where individual right is involved, decide upon the legality of an act of the Supreme Executive power, as well as upon the validity of legislative acts. (*Ibid.*)

§ 252. Where the constitution prescribes the qualifications for an office, the legislature cannot add others not therein prescribed. It was accordingly held, that where the constitution provided that "all civil officers of the commonwealth at large shall reside within the State, and all district, county or town officers within their respective districts," it was not competent for the legislature to require the Secretary of State to reside at the seat of government. (*Ibid.*) In the same case it was further held that, by the common law, ministerial officers may generally appoint deputies to act in the name and place of the principal, and whose acts within the scope of their appointment, will be held valid.

§ 253. An office may be abandoned by removal from the State, county or district to which the officer is restricted by the law of his office; or by accepting an incompatible office; or by the relinquishment of any express qualification; or by the assumption of any absolute disqualification, or by resignation, (*Ibid.*)

§ 254. Where an officer is commissioned for a certain term of years "if he shall so long behave himself well," he cannot be removed for misbehavior without notice and a trial. The conviction of misbehavior in our government implies a right to notice, defense, and proof, on the part of the officer, and is a judicial question. The executive, therefore, cannot determine that the Secretary of State, or any other officer, holding during good behavior, has been guilty of misbehavior and thereupon remove such officer. [*Ibid.*]

§ 255. The doctrine of *Page vs. Hardin*, was approved and adopted by the Supreme Court of New Jersey, in the recent case of *The State vs. Prichard and others*, (*Am. Law Register, New Series*,) *Vol.* 12, *p.* 514.) And in this latter case the Court went further, and held that even if the incumbent of an office be convicted of an infamous crime, this does not, *ipso facto*, work such a forfeiture of his office as to make it vacant. It was determined that in the absence of any statute expressly declaring that such conviction shall create a vacancy in the office, it is not within the power of the executive to give it this effect, and to appoint a successor to the person convicted. The right to remove a public officer for misbehavior in office does not appertain to the executive, but such is a judicial act, and belongs to a Court,—in New Jersey to the Court of impeachments. Because the conviction of an officer of an infamous crime deprives him of the right to testify as a witness and of the right to vote, it does not follow that it also deprives him of his office. Says the Court in the case just cited: "Because as a punishment the law has denounced a loss of two of the rights of citizenship, it does not follow that a third right is to be withheld from the delinquent. Indeed, the reverse result is the reasonable deduction, because it is clear on common principles that no penalty for crime but that which is expressly prescribed, can be exacted. The fact that severe penal consequences are annexed by statute to the commission of a breach of law, cannot warrant the aggravation by the judicial hand of the punishment prescribed." It may not be out of place here to remark, that while the law is no doubt as laid down in the case just cited, it would, as the judge delivering the opinion clearly intimates, be well for the legislatures of the several States to provide by statute that the conviction of a public officer of any official delinquency, or of the commission of any infamous crime, shall *ipso facto* work a forfeiture of his office, and that the record of such conviction by a Court of competent jurisdiction shall be sufficient to authorize the proper authority to declare and to fill the vacancy. For it is plain that in the absence of such legislation, according to the law which seems well settled, a convicted felon may, for a time at least, continue to exercise the functions of a public office, unless indeed by imprisonment, he be deprived of the power to do so.

§ 256. The constitution of Kentucky provides, that "any person who shall after the adoption of this constitution, either directly or indirectly, give, accept, or knowingly carry a challenge to any person or persons to fight in single combat with a citizen of this State, with any deadly weapon, either in or out of the State, shall be deprived of the right to hold any office of honor or profit in this commonwealth, and shall be punished otherwise in such manner as the General Assembly may prescribe by law." It has been held by the Board for the determination of contested elections in that State, that this constitutional provision does not require a conviction of the crime of giving, accepting or carrying a challenge in order to disqualify the offender. [*Cochran vs.*

Jones, 14 *Am. Law Reg. N. S.*, 222.] It was held in this case that under the constitutional provision above quoted, the doing of any of the acts named therein, disqualifies the person so acting for any office of honor or profit under the State, besides subjecting him to such punishment as may be prescribed by law. That the disqualification and the offence against the laws are separate subjects, and that the contested election board has jurisdiction to decide the former, without reference to the latter. This decision is based upon the theory that the constitution does not declare the giving, accepting or carrying a challenge, a penal offence: that it does not make these acts crimes, but simply prescribes as among the qualifications for office, that persons who have so acted shall not be eligible. This view is ably supported in the opinion, and yet its soundness is somewhat questioned by the author of the note to the case, published with the report *supra*. The question presented is, [and it is one not free from doubt] whether the disqualification of duelists under the constitution of Kentucky is a *punishment*. If it be in the nature of a punishment for a penal offence, then a judgment of conviction by a court of competent jurisdiction, would be necessary to enforce it. The better opinion, however, would seem to be that the constitutional provision in question was designed to execute itself; that it was not to be left to the legislature to provide by statute for the indictment and punishment of persons guilty of dueling before such persons could be excluded from holding office, and that the board, for the determination of contested elections, had therefore jurisdiction to inquire whether the claimant for office before them had done any of the acts, which, if done, would render him ineligible. It would seem to be a rule admitting of but few exceptions, that a tribunal clothed with power to try the title to an office, must be permitted to inquire into the *qualifications* of all claimants, and to ascertain and consider all such facts as relate to the question of eligibility. This view of the constitutional provision above quoted, is strengthened by the consideration that the same constitution in which it is found, imposes a number of disqualifications, in respect to some of which a *conviction* is in terms required, and in respect to others no previous conviction is made necessary,—the disqualification on account of dueling being of the latter class. Thus it is provided that "every person shall be disqualified from holding any office of profit or trust * * * who shall be *convicted* of having given or offered any bribe or treat to secure his election." The argument is, that the requirement of conviction was inserted with respect to some acts and omitted as to others, by the framers of the constitution, for a purpose, and that purpose must have been to dispense with the necessity for a conviction in the cases where it is not in terms required. (*h*)

§ 257. It seems that the power given by the constitution of the United States to the executive of any State, to make temporary appointments to fill vacancies which may happen during the recess of the legislature, does not empower such executive to *anticipate* a vacancy, and make an appointment to

(*h*) But see decision in same case by court of appeals of Ky. *14 Am. Law Reg.*, *373*.

fill it, before it happens. (*Case of James Lanman, Cl. & H.*, 871.) Such appears to have been the ground upon which Mr. Lanman was refused a seat in the Senate, although it does not very clearly appear, either from the report of the committee or the debate in the Senate, what were the reasons for the decision. The record, however, discloses no objection to the validity of the appointment, other than the fact that it was made before the vacancy happened. And in the course of the discussion of a subsequent case in the Senate, (that of *Potter vs. Robbins*,) this case was frequently referred to as having been decided upon the ground above stated. In the latter case Mr. Bibb, Senator from Kentucky, said, referring to the case of Lanman: "The Governor had thought fit to appoint Mr. Lanman to a vacancy which *would* occur, not one which *had* occurred. This (the Governor's) act was consequently declared void." (See *Cl. & H.*, 886.)

§ 258. As we have seen, the question of eligibilty to be elected to, or to hold an office, is generally to be determined by the construction of some statutory or constitutional provision, fixing the qualifications therefor. But cases have arisen where both the constitution and statute are silent. Thus in Wisconsin there is no statutory or constitutional provision to determine whether an alien may be elected to or hold office. In *State vs. Smith*, (14 *Wis.*, 497,) the question arose whether an alien could hold the office of sheriff. In that case the defendant was an alien, and had entered upon the discharge of the duties of his office, without having become an elector, which he might have done by declaring his intention to become a citizen. Up to the time of the commencement of the action he had not become a voter, so that the case presented simply the question of the right of an alien, not a voter, to *hold* the office. The Court held that he could not hold it, and the decision was put upon the ground that a person cannot lawfully hold such an office unless he is a qualified elector of the State. The Court, by Dixon, C. J., said: "It is an acknowledged principle which lies at the very foundation, and the enforcement of which needs neither the aid of statutory or constitutional enactments or restrictions, that the government is instituted by the citizens for their liberty and protection, and that it is to be administered, and its powers and functions exercised by them, and through their agency." This case, however, went no further than to hold that a person not an elector, is ineligible, in the absence of any statutory or constitutional provision on the subject, to *hold* an office. It left open the question whether a person not an elector, may, in the absence of such statutory or constitutional provision, be *elected* to an office, and be entitled to enter upon and discharge its duties, provided his disability is removed before the commencement of the term, for which he is elected. This latter question, however, did arise in the same State, in the more recent case of *State vs. Murray*, (28*th Wis.*, 96,) and was decided affirmatively. In this case the distinction is clearly made between ineligibility to *hold* an office, and ineligibility to be elected to an office for a term to commence in the future, and for the duties of which the person chosen may qualify himself before the term begins. It may here be added that it has been the constant practice of the Congress of the United States since the rebellion, to admit persons to seats in that body who were ineligible at the date of their election, but whose disabilities had been subsequently removed.

§ 259. Where the constitution of a State fixes the tenure of an office at four years, an act of the legislature of such State providing for an election to that office, and limiting the term of the person to be elected, to two years, is void, in so far as it relates to the length of the term. But in other respects it is constitutional and valid, and the person chosen under it will be entitled to hold the office for the constitutional term of four years. (*Westbrook vs. Roseborough*, 14 *Cal.*. 180.)

§ 260. Where the law requires an officer resigning to do so by a written resignation, to be sent to the governor, it is not necessary that the governor should signify his acceptance of a resignation to make it valid. The tenure of office, in such a case, does not depend upon the will of the executive, but of the incumbent. A civil officer has the absolute right to resign his office at pleasure, and it is not within the power of the executive to compel him to remain in office. [*People vs. Porter*, 6 *California*, 26. *And see also* 1, *McLean's Reports*, 512.]

§ 261. The Constitution of Kansas provides, that "in case of any vacancy in any judicial office, it shall be filled by appointment by the Governor, until the next regular election that shall occur more than thirty days after such vacancy shall have happened." Where the Governor acting under the power here conferred, to fill a vacancy, appointed a person to the office of Justice of the Peace, made vacant by the resignation of the incumbent, it was held that the person appointed could hold only until the first election thereafter, which occurred more than thirty days after the happening of the vacancy, and if that election occurred before the expiration of the original term, the person chosen thereat could hold only for the remainder of the original term. Where the law fixes the term of an office, and provides when it shall be filled, as, for example, at the regular election in each alternate year, the term is not affected by the death, resignation or removal of the incumbent. The regular election for the full term must take place precisely as if no vacancy had occurred. The recitals in a certificate of election, as to the duration of the term, are at best but *prima facie* evidence of such duration, and can always be overthrown by competent testimony. It has been therefore held that where a person was elected at an election occurring in the middle of the original term of two years, the fact that he received a certificate declaring that he was chosen for two years, made no difference as to his rights. (*Hale vs. Evans*, 12 *Kansas*, 582.)

§ 262. It is essential to the validity of an election to office, that it be authorized by some statute in force at the time. By a statute of California it was provided as follows; "Harbor commissioners are elected and appointed, and hold their office as prescribed in the title VI, of part III, of this code." On referring to that portion of the code it was discovered that no provision for such election had been made. It was accordingly held that where a Harbor commissioner resigned the office, no successor could be chosen by the people, until the passage of a law to authorize them so to do. It was further held that inasmuch as the Governor had power to fill all vacancies, the person appointed to fill the vacancy in the office of Harbor commissioner, occasioned by the resignation of the incumbent, would hold until the next legal or authorized election by the people. (*People vs. Matthewson*, 47 *Cal.*, 442.)

§ 263. In *State vs. Jones*, (19 *Ind.*, 359,) the following propositions were laid down:

1. "Where it appears *prima facie* that acts or events have occurred subjecting an office to judicial declaration of being vacant, the authority authorized to fill such vacancy, supposing the office to be vacant, may proceed before procuring a judicial declaration of the vacancy, and appoint or elect, according to the forms of law, a person to fill such office; but if, when such person attempts to take possession of the office, he is resisted by the previous incumbent, he will be compelled to try his title and oust such incumbent, or fail to oust him in some mode prescribed by law.

2. If such elected or appointed person finds the office in fact vacant, and can take possession uncontested by the former incumbent, he will be officer *de facto*, and should the former incumbent never appear to contest his right, he will be regarded as having been an officer *de facto* and *de jure*; but should such former incumbent appear after possession has been taken against him, the burden of proceeding to oust the then actual incumbent will fall upon him, and if

in such proceeding it is made to appear that facts had occurred before the appointment or election, justifying a judicial declaration of a vacancy, it will be then declared to have existed and the election or appointment be held to have been valid."

And it is doubtless true as here stated, that no judicial declaration of a vacancy is absolutely necessary, and that if a vacancy *in fact* exists, the proper authority may fill it. But where the whole body of the electors constitute the proper authority to fill a vacancy, if they proceed upon the idea that its existence is a matter of general notoriety, and without any notice or proclamation of the same, it must appear that it was notorious and that the whole body of the electors, or at least the principal part of them were aware of it, and took part in the election to fill it, or had an opportunity to do so.

CHAPTER VI.

PRACTICE AND EVIDENCE IN CONTESTED ELECTION CASES.

§ 264. At common law the proper remedy against a person claiming to exercise an office, and who was believed to be not entitled thereto, was by the writ of *quo warranto*, which was issued upon proper application for the purpose of inquiring into the authority of such person, and ousting him from such office, in case no authority should be shown. In modern practice an *information* in the nature of a *quo warranto*, is resorted to, in the absence of any statutory proceeding. (*Walker's American Law, p.* 566. *Blackstone's Comm., Vol.* 3, *p.* 263.) And in fact where there are special proceedings authorized by statute, they partake of the nature and retain most of the substance of the common law proceeding by *quo warranto*.

§ 265. According to the common law of England the information was filed in the Court of King's Bench, by the Attorney General. In this country it should be filed by a law officer of the government, and presented to a Court having the necessary common law jurisdiction. The proceeding was originally of a *quasi* criminal character, being intended to secure the punishment of the usurper by a fine as well as to oust him, or seize the office or franchise for the crown. But "it hath," says Blackstone, "long been applied to the mere purposes of trying the civil right, seizing the franchise, or ousting the wrongful possessor; the fine being nominal only."

§ 266. In an information setting forth that the respondent has usurped an office which is claimed by other persons, their claims should be set forth, and the judgment may order the ouster of the usurper, as well as the admission of the rightful claimant. (*Gaud vs. The State*, 10 *Ohio State*, 237.) Leave of Court must be had to file an information of this character, under the common law, though the Attorney General of England it seems might file it at his will. (4 *Blackstone*, 311.)

§ 267. On the trial of a contested election before a board or legislative body, the members returned as elected are not competent to vote upon the question of the validity of their own election. (*Commonwealth vs. McKloskey*, 2 *Rawle*, 369. *Brightley's Election Cases*, 196.) This rule grows out of the doctrine that no man should have a voice in deciding his own case. At common law it is held that even an act of parliament cannot require anything so repugnant to natural justice, as that the same person may be a party and a judge. (*Davy vs. Savadge, Hobart*, 87, 12 *Mad.*, 687.) Out of this principle grows also the parliamentary rule which forbids a member of a parliamentary body to vote upon any question in which he is directly interested. The Court in *Commonwealth vs. McKloskey*, *supra*, does not put it too strongly when it says "for a man to constitute himself a judge in his own cause is indelicate and indecent." To the same effect are the following authorities: *Rice vs. Foster*, 4 *Harrington*, 485. *Carson's Case*, 2 *Lloyd's Debates*, 23. *Stockton's Case, U. S. Senate, Cong'l Globe*, 1865–6–*page* 1635. *Cushing's Election Cases*, 97.

§ 268. It is true that the Senate of the United States permitted Hon. B. F. Wade, Senator from Ohio, to sit as one of the judges for the trial of Andrew Johnson, President of the United States, upon articles of impeachment, and that he voted upon the same, notwithstanding the fact that being President *pro tempore* of the Senate, and ex-officio Vice President of the United States, he would have become President, had the President been convicted. (2, *Johnson's trial*, 486–7, 496, 3 *ibid*, 360.) The question of Mr. Wade's right to be sworn as a member of the Court of impeachment was raised by Senator Hendricks of Indiana, and was debated at some length, and then withdrawn, so that it was not formally decided. If, however, it had been decided in his favor, it could only have been upon the ground that it did not come within, or that it constituted an exception to, the rule we have stated. It was contended that the State of Ohio, in the person of her two Senators, had a right to be heard in the decision of the great case of impeachment then pending, notwithstanding the contingent interest which one of the Senators had in the result, and that the importance of giving to each State an equal voice in that decision, was sufficient to justify what was at least an apparent departure from, or an exception to, that rule. Whatever may be thought of the soundness of this argument, it is sufficient for our present purpose to say that it does not involve any question as to the soundness of the general rule, that no man shall be a judge in a matter in the decision of which he is directly and personally interested.

§ 269. In *ex parte Murphy* (7 *Cowen*, 153,) it was held that the mere circumstance that improper votes were received at an election will not vitiate it. In that case, one candidate had received a majority of two votes, and it was charged that two illegal votes were cast, but there was no allegation that they were cast for the candidate having the majority. The motion for *quo warranto* was denied, the Court saying, "For all that appears the spurious ballots were for the ticket which was in the minority." This ruling, however, should be explained and probably qualified. If it goes no further than to hold that the information in that particular case was insufficient to warrant the allowance of a *quo warranto*, it may be accepted as correct, but, if it is construed as asserting the doctrine, that in all cases it is necessary to show that the person declared elected was, in fact, defeated, before the election can be set aside, then it goes too far. An election may be set aside, declared void, and a new election be ordered, upon the introduction of such proof as renders it impossible to determine who has been chosen by a fair majority, but the contestant can, in no case, be declared entitled to the office until he shows, affirmatively, that he has received a majority of the legal votes cast.

§ 270. It often appears in the course of the trial of a case of contested election that votes have been cast by persons not qualified to vote, and in such cases it becomes very important to ascertain for whom such votes were cast. A question of much importance has arisen as to whether the declarations of illegal voters made not under oath, should be received to show the fact that they voted, or that they were not legally qualified to vote. The English authorities, though not entirely uniform, are generally in favor of admitting such declarations, and perhaps the weight of authority in this country is the same way, though it cannot be denied that the tendency in the more recent, and we think also the better considered cases, is to exclude this evidence as hearsay. (*State vs. Ohio*, 23 *Wis.*, 319. *The New Jersey Case*, 1 *Bartlett*, 19. *Vallandigham, vs. Campbell, do* 230, *and cases there cited.*)

§ 271. The soundness of the rule which admits this species of evidence, is seriously questioned in the late case of *Cessna vs. Myers*, 42*d Congress*. The report in that case presents the following objections to the rule 6.

"The general doctrine is usually put upon the ground that the voter is a party to the proceeding, and his declarations against the validity of his vote are to be admitted against him as such. If this were true, it would be quite clear that his declarations ought not to be received until he is first shown, *aliunde*, not only to have voted, but to have voted for the party against whom he is called. Otherwise it would be in the power of an illegal voter to neutralize wrongfully two of the votes cast for a political opponent: 1st, by voting for his own candidate; 2d, by asserting to some witness afterward that he voted the other way, and so having his vote deducted from the party against whom it was cast.

But it is not true that a voter is a party in any such sense as that his declarations are admissible on that ground. He is not a party to the record. His interest is not legal or personal. It is frequently of the slightest possible nature. If he were a party, then his admissions should be competent as to the whole case—as to the votes of others, the conduct of the election officers, &c., which it is well settled they are not. Another reason given is, that the inquiry is of a public nature, and that it should not be limited to the technical rules of evidence established for private causes. This is doubtless true. It is an inquiry of a public nature, and an inquiry of the highest interest and consequence to the public. Some rules of evidence applicable to such an inquiry must be established. It is nowhere, so far as we know, claimed that in any other particular the ordinary rules of evidence should be relaxed in the determination of election cases. The sitting member is a party deeply interested in the establishment of his right to an honorable office. The people of the district especially, and the people of the whole country, are interested in the question, who shall have a voice in framing the laws? The votes are received by election officers, who see the voter in person, who act publicly in the presence of the people, who may administer an oath to the person offering to vote, and who are themselves sworn to the performance of their duties. The judgment of these officers ought not to be reversed, and the grave interests of the people imperiled by the admissions of persons not under oath, and admitting their own misconduct.

The practice of admitting this kind of evidence originated in England. So far as it has been adopted in this country, it has been without much discussion of the reasons on which it was founded. In England, as has been said, the vote was *viva voce*. The fact that the party voted, and for whom, was susceptible of easy and indisputable proof by the record. The privilege of voting for members of Parliament was a franchise of considerable dignity, enjoyed by few. It commonly depended on the ownership of a freehold, the title to which did not, as with us, appear on public registries, but would be seriously endangered by admissions of the freeholder which disparaged it. An admission by the voter of his own want of qualification was, therefore, ordinarily an admission against his right to a special and rare franchise, and an admission which seriously imperiled his title to his real estate. An admission so strongly against the interest of the party making it would seldom be made unless it were true. It furnishes no analogy for a people who regard voting, not as a privilege of a few, but as the right of all, where the vote, instead of being *viva voce*, is studiously protected from publicity, and where such admissions, instead of having every probability in favor of their truth, may so easily be made the means of accomplishing great injustice and fraud, without fear either of detection or punishment.

It may be said that the principle of the secret ballot protects the voter from disclosing how he voted, and in the absence of power to compel him to testify and furnish the best evidence, renders the resort to other evidence necessary.

"The committee are not prepared to admit, that the policy which shields the vote of the citizen from being made known without his consent, is of more importance than an inquiry into the purity and result of the election itself. If it is, it cannot protect the illegal voter from disclosing how he voted. If it is, it would be quite doubtful whether the same policy should not prevent the use of the machinery of the law to discover and make public the fact, in whatever way it may be proved. It is the publicity of the vote, not the interrogation of the voter in regard to it, that the secret ballot is designed to prevent. There would seem to be no need to resort to hearsay evidence on this ground, unless the voter has first been called, and, being interrogated, asserts his privilege and refuses to answer. Even in that case, a still more conclusive objection to hearsay testimony of this character is this: it is not at all likely to be either true or trustworthy.

"The rule that admits secondary evidence when the best cannot be had only admits evidence which can be relied on to prove the fact, as sworn copies when an original is lost, or the testimony of a witness to the contents of a lost instrument. Hearsay evidence is not admitted in such cases, and is only admitted in cases where hearsay evidence is, in the ordinary experience of mankind, found to be generally correct, as in matters of pedigree and the like. But a man who is so anxious to conceal how he voted as to refuse to disclose it on oath, even when the disclosure is demanded in the interest of public justice, and who is presumed to have voted fraudulently—for otherwise, in most cases, the inquiry is of no consequence—would be quite as likely to have made false statements on the subject, if he had made any. To permit such statements to be received to overcome the judgment of the election officers, who admit the vote publicly, in the face of a challenge, and with the right to scrutinize the voter, would seem to be exceedingly dangerous."

§ 272. In *Newland vs. Graham*, (1 *Bartlett*, 5,) the declarations of voters made after the election, of their having voted for the sitting member, were held inadmissible, and were excluded, although it was shown that, by the statute of North Carolina, where the election took place, voters were not compellable to give evidence for whom they voted. The Committee did not in their report state the ground of their decision, but we may fairly presume that it was held that an illegal voter could not refuse to answer for whom he cast his vote, and shield himself under the statute made to preserve the secrecy of an honest ballot, and that, therefore, since all such persons can be compelled to state for whom they voted, they should be called as witnesses, and their declarations not under oath, should not be received.

§ 273. And again in the recent case of *Gilliland vs. Schuyler*, (9 *Kansas*, 569,) it was held that statements of third parties as to the number of times and the names under which they voted was hearsay and incompetent. The Court said: "It is the testimony of what other persons told the witness, persons not parties to the suit, so that their admissions could be receivable. These declarations were not made at the polls by persons conducting the election, and so as to make part of the *res gestæ*; nor do they accompany a principal fact, so as to qualify or explain it." The Court also says: "We have examined the cases of *People vs. Pease*, 27 *N. Y.*, 45, *State vs. Olin*, 23 *Wis.*, 319, and the note to 3 *McCord*, 230, and so far as they enunciate any principle contrary to the doctrine here announced we disapprove them."

§ 274. Where the statute required that the return of the vote of each town should consist of a copy of the town record, signed by the selectmen and attested by the clerk, it was held that a certificate which did not on its face purport to be a copy of the town record, and which was attested by James N. Tilton, without anything to show that he was town clerk, was void, and could not be received by the canvassing board. (*Luce vs. Mayhew et. al.*, 13 *Gray*, *Mass.* 83.) And of course if the proper officers omit altogether to sign a return, though it may be otherwise formal, it is void, and proves nothing. (*Barnes vs. Adams*, 2 *Bartlett*, 771.)

§ 275. Where the statute provides for a list of voters to be prepared by the selectmen of a town and used at the election, such list is to be regarded as an official document, and is itself the best evidence upon the question whether the name of a particular voter is upon it. It is therefore not competent for a party to show by parol that his name was on such voting list, without first giving notice to produce the list. (*Harris vs. Granville, Whitcomb, et. al.*, 4 *Gray, Mass.* 433.) And it was further held in the same case that the fact that a person's name is on the voting list, is only *prima facie* evidence of his right to vote, and the selectmen may strike off the name and reject the vote, if they can prove that he was not entitled to vote. See also *Humphrey vs. Clingman*, 5 *Metcalf*, 168.

§ 276. A statutory provision requiring notice of contest to be given within a given time, from the date of the official count, or from the declaration of the result, or the issuing of the certificate of election or the like, is peremptory, and the time cannot be enlarged. (*Bowen vs. Hixon*, 45 *Mo.*, 340.) "It has always been held," says the Court in that case, "that where the jurisdiction of a Court is made to depend upon the time, either of giving notice or of taking appeals, the requirement is peremptory." And see also *Castello vs. St. Louis Circuit Court*, 28 *Mo.*, 278. And it may be added that there is the strongest reason for enforcing this rule most rigidly in cases of contested election, because promptness in commencing and prosecuting the proceedings, is of the utmost importance to the end, that a decision may be reached before the term has wholly, or in great part, expired.

§ 277. Where, as is the case in several of the States, the statute provides a mode of preserving the identical ballots cast at an election, for the purpose of being used as evidence in case of contest, such statute, and particularly those provisions which provide for the safe keeping of such ballots, must be followed with great care. The danger that after the count is made known, (especially if the vote is very close,) the ballots may be tampered with, is so great, that no opportunity for such tampering can be permitted. Such ballots, in order to be received in evidence, must have remained in the custody of the proper officers of the law, from the time of the original official count, until they are produced before the proper court or officer, and if it appear that they have been handled by unauthorized persons, or that they have been left in an exposed and improper place, they cannot be offered to overcome the official count. See *Gooding vs. Wilson,* (42*d Congress.*) *Butler vs. Lehman,* (1 *Bartlett,* 354.) *Kline vs. Verree,* (*ibid, page* 381.) In *Butler vs. Lehman* the House of Representatives, after a full discussion, sustained the minority of the committee in rejecting a recount, upon the ground that the ballot boxes had not been so kept as to rebut a reasonable presumption, that they had been tampered with.

§ 278. In California there was a statute requiring the preservation of the ballots in the clerk's office for six months. In the same act was a provision requiring the preservation of the poll list and tally paper, with the certificates of the officers attached. Under this statute the case of *People vs. Holden*, 28*th California*, 123, arose. The defendant in that case was returned as elected county judge by five majority, and the relator as defeated by that number. Upon an inspection of the ballots cast at one of the precincts and preserved in the clerk's office, under the law, it appeared that thirty-one democratic tickets had been cast, and that the name of Holden was on all of them except two, from which as appeared upon inspection, his name had been torn off. Several ballots containing Holden's name having been thrown out for other causes, the case turned upon the two ballots, from which his name had been torn, and the question was whether the name was torn off after, or before, the ballot was placed in the box. There was no evidence upon this point and the court held, that the presumption was that the ticket had not been mutilated, and that the name had been torn off by the voter before voting. The evidence consisted of the certified returns and poll list, on the one hand, and the ballots on the other. Here was a case of presumption against presumption. The law presumed that the returns were correct, and it also presumed that the ballots had not been tampered with. The temptation to tear the name of Holden from a few tickets, and thus change the result, was unquestionably very great, while it could hardly have been supposed by the officers, who certified the township returns, that to change two or three votes would change the result. The soundness of the ruling is seriously doubted, by Mr.

Brightley, in his note to this case, [*Brightley's Election Cases*, 484,] and it is quite certain that the precedent is quite an unsafe one. Before the ballots should be allowed in evidence to overturn the official count and return, it should appear *affirmatively* that they have been safely kept by the proper custodian of the law,—that they have not been exposed to the public, or handled by unauthorized persons, and that no opportunity has been given for tampering with them. If this is believed to be a rule, founded upon the presumption that a fraud or a crime has been committed, the answer is that the rule does no more than to make choice between two presumptions of law, which in this instance come in conflict, and cannot both prevail. In such a case the question is, which is the stronger, the more reasonable, and the safer presumption? And inasmuch as the ballots are counted by the board of canvassers, immediately upon the closing of the polls, and generally before there has been an opportunity for tampering, and when it cannot be known that the changing of a few votes will change the result, and in most cases by a board composed of friends of each of the competing candidates, it is believed that in the absence of all proof, in case of a conflict between the tally sheets and returns on one side, and the ballots as they are found to be at some period after the election is over, and after the state of the vote as returned has been made known on the other; the correctness of the original official canvass, made by sworn officers at the time of the election should be presumed.

§ 279. The case of *Archer vs. Allen*, (1 *Bartlett*,

169,) is another case in which there was a recount of the ballots, after the official count had been made and the result announced. The official canvass showed the election of the incumbent by a majority of only one vote. The recount, which was made by officers of the election, some *four months* after the day of election, resulted in the alleged discovery of a mistake of two votes in favor of contestant, just sufficient to change the result. The necessity for proving affirmatively that the ballots had not been tampered with, seems to have been felt and conceded by the contestant, and a good deal of testimony was taken upon that point, enough, according to the report of the majority of the committee, to make it clear that the ballots counted at the second and unofficial canvass, were the identical ballots originally deposited in the box. The minority of the committee, however, took the opposite view, and insisted that the proof of identity was insufficient.

After an elaborate debate in the House, the report of the majority declaring the incumbent not duly elected, was adopted, but the resolution giving the seat to the contestant was lost, and the seat thereby became and was declared vacant.

§ 280. An application for a recount of the ballots cast at an election, will not be granted unless some specific mistake or fraud be pointed out in the particular box, to be examined. Such recount will not be ordered upon a general allegation of errors in the count of all, and giving particulars as to none of the boxes. [*Kansas Case*, 2 *Parsons*, 599. *Thompson vs. Ewing*, 1 *Brewst.*, 67, 97.] These rulings were made in cases of applications to the

Court to order a recount of ballots. Of course such an order might be accompanied with proper provisions for securing fairness and accuracy, and the result might and would be rejected in case of doubt as to the identity of the ballots, but before ordering it the Court held that there must be charges of mistake or fraud sufficiently precise to induce the Court to entertain the complaint, and that a general allegation of errors believed to exist, was not enough to authorize the perilous experiment of testing the election return by the result of a recount.

§ 281. In *Skerret's Case*, (2 *Parsons*, 509,) the Court of Common Pleas of Philadelphia, had occasion to discuss the requisites of a petition to contest an election. The statute of Pennsylvania provided as follows: "That the returns of the elections under this act shall be subject to the inquiry, determination and judgment of the Court of Common Pleas of the proper county, upon complaint in writing, of thirty or more of the qualified electors of the proper county, of the undue election or return of such officer, two of whom shall take and subscribe an oath or affirmation that the facts set forth in said complaint are true," &c. And it was held that the complaint must set forth the facts with particularity and precision, and they must be such as if true to render it the duty of the Court either to vacate the election or to declare another person than the one returned, to have been duly elected. It was further held that unless the petition be thus verified and set forth facts that if true would have changed the result, it will be quashed on motion.

No doubt it would also be held bad on demurrer. There is no doubt as to the soundness of this ruling. It is not desirable to encourage groundless or frivolous contests. If the complainants have a solid basis for their complaint, they can readily specify the facts upon which they rely, and if they have not such solid basis, it is better that they be not permitted to proceed. "The true rule," says King P. J., in Skerret's case, *supra*, "regulating such proceedings, should be defined so as to advance on the one hand, substantial and meritorious, and to arrest on the other, futile and querulous complaints." It is not sufficient to state generally that A. received a majority of votes while the certificate was given to B., and therefore the complainants charge that there was an undue election. This is but a conclusion, and it is not for the pleader to state conclusions but facts, from which the Court may draw conclusions. If fraud is alleged, the petition must state the manner in which the fraud was effected, and the number of votes fraudulently received or fraudulently rejected." Upon this general subject see *Carpenter's Case*, 2 *Parsons*, 537. *Lelar's Case*, 2 *Parsons*, 548. *Kneass' Case*, 2 *Parsons*, 553.

§ 282. Where some of the grounds set out in the petition are mere irregularities, which, if sustained by proof, would not vitiate the election, they will be stricken out on motion, and the respondent will not be put to the trouble of taking proof to rebut them. *Kneass' Case*, *supra*, and see *Batturs vs. Megary*, 1 *Brewst.*, 192. And it is not necessary to give the names of the persons who are alleged to have voted illegally. (*Gibbons vs. Sheppard*, 2 *Brewst.*, 2, 65 *Pa. St. R.*, 36. *Batturs vs. Megary*, 1 *Brewst.*, 162.)

§ 283. It was held by the Supreme Court of Pennsylvania, in *Gibbons vs. Sheppard, supra*, that certainty to a common intent is all that is required, and that some of the rulings above referred to were too stringent; that the rule must not be held so strictly as to afford protection to fraud, by which the will of the people is set at naught, nor so loosely as to permit the powers of sworn officers chosen by the people, to be inquired into without well defined cause. (65 *Pa. St. R.*, 36–7.)

Undoubtedly the same rule should be applied to a pleading of this character that is applied to all other similar pleadings. It should state in a legal and logical form, the facts which constituted the ground of the complaint; nothing more is required; nothing less will suffice.

§ 284. In most of the States of the Union, there are statutes to regulate pleadings under which Courts are authorized to allow amendments where petitions or other pleadings are found to be defective, and under most of these statutes a petition in a contested election case may be amended. And in the absence of any statute of this character, the Court trying a case of contested election may, under its general common law power, permit such a petition to be amended. And an amendment ought to be allowed whenever the Court in the exercise of a sound discretion shall be of opinion that the ends of justice will be thereby promoted. (*Kneass' Case*, 2 *Parsons, Philadelphia*, 553. *Brightley's Election Cases*, 337.)

§ 285. There is, however, a very strong reason for requiring any such amendment to be made *in-*

stanter, and for bringing an election case to a prompt and speedy trial and determination, and it is this. The subject matter of the controversy is daily growing less, and of less importance and value. The office in question is usually for a short term of one or perhaps several years only, and if the "laws delays" are to be allowed in these as in other cases, the term would often expire before a decision could be reached. And if an amendment of a petition would necessarily result in a continuance, or in considerable delay, it ought not to be permitted, because it is better that he whose fault it is that the original petition is insufficient should suffer, than that an innocent party should be deprived of his right to a speedy trial. In such a case the furtherance of justice requires that leave to amend should be refused. See also *Gibbons vs. Sheppard*, 65 *Pa, St. R.*, 20, 35. *Mann vs. Cassiday*, 1 *Brewst.*, 32. *Thompson vs. Ewing*, *ibid*, 68, 97, 101.

§ 286. Where an election district is composed of several sub-divisions or voting precincts, a failure of the officers of one of such sub-divisions to make a return, no matter from what cause, will not invalidate the election unless it be shown that the votes not returned would have changed the result. It was so held by the Supreme Court of New York, in *ex parte, Heath and others*, (3 *Hill*, 42,) which was a case involving the validity of an election of ward officers in the sixth ward of the City of New York. The ward was composed of four districts, from three of which the returns were regular, but as to the remaining ward (the first,) the inspectors certified thus: "It is impossible for us to declare what persons were by the greatest number of votes elected, by reason of lawless violence committed upon the inspectors of the first district, &c., and the dispersion of the ballots before they were counted, &c." There was no evidence to show that votes not returned from the first district would have changed the result as shown by the returns from the other three, and accordingly it was held that the persons receiving the highest number of votes as shown by the returns from the three districts, were entitled to qualify; and a mandamus was granted, commanding the Mayor to administer the oath of office to them. In the course of his opinion in the case, Cowan J. says, "In no case we are aware of has it ever been held that the accidental loss of the ballots in a single sub-division of an election district, even though it prevent a return, shall, of itself, defeat, or indeed detract from the election as it stands on the votes which are properly returned. Once admit the principle that the loss of a part of the votes out of the number which may or should be given at an election, avoids the whole, and it is difficult to conceive how a system of government so entirely elective as ours, could be carried on. That a part of the votes given are lost, is never allowed *per se*, even in a private corporate election, as a ground for setting the election aside. It is not enough to say the result is therefore uncertain. (*Ex parte Murphy*, 7*th Cowan*, 153.) Yet the contrary rule would be much more tolerated in the case of private corporations than in that of large municipal and civil divisions. To give the loss any effect, it must at least be shown that without its happening the result would have been different. *The People, ex rel, &c., vs. Vail,* 20 *Wend.*, 12."

§ 287. In all legislative bodies which have the power to judge as to the election and qualification of their own members, the rule is well settled that when the right of the sitting member is called in question, the body will look beyond the certificate of the returning officers, and determine the question upon the actual merits. The certificate is *prima facie* evidence only in such a controversy. The rule is the same in the Courts, and in trials of contested election cases before a jury. (*The People vs. Vail,* 20 *Wend.*, 12.) But it is, as elsewhere shown, equally well settled, that the returning board or officer whose duty it is to open returns, ascertain the result, and issue commissions, cannot go behind the returns. And if a party wishes to go behind the returns and set them aside, he must in his pleading make specific allegations, showing wherein they are false. (*State ex rel vs. Townsley,* 56 *Mo.*, 107.)

§ 288. Under the statute of Pennsylvania, conferring jurisdiction upon the Court of Quarter Session, to hear and determine election contests, and making its decision final and conclusive, it was held that an issue to a jury could not be directed to try the question of an alleged fraud in an election. The chief reason given was that a trial by jury if conceded to one contestant, must be conceded to all, and that "delay must take place in preparing and setting down such an issue for trial; after trial of the most tedious and expensive kind the jury may disagree, (one dissenter from the rest being adequate to produce that result,) and their consequent discharge.

Another and another trial may follow with like results, until one of the parties weary with delay, or bankrupt in prosecuting his rights abandons them in despair," and by bills of exceptions and writs of error the proceedings might be still further prolonged. This would operate most unjustly to the contestant, if in the end it should appear that he was rightly entitled to the office. (*Kneass' Case*, 2 *Parsons*, 599. *Brightley's Election Cases*, 260.)

§ 289. The same point was decided in the same way, by the Supreme Court of Pennsylvania, in *Ewing vs. Filley*, 43 *Pa. St. R.*, 389. And in that case the Court also held that an act providing for the trial of a case of contested election without the intervention of a jury, is not for that reason unconstitutional. "It is not," says Lowrie, C. J., in that case, "in the act of organization of the State, nor in the perpetuation of its organic succession, but in the administration of rights under the organization, that the constitution secures the trial by jury. The jury is the proper element in the determination of rights which need enforcement by means of the State organization, but there is a much larger popular element in our elections, the votes of all the people, and all our political practice shows that we have not considered a jury an essential means in deciding contested elections of public officers.

§ 290. The returns and other election papers though conclusive upon the canvassers, may be impeached upon a *quo warranto*, or other form of contested election. The very question to be determined in such a contest is frequently the truthfulness and reliability of the returns, poll books, &c., and the duty of the tribunal trying the case, is to ascertain not who was returned as elected, but who was in fact elected. (*People vs. Vail*, 20 *Wend.*, 12. *Commonwealth vs. Commissioners*, 5 *Rawls.*, 77.) And in accordance with this rule it was decided in *Howard vs. Shields*, (16 *Ohio, State Rep.*, 184,) that parol evidence is admissible, not only to impeach, but also to correct omissions in the poll books and tally sheets, and that these documents when so corrected are sufficient *prima facie* evidence of the result of the election. In that case the judges and clerks of the election had omitted to sign the poll books and tally papers at the proper place, and had also omitted to fill the blanks in the caption, or to state the aggregate number of the voters, and parol evidence was held to be admissible to correct these errors.

§ 291. In the case last named it was also held that the tally sheet kept by the officers of the election, is competent evidence in an election contest to show the true state of the vote. It is good until impeached, and affords *prima facie* evidence of the number of votes cast for each candidate. And see also *Powers vs. Reed*, 19 *Ohio State R.*, 189. The ballots themselves are, however, (when fully identified,) better evidence of the number of votes cast, and for whom cast, than the tally lists made from them by the officers of election. (*People vs. Holden*, 28 *Cal.*, 123.) But unless the law has provided means for preserving and identifying the very ballots cast, and unless the law in that respect has been strictly pursued, the ballots may not afford evidence as reliable as the other election papers.

§ 292. It has been held that for the purpose of

showing that a person voted the poll list is admissible in evidence, though not signed by the inspectors or clerks having no heading to denote its character, and never having been filed in the clerk's office. (*People vs. Pease*, 27 *N. Y.*, 45.) But it would, of course, be necessary to prove by evidence *aliunde*, that such a paper was the poll list, which was actually kept by the officers of the election, since it would not prove itself.

§ 293. And where a voter refuses to disclose, or fails to remember for whom he voted, it is competent to resort to circumstantial evidence, to raise a presumption in regard to that fact. *Ibid.* And see *Cushing's Am. Parl. Law, Sec.* 199, 210. And within this rule it was held in *People vs. Pease,* to be proper to ask the voter for whom he intended to vote; also to prove that he was an active member of a particular political party, or obtained his ballot from a person who was actively supporting a particular candidate or a particular ticket. (*d.*)

§ 294. It seems to be quite well settled that where one who is alien born has voted at an election, the law presumes that he has been naturalized until the contrary is shown. To presume the reverse would be to presume that a crime has been committed, but the law always presumes innocence. It is true this involves the necessity of proving a negative, a very difficult thing to do, but often necessary in order to charge a party with a criminal offense. (*New Jersey Case*, 1 *Bartlett*, 24.) The very great difficulty

(*d.*) Notwithstanding the high authority of *People vs. Pease*, it is apparent that the distinction between asking a voter for whom he voted and asking him for whom he *intended* to vote, is very narrow, and probably not substantial.

however, of proving that a person has not been naturalized, would seem to require that slight proof ought to be sufficient to shift the burden. Thus, if it be shown that he claimed that aliens had the right to vote, or if he has made declarations or admissions to the effect that he has not been naturalized; or if he produces as the evidence of his citizenship, a paper showing that he has declared his intention to become a citizen only; or perhaps, if when he is called as a witness, he refuses to answer whether he has been naturalized or not, or to say when or where, or by what Court, he was naturalized—in any of these cases, the presumption that such a voter was duly naturalized ought to be regarded as so far overcome as to require the party seeking to sustain his vote, to produce affirmative evidence of naturalization, a thing not very difficult to do, since there is always a record, and the voter must be presumed to know where it is. There are in the United States many hundreds of Courts possessing the power to grant naturalization, and to require in any case that affirmative proof be offered that no one of such Courts has ever granted naturalization to a particular person, would be to require what is practically impossible.

§ 295. The charters of most municipal corporations contain a provision to the effect that the council or other legislative body thereof shall be "the judge of the election and qualification of its own members." And an important question has arisen as to whether the jurisdiction of a city council, or other similar body, is under such a charter exclusive of that given to the courts of justice or only concurrent with it. In *State vs. Funck*, (17 *Iowa*, 365,) it was held that inasmuch as the city had passed no ordinance defining the method by which an election of one of its members may be contested, the claimant could resort to the proceeding provided by statute for trying title to a public office, but no opinion was expressed as to what the law would be in a case where provision is made by ordinance for such trial. An examination of the adjudged cases in this country will, however, show that the jurisdiction of the Courts to inquire into the regularity and the validity of elections—a jurisdiction which belongs to all Courts of general and original jurisdiction, is not to be regarded as taken away by any merely negative words. Their jurisdiction remains unless it "appears with unequivocal certainty that the legislature intended to take it away." (*Dillon on Municipal Corporations, Sec.* 144.) It follows that a charter provision that the council of a city "shall be the judge of the election, qualifications and returns of its own members," does not oust the courts of justice of their jurisdiction. The two tribunals have concurrent jurisdiction in such a case; but if the provision be that no court shall take cognizance of cases of this character, or that the council shall be the *sole* or the *exclusive*, or final judge, &c., then the courts are shorn of their power in the premises. Upon this general subject see the learned and exhaustive discussion by Judge Dillon, in his work on *Municipal Corporations, Sec.* 139 *to* 142. And see also *State vs. Fitzgerald*, 44 *Mo.*, 425. *Commonwealth vs. Carrigues*, 28 *Pa. State R.*, 9. *Ewing vs. Filley*, 43 *Pa. State*, 384. *Commonwealth vs. Leach*,

44 *Pa. State*, 332. *Cooley on Const. Limitations*, 276, 623, 634, *note*. *Smith vs. New York*, 37 *N. Y.*, 518. *People vs. Mulvaney*, 13 *Mich.*, 481. *Ex parte Heath*, 3 *Hill, N. Y.*, 42, and cases cited by Cowan, Judge. The true doctrine seems to be that a special remedy given by statute is cumulative, and not exclusive of the ordinary jurisdiction of the courts, unless the manifest intention of the statute be to make such special remedy exclusive, and such intention must be manifested by affirmative words to that effect.

§ 296. A statute of New York directed that one of the inspectors of election who shall actually preside at such election, to be appointed by the major part of the inspectors, shall in person deliver to the clerk a copy of the statement of votes. It was held that the appointment of the inspector to deliver the statement to the clerk need not necessarily be in writing. An appointment by writing, in such a case, is to be preferred, but is not indispensable, since the statute is silent as to the mode of appointment, and it was therefore error to exclude a statement of the vote at a given precinct, because the inspector presenting it did not produce WRITTEN evidence of his appointment to discharge that duty. (*The People vs. Van Slyck*, 14 *Cowan*, 297.)

§ 297. It is very clear that the rule which upon grounds of public policy protects the legal voter against being compelled to disclose for whom he voted, does not protect a person who has voted illegally from making such disclosure. To give to that rule this wide scope, would be to make it shield alike the right and the wrong, the honest and the dishonest. It was intended to protect the inviolable secrecy of an honest ballot, and thus the purity of the ballot box. It was not intended to be used in aid of the schemes of corrupt men to defeat the will of the people. It follows, that having proven that A. voted at the election in question, and that he was not a legal voter, he may be required to testify as to the person or persons for whom he voted. (*McDaniel's Case*, 3 *Pa. Law Journal*, 310. *Brightley's Election Cases*, 248.)

§ 298. If an illegal voter, when called as a witness, swears that he does not know for whom he voted, and it is impossible to determine from any evidence in the case, for whom he voted, his vote is not to be taken from the majority. *Ibid.* But it does not follow that such illegal votes must necessarily be counted in making up the true result, because it cannot be ascertained for whom they were cast. In purging the polls of illegal votes, the general rule is, that unless it be shown for which candidate they were cast, they are to be deducted from the whole vote of the election division, and not from the candidate having the largest number. (*Shepherd vs. Gibbons*, 2 *Brewst.*, 128. *McDaniel's Case*, 3 *Penn., L. J.*, 310. *Cushing's Election Cases*, 583.) Of course, in the application of this rule such illegal votes would be deducted proportionately from both candidates, according to the entire vote returned for each. Thus, we will suppose that John Doe and Richard Roe are competing candidates for an office, and that the official canvass shows

For John Doe,	625	votes.
For Richard Roe,	575	votes.
Total vote,	1200	

Majority for Doe,——50

But there is proof that 120 illegal votes were cast, and no proof as to the person for whom they were cast. The illegal vote is ten per cent. of the returned vote, and hence each candidate loses ten per cent. of the vote certified to him. By this rule John Doe will lose 62½ votes, and Richard Roe 57½ votes, and the result as thus reached is as follows:

Doe's certified vote,	625
Deduct illegal votes,	62½
Total vote,	562½

Roe's certified vote,	575
Deduct illegal votes,	57½
Total vote,	517½

Majority for Doe,——45.

§ 299. This is probably the safest rule that can be adopted in a court of justice, where there is no power to order a new election, and where great injury would result from declaring the office vacant; but it is manifest that it may sometimes work a great hardship, inasmuch as the truth might be, if it could be shown, that all the illegal votes were on one side, while it is scarcely to be presumed that they would ever be divided between the candidates in exact proportion to their whole vote. But the rule which in the absence of proof as to how illegal votes were cast, would deduct them all from the majority candidate, is much more unreasonable and dangerous. Of the two evils the least should be chosen. We see here, however, how important it is that it should, if possible, be made to appear either by direct or circumstantial evidence, for whom each illegal vote was cast.

In a legislative body having power to order a new election, and in any other tribunal having the same power, it will doubtless, generally, be regarded as safer and more conducive to the ends of justice, to order such new election, than to reach a result by the application of the rule above stated.

§ 300. It would seem, therefore, that in a case where the number of bad votes proven is sufficient to affect the result, and in the absence of any evidence to enable the court to determine for whom they were cast, the court must decide upon one of the three following alternatives, viz:

1. Declare the election void.
2. Divide the illegal votes between the candidates in proportion to the whole vote of each.
3. Deduct the illegal vote from the candidate having the highest vote.

And it is clear, also, that where in such a case no great public inconvenience would result from declaring the election void, and seeking a decision by an appeal to the electors, that course should be adopted. And in a case where it is essential that one or the other party to the contest be confirmed in the office to prevent such public inconvenience, then the second alternative above named should be adopted, but the third should in no event be adopted. Let it be understood that we are here referring to a case where it is found to be impossible by the use of due diligence to show for whom the illegal votes were cast. If in any given case it be shown that the proof was within the reach of the party whose duty it was to produce it, and that he neglected to produce it, then he may well be held answerable for his own neglect, and because it was his duty to show for whom the illegal votes were cast, and because he might, by the use of reasonable diligence, have made this showing, it may very properly be said that he should himself suffer the loss occasioned by deducting them from his own vote.

This is the principle involved in the case of *Duffey*, (4 *Brewster*, 531,) where the court laid down the following rules:

1. It is the right of petitioners contesting an election, and also the right of the respondent, to examine the election papers on file in the proper office, and if it be apparent from them that persons have voted in any district whose names were not on the "registry list," without being vouched according to law, then *prima facie* all such votes are illegal.

2. When a contest has been inaugurated and complaint made and notice given that such votes have been received, the burden of proof falls upon the candidate advantaged by the general count in such district to show either that the persons so voting possessed severally every qualification, or if this be not so that they voted for his opponent; he must lift the curse which the law imposes upon such ballots; otherwise it will be presumed that they were polled and counted for him; and thereupon the poll will be purged by striking the whole number of such votes from his count.

To the first of these propositions no exception can be taken, and we apprehend that the same ruling will be made in all our States which have registry laws requiring persons not registered to file with the judges of the election affidavits of themselves or others, in proof of their right to vote. The second proposition can be maintained if at all, only upon the ground that it is in the case stated practicable to show for whom the illegal votes were cast. It is said in the course of the opinion: "The number of these illegal votes was easy of ascertainment; the names of the persons polling them had but to be read to be known." Upon the theory that the illegal voter can be called as a witness and compelled to disclose for whom he voted, (which is beyond doubt the true theory,) it would be easy in such a case as the one stated, to call the illegal voters and require them to testify to the fact. It still remains, however, a question whether they shall be called at the instance of the contestant upon the theory that the burden of proof is upon him to make out his case, or at the instance of the respondent upon the theory that because he is advantaged by the general result he must show that all illegal votes were cast for his opponent, or suffer them to be deducted from his own vote. The court adopted the latter theory, but we think the safer rule would be for the contestant to show not only that a certain number of illegal votes were polled, but also to show if he can, that they were cast for his opponent. It is not intended by this to assert that the rule above quoted from Duffey's case is positively erroneous, but only to intimate a doubt, and to express the opinion that the ordinary principle which requires the party holding the affirmative to prove the facts, and all the facts, necessary to make out his case, is the better rule, and that it will in all cases be safer to follow it. Of course, if by the use of due diligence it be impossible to find the illegal voters, or if upon being found it shall be impossible to ascertain from their testimony how they voted, the contestant should not suffer. This would present the question, what is to be done with illegal votes when it is found to be impossible by due diligence to show for whom they were cast, a question which is discussed in the preceding sections.

§ 301. A person who votes without being qualified is a mere intruder, and not entitled to the privileges which belong to legal voters. But such a person will not be compelled to testify as to the person for whom he voted, until it is clearly shown that he voted illegally. So long as the question as to the legality of his vote is in doubt, he cannot be compelled to make the disclosure. (*Case of Locust Ward Election*, 4 *Penn.*, *L. J.*, 349. *People vs. Cicott*, 16 *Mich.*, 283. *State vs. Hilmantel*, 23 *Wis.*, 422.) An illegal voter may, however, decline to answer for whom he voted, on the ground that his answer might criminate himself, but in such case the contents of the ballot may be shown by other testimony. (*State vs. Ohio*, 23 *Wis.*, 309.)

And a legal voter may waive his privilege and voluntarily testify as to the persons for whom he has voted. (*Reed vs. Kneass*, 2 *Parsons*, *Philadelphia*, 584. *Brightley's Election Cases*, 366.)

§ 302. While a mere irregularity which does not effect the result, will not vitiate the return, yet where the provisions of the election law have been entirely disregarded by the officers, and their conduct has been such as to render their returns utterly unworthy of credit, the entire poll must be rejected. In such a case the returns prove nothing. But it does not follow that legal votes cast at such poll must be lost. They may be proven by secondary evidence, (the return being, until impeached, the primary evidence,) and when thus proven may be counted. (*Littlefield vs. Green*, 1 *Chicago Legal News*, 230. *Brightley's Election Cases*, 493. *McKenzie vs. Braxton*, 42*d Congress*. *Giddings vs. Clark*, 42*d Congress*.)

§ 303. The question, under what circumstances the entire poll of an election division may be rejected, has been much discussed, and conflicting views have been expressed by the courts. The power to reject an entire poll, is certainly a dangerous power, and though it belongs to whatever tribunal has jurisdiction to pass upon the merits of a contested election case, it should be exercised only in an extreme case, that is to say, a case where it is impossible to ascertain with reasonable certainty, the true vote. It must appear that the conduct of the election officers has been such as to destroy the integrity of their returns, and to avoid the *prima facie* character which they ought to bear as evidence, before they can be set aside, and other proof demanded of the true state of the vote. (*Mann vs. Cassiday*, 1 *Brewst.*, 60.) And it is truthfully said in *Thompson vs. Ewing*, (*Ibid*, 107,) "that the whole conduct of election officers may, though actual fraud be not apparent, amount to such gross and culpable negligence, such a disregard of their official duties, as to render their doings unintelligible or unworthy of credence, and their action entirely unreliable for any purpose." See also *Weaver vs. Given*, [*Ibid* 140.]

Batturs vs. Megary, [*Ibid*, 162.] *Gibbons vs. Stewart*, 2 *Brewster*, 1.

§ 304. It was said by the Supreme Court of Pennsylvania, in *Chadwick vs. Melvin*, (*Brightley's Election Cases*, 551,) that "there is nothing which will justify the striking out of an entire division, but an inability to decipher the returns, or a showing that not a single legal vote was polled, or that no election was legally held." Undoubtedly the general rule is that if legal votes have been cast in good faith by honest electors, it is the duty of the court or tribunal trying a contest to ascertain their number and give them due effect, notwithstanding misconduct or even fraud on the part of the election officers. Such fraud or misconduct may destroy the value of the officer's certificate, and may subject him to severe punishment, but the innocent voter should not suffer on that account, if by any means his rights can be upheld. And yet the statement just quoted from *Chadwick vs. Melvin*, is too sweeping. The question is not whether a single legal vote has been polled, but whether the voice of the majority has been fairly expressed. In *Biddle and Richard vs. Wing*, (*Cl. & H.*, 504,) the rule is more correctly stated as follows: "Indeed nothing short of the impossibility of ascertaining for whom the *majority of votes* were given, ought to vacate an election, especially if by such decision the people must, on account of their distant and dispersed situation, necessarily go unrepresented for a long period of time."

§ 305. Although the fact that the officers of an election were not sworn, will not of itself, and in the absence of fraud, render the election null and void;

yet if fraud be proven, or it appear that such officers have wilfully disobeyed the law or disregarded their duty, the fact that they were not sworn, may become an important fact in determining whether or not the poll shall be entirely rejected. It is impossible to define exactly the degree of irregularity and illegality in the conduct of an election which will render it void, but perhaps the best rule upon the subject is this. If the voice of the electors can be made to appear from the returns, either alone or aided by extrinsic evidence, with reasonable clearness and certainty, then the election should stand; but not otherwise. This rule has made necessary another, viz: That if it appear that illegal votes have been admitted, it is the first duty of the tribunal trying the contest to purge the poll of such illegal votes, if there is evidence upon which this can be done, and effect should be given to the majority of the good votes.

§ 306. The general rule is that the ordinary rules of evidence apply as well to election contests as to other cases. The evidence must therefore be confined to the point in issue, and must be relevant. The burden of proof is always upon the contestant or the party attacking the official return, or certificate. The presumption is that the officers of the law charged with the duty of ascertaining and declaring the result, have discharged that duty faithfully. In a contested election case, however, where the question is who received the highest number of votes, this presumption may be rebutted and overcome by proof. If a disqualified voter declines to answer as to how he voted, or if he cannot be found so as to be examined as a witness, a good deal of latitude should be allowed in showing the fact by circumstantial evidence. It may be shown that an illegal voter asked for a particular ticket at the poll; that no scratched tickets were voted, and the like. [*Thompson vs. Ewing*, 1 *Brewst.*, 68–9.]

§ 307. A statute which confers upon any elector of the proper county the right to contest, at his option, the election of any person who has been declared to be duly elected to a public office, to be exercised in and for such county, does not oust the jurisdiction of the proper court, on information in the nature of a *quo warranto*, to inquire into the authority of any person who assumes to exercise the functions of a public office or franchise, and to remove him therefrom if he be a usurper, having no legal right thereto. [*People vs. Holden*, 28 *Cal.*, 123.] "The two remedies are distinct," says the court in that case, "the one belonging to the elector in his individual capacity, as a power granted, and the other to the people, in the right of their sovereignty." See also, *People* vs. *Jones*, (20 *Cal.*, 50.)

§ 308. It seems to be settled that the title to an office confers upon the person elected a right to the fees and emoluments thereof, from the commencement of his legal term. And, accordingly, it has been frequently held that an action for money had and received will lie by the officer *de jure* against one who has intruded into the office by color of a certificate of election, to recover fees received during the time of such intrusion. (*Arris* vs. *Stukely*, 2 *Mod.*, 260. 1 *Selw.*, *N. T.* 68, *Crosbie* vs. *Hurley*, 1 *Ale & Nap.*, 431. *Mayfield* vs. *Moore*, *Brightley's Election Cases*, 605.)

The fees and emoluments "are incident to and as clearly connected with the office as are rents and profits to real estate, or interest to bonds and such like securities." (*Glascock* vs. *Lyons*, 20 *Ind.*, 1. *Petit* vs. *Rosseau*, 15 *La.*, 239. *People* vs. *Smythe*, 28 *Cal.*, 21. *People* vs. *Tiernan*, 30 *Barb.*, 193. *People* vs. *Pease*, 27 *N. Y.*, 56. *Hunter* vs. *Chandler*, 45 *Mo.*, 453. *United States* vs. *Addison*, 6 *Wall.*, 291. *Mott* vs. *Connolly*, 50 *Barb.*, 516.) In *Mayfield* vs. *Moore*, (*supra*,) it was held, however, that if the incumbent received his commission *bona fide*, he will be allowed in such action his reasonable expenses in executing the duties of the office, but otherwise, if his intrusion was without pretense of legal right.

§ 309. In the case of *United States* vs. *Quinn*, [*Brightley's Election Cases*, 592,] Judge Woodruff of the United States Circuit Court, for the southern district of New York, had occasion to discuss the constitutionality of the 20th section of the act of Congress of May 31, 1870, punishing a fraudulent registration for the purpose of voting for a member of Congress. In a very clear and able opinion he demonstrates, that Congress has power to punish frauds perpetrated in an attempt to prevent a fair election of a member of that body. This is not an attempt to fix the qualifications of electors for Representatives in Congress. These are fixed by the State, and are the same as those belonging to electors for members of the most numerous branch of the State legislature. It only provides in effect that "it shall be an offense against the laws of the United States, to contribute by fraud or violation of the

State registry laws, to the sending of a Representative to the Congress of the United States, who is not clothed with the authority which a true expression of the popular will would give; and that is all." It would indeed be a strange anomaly if the government of the United States could be obliged to look upon commission of frauds and crimes perpetrated for the purpose of putting into the halls of Congress men who have no right there, and who owe their seats to corruption, and yet remain powerless to prevent or punish it. If it be said that it is the exclusive prerogative of the States to punish election frauds, whether committed in the effort to elect State officers simply, or members of the National legislature, or Presidential electors, the answer is, that the States have the power, but not the exclusive power, to punish frauds appertaining to the election of federal officers. The power to punish such frauds against itself belongs to the United States Government, and is nothing more nor less than the power of self protection.

§ 310. The House of Representatives of the United States will not grant to a sitting member whose seat is contested, an extension of time in which to take testimony, unless it appear that he has not by the use of great diligence, been able to procure his testimony within the time allowed by the law. The reason for this rule is thus stated in the report of the Committee of Elections, in the case of *Giddings* vs. *Clark*, in the 42d Congress.

"It must be borne in mind that the party now asking an extension is the sitting member. He is now, and has been during a large part of the term, exercising the functions and receiving the emoluments of the office in question. In a litigation of this character the thing in controversy grows daily less, and does not, as in most ordinary law suits, remain intact to be recovered by the successful party in the end. In this particular case the extension asked for would be very nearly equivalent to a final decision of the case in favor of the sitting member upon the merits. We are now near the close of the second session of the Congress. If the parties are to be sent back to Texas to take further testimony, of course no further action can be taken until the opening of the third and last session, which is of but ninety days' duration, and would be necessarily far spent before a final decision could be reached. It does not follow from these considerations that a sitting member can in no case be allowed an extension after the time allowed by law for taking testimony expires, but your committee think it does follow that no such extension should ever be granted to a sitting member, unless it clearly appears that by the exercise of great diligence he has been unable to procure his testimony, and that he is able, if an extension be granted, to obtain such material evidence as will establish his right to the seat, or that by reason of the fault or misconduct of the contestant he has been unable to prepare his case."

§ 311. In a contested election case in Congress an application by the sitting member for an extension of time to take testimony, made after the time allowed by law for taking testimony has expired, and after the term of office contested for has well nigh expired, it is necessary, in addition to showing great diligence, to state on oath the names of the witnesses whose testimony is desired, and the particular facts which can be proven by them. And the affidavits of such witnesses themselves should be produced, or a sufficient reason given for failing to produce them. *Ibid.* (See same report for discussion as to what constitutes the proper degree of diligence in such a case.)

§ 312. Where the statute makes it a misdemeanor for any officer of elections to place any number or mark upon the ballot of a voter, but does not declare that ballots so marked or numbered by such officer, shall be rejected—the true rule is to receive and count them. To reject such ballots would be to establish a rule under which an officer of election could destroy the effect of a ballot cast in good faith by a legal voter, by placing a number or mark upon it. For a full consideration and discussion of this point, see the cases of *McKenzie* vs. *Braxton*, and *Giddings* vs. *Clark*, in the 42d Congress. The report in the latter case says:

"By reference to the statute here referred to, it will be seen that it is made a misdemeanor for any judge of election to place any number or mark upon the ticket of any voter; but it is not declared that the vote of a legally qualified voter shall be rejected because his ballot is marked by the judges. We should not be inclined to put a construction upon this statute which would enable an officer of election to destroy the effect of a ballot cast in good faith by a legal voter, by placing a number or mark upon it. A ballot may be thus marked or numbered without the knowledge or consent of the voter, and it would be manifestly unjust that he should, in this way, be deprived of his vote."

"We think it plain that, inasmuch as the statute affixes a penalty for marking a ballot, and does not expressly declare that a marked ballot shall be thrown out, the board erred in rejecting the vote of this county upon this ground."

§ 313. The House of Representatives of the United States, in construing a State law, will follow the construction given it by the authorities of the State, whose duty it is to construe and execute it. Where a given construction has been adopted and acted upon by the State authorities, the federal government should abide by and follow it. It was so held by the House of Representatives of the United States, in the matter of the election of Representative from the State of Tennessee. (42*d Congress.*) The report of the committee has this language:

"It is a well established and most salutary rule, that where the proper authorities of the State government have given a construction to their own constitution or statutes, that construction will be followed by the Federal authorities. This rule is absolutely necessary to the harmonious working of our complex governments, State and National, and your committee are not disposed to be the first to depart from it."

And in the case of *Birch* vs. *Van Horn*, (2 *Bartlett*, 205,) the House refused to go into an inquiry as to the validity of the new constitution of Missouri, upon the ground that it had been recognized as valid by the people, and by all the departments of the State government.

§ 314. The officers authorized to take testimony in contested election cases, in the House of Representatives, derive their authority from the act of Congress, and not from State laws. Hence the Mayor of a city may take such testimony outside of the limits of the city of which he is Mayor, although by the State law he has no power to administer an oath elsewhere than within such city. (*Washburn* vs. *Voorhies*, 2 *Bartlett*, 54.)

§ 315. In Wisconsin it is held that the complaint in a contested election case, brought in the Courts of that State, is sufficient, if it states the number of votes in favor of the defendant which were illegally polled, without specifying the names of the persons by whom such illegal votes were cast. (*Doerflinger* vs. *Helmantel*, 21 *Wis.*, 566.) And this is in accordance with the general tenor of judicial decisions in this country.

§ 316. A contested election case, whatever the form of the proceeding may be, is in its essence a proceeding in which the people—the constituency—are primarily and principally interested. It is not a suit for the adjudication and settlement of private rights simply. It follows that the parties to the record cannot, by stipulation or otherwise, discontinue or compromise a case of this character without the consent and approval of the court or tribunal trying it. Nor should such consent ever be given, unless the Court giving it is sufficiently advised to be able to say that it is for the interest of the public to do so. (*Mann* vs. *Cassiday*, 1 *Brewster*, 43. *Peo-*

ple vs. *Holden*, 28 *Cal.*, 139. *Kneass' Case*, 2 *Parsons*, 570. *Collings' Case*, *Brightleys' Election Cases*, 513.)

§ 317. Mandamus is not the proper remedy for obtaining possession of an office, or for ousting one who usurps an office. There are cases perhaps where there is no doubt as to the duty of a public officer to issue a commission to a person elected, and in which, therefore, a mandamus may issue to compel the performance of that duty. But when it is a question of any doubt, a court should not interfere by *mandamus*, but should put the party in the first instance to an information in the nature of a *quo warranto*, or to such remedy as may be specifically provided by statute. (*Commonwealth* vs. *Commissioners*, 5 *Rawle*, 75.)

§ 318. And it has been held also that a court of chancery should not interfere by injunction to restrain the officers of election from counting illegal votes, or from issuing certificates of election to persons not entitled to them. The reason is that a court of chancery will not interfere collaterally and in advance of a contest to pass upon the claims of conflicting claimants of an office. (*Lawrence* vs. *Knight*, 1 *Brewster*, 69, *Brightley's Election Cases*, 617.) And to the same effect is *Hulseman* vs. *Rems*, (41 *Pa. State R.*, 296.) But this ruling, though evidently sound and supported by the weight of authority, has not been altogether uniform. In *Miller* vs. *Lowery*, (5 *Phila.* 202,) the Court of Common Pleas of Philadelphia granted an injunction to restrain a candidate who had received a certificate of election, regular upon its face, from taking possession of the office, upon the ground that the certificate had been fraudulently issued. And see also *Peck* vs. *Weddell*, (17 *Ohio State R.*, 271.)

§ 319. Where the application is for an injunction to restrain the officers of election from receiving votes from a class of persons who are clearly disqualified, the same rule does not apply, and an injunction may well be granted, for in such a case, the object would be, not to decide prematurely and collaterally, a contested election case. *McIlvain* vs. *Christ Church, of Reading*, [28 *Legal Int.*, 126.]

§ 320. A case may have arisen in which a court having, in a proper action, decided upon the result of an election, may have issued upon proper application, a writ of mandamus; to compel the proper election officers to issue a certificate of election in accordance with that decision. But, ordinarily the writ of mandamus will only issue to compel a certificate to issue upon the returns, and in accordance with the result as it appears therefrom. When it becomes necessary to go beyond the returns and consider questions touching the legality of the election, or of fraud, illegal voting, or the like, then mandamus is not the proper action, and it is necessary to resort to *quo warranto*, or to such statutory proceeding as may be provided in such cases. (*State* vs. *Churchill*, 15 *Minn.*, 455.)

§ 321. Mandamus will lie to compel a board of returning officers to declare the result and issue certificates in accordance therewith, where these duties are by statute required of such board. As such duties are purely ministerial, the board may be compelled by mandamus to perform them. (*Clark* vs.

McKenzie, 7 *Bush.*, [*Ky.*] 523.) And in West Virginia it has been held that the Circuit Court can by mandamus compel a board of supervisors of a county to issue certificates of election to township officers adjudged by the Court to have been duly elected at a valid election. (*Bush* vs. *Monroe Co.*, 4 *W. Va.*, 371.) But of course this latter case must have been one in which the election returns and all proper evidence as to the result, came legitimately before the Court for consideration. If otherwise, the case is not good authority, for it is quite well settled that mandamus will not lie to try and finally determine the title to an office.

§ 322. It is well settled, as a general rule, that the writ of mandamus will not be granted in any case where another adequate and specific remedy is provided, and it follows that the cases are rare in which the courts will interfere by mandamus, with questions touching the title to and possession of a public office. The courts have almost uniformly refused to grant the writ of mandamus in cases of this kind, upon the ground that an information in the nature of a *quo warranto* is the appropriate remedy for testing the title to an office, as well as for determining the right to the possession thereof. Where a party is in possession of an office as its actual incumbent, exercising its functions *defacto*, and under color of right, mandamus will not lie to compel him to vacate and give place to another. In all such cases the party aggrieved will be left to his common law remedy by *quo warranto*, or to such other remedy of like nature, as may be specifically provided by statute. (*High on Extraordinary Legal Reme-*

dies, Sec. 49. *People* vs. *Corporation of New York,* 3 *Johns Cas.,* 79. *People* vs. *Supervisors of Greene,* 12 *Barb.,* 217. *Anderson* vs. *Colson,* 1 *Neb.,* 172. *Bonner* vs. *State of Georgia,* 7 *Geo.,* 473. *St. Louis Co. Court* vs. *Sparks,* 10 *Mo.,* 118. *State* vs. *Rodman,* 43 *Mo.,* 256. *People* vs. *Common Council of Detroit,* 18 *Mich.,* 338. *Underwood* vs. *White,* 27 *Ark.,* 382. *People* vs. *Forquer, Breese* 68. *State* vs. *Dunn, Minor's,* [*Ala.*] 46. *Commonwealth* vs. *Commissioners,* 6 *Whart.,* 476.) And the same doctrine is maintained in the courts of England, (*King* vs. *Mayor of Colchester,* 2 *T. R.,* 260. *Queen* vs. *Derby,* 7 *Ad. & E.* 419. *King* vs. *Winchester, Ib.,* 215.) A few cases may be found which seem to hold a contrary doctrine. (*Conlin* vs. *Aldrich,* 98 *Mass.,* 557. *Harwood* vs. *Marshall,* 9 *Md.,* 83.) But it is safe to say that the rule as above stated is sustained by the overwhelming weight of authority.

§ 323. And the rule is quite as well sustained by reason. Mr. High, in his excellent work on Extraordinary Remedies, well says: (*Sec.* 50.) "Aside from the existence of another adequate remedy by proceedings in *quo warranto,* to test the title of an incumbent to his office, it is a sufficient objection to relief by mandamus in such a case, that the granting of the writ would have the effect of admitting a second person to an office already filled by another, both claiming to be duly entitled thereto, and resort must still be had to further proceedings to test the disputed title. And the rule finds still further support in the fact that ordinarily the determination of the question of title to a disputed office upon proceedings in mandamus would be to determine the rights of the *de facto* incumbent in a proceeding to which he is not a party."

§ 324. "Where the office is already filled," says the court in *People* vs. *Corporation of New York, supra,* "by a person who has been admitted and sworn and is in by color of right, a mandamus is never issued to admit another person, because the corporation being a third party may admit or not, at pleasure, and the rights of the party in office may be injured without his having an opportunity to make a defense. The proper remedy in the first instance is by an information in the nature of a *quo warranto,* by which the rights of the parties may be tried."

§ 325. While it is well settled that mandamus will not lie for the purpose of settling disputed questions concerning title or possession of an office, cases have arisen in which this writ has been granted to compel the proper officer to swear in the person elected to an office. This is simply to compel the qualifying officer to discharge a duty enjoined upon him by law, and is therefore within the proper scope of this writ. (*King* vs. *Clark,* 2 *East,* 75. *Churchwarden's Case, Carth.,* 118. *King* vs. *Rees, Ib.,* 393. *Ex parte Heath,* 3 *Hill,* 42. *High on Extraordinary Remedies, Sec.* 53, *and cases cited.*)

§ 326. But it is not competent, or at least not proper, for a court in the exercise of this power, to compel the swearing in of the person elected to go further, and in cases of disputed and contested elections, to compel the qualifying officer to swear in either one of such parties before a judgment of ouster has been rendered in a proper proceeding. "In all cases of doubt," says Mr. High, in his work above cited, (Sec. 53,) "as to the election of officers where the validity of the election is the chief point in controversy, the courts will not interfere by mandamus, but will put the aggrieved party in the first instance to an information in the nature of a *quo warranto*. And before a mandamus will be granted to compel the recognition of one as an officer, the court will require that judgment of ouster shall have been given against the incumbent *de facto*." (*Commonwealth* vs. *County Commissioners*, 5 *Rawle*, 75.)

§ 327. The Supreme Court of Massachusetts, in *Ellis* vs. *County Commissioners*, (2 *Gray*, 370,) held that where the law imposed upon the County Commissioners, the duty of certifying as to who received the highest number of votes for County Treasurer, mandamus will lie to compel such commissioners to certify that the petitioner had a majority of such votes, [if such was the fact,] although another person had been declared by them to be County Treasurer, and put in possession of the office. This was a case, however, which turned upon a single question of law, and all the facts were, by the return to the alternative writ fully stated. And while holding that the court might, if satisfied that petitioner actually received a majority of all the legal votes cast, command the board to so certify, the opinion is clearly intimated that after obtaining such a certificate it would be necessary to resort to *quo warranto* in order to remove the incumbent from the office and place the petitioner in possession; and it is therefore evident that the latter action is, in the absence of statutory regulations the more appropriate remedy, and that it should be adopted in the first instance. Indeed it is impossible to reconcile this case with the general current of authority upon this subject, and it is quite clear that no action should be had in a mandamus proceeding, to which the incumbent of the office is not a party, which may directly or indirectly affect his rights, or pre-judge his claims.

§ 328. While mandamus will not lie to compel admission to a disputed office, or to determine disputed questions of title to an office, it is sometimes the proper remedy for a failure of election officers to perform certain merely ministerial duties in connection with elections. By it the proper board or officer can be compelled to canvass the election returns; to determine and declare the result; to issue certificates to the persons entitled thereto. The writ may also be sought merely for the purpose of swearing in the person elected. (*Ex parte Heath*, 3 *Hill*, 42.) But the effect of a mandamus to swear one into an office is not to create or confer any title not already existing. (*High on Extraordinary Remedies*, § 52, and cases cited.)

§ 329. It is also clear that after there has been a judgment of ouster given against the incumbent *de-facto*, in a regular proceeding by *quo warranto*, a mandamus will be granted to compel the recognition of such person as such officer unless some other process is provided by law. (*Commonwealth* vs. *County Commissioners*, 5 *Rawle*, 75,) And when mandamus is asked to compel the issuing of a commission to a person duly elected to an office, it is essential that the relator should show a clear title to the office claimed. (*State* vs. *Albin*, 44 *Mo.*, 346.)

§ 330. Mandamus will lie to compel the making

of an appointment to fill an office if the person who is properly vested with the power of appointment fails or refuses to act. But the writ will not be granted to compel the making of an appointment to an office where it is apparent that the appointing power is about to proceed in the matter, and where it is not shown that there is an attempt to evade the law by unnecessary delay. [*People* vs. *Regents of University*, 4 *Mich.*, 98.]

§ 331. The rule is, that mandamus will lie to compel election officers to discharge purely ministerial functions as contra-distinguished from such duties as are *quasi* judicial in their character. The duties of returning officers are chiefly ministerial, but in the nature of the case they must exercise a sort of judicial function in determining whether the papers received by them and purporting to be returns, are in fact such, and are genuine and intelligible and substantially as required by law. But after these questions are determined, the duty of counting the votes as returned, and declaring the result is a ministerial duty which the proper officers are bound to perform, and the performance of which may be compelled by mandamus. And it is not doubted that even as to questions concerning which returning officers exercise a discretion, they can be compelled by mandamus to act and to decide, though their discretion cannot be controlled by this means, and they cannot, therefore, be directed by mandamus as to how they shall decide. If they decide any such questions wrongfully or erroneously, the party injured has his remedy by *quo warranto*, or by such other form of remedy as may be provided by statute.

§ 332. And of course it will be understood from what has already been stated, that where, as is sometimes the case, large judicial powers are conferred by law upon canvassing boards, mandamus will not lie to direct or control them in the exercise of their judicial or discretionary functions. It must be constantly borne in mind that the office of this writ is to compel the performance of acts which are purely ministerial in their nature, though it may, as we have said, be employed to compel, but not to control, the exercise of judicial functions. This rule being kept in view, no serious difficulty can arise upon this subject. [*Grier* vs. *Shackleford*, 2 *Brev.*, [2*d Ed.*] 549. *Mayor &c.*, vs. *Rainwater*, 47 *Miss.*, 547.]

§ 333. In proceedings by mandamus involving collaterally the rights of contesting claimants to an office, the court will not review the decision of a board of canvassers, for the reason that such decision is to be treated as conclusive, except in proceedings by *quo warranto*. [*People* vs. *Stevens*, 5 *Hill*, 616. *High on Extraordinary Remedies*, *Sec.* 57.] In accordance with this doctrine it has been held that where the statute directs the board of County Commissioners to order an election for county officers, provided a certain number of qualified electors petition therefor, and it is made the duty of said board to ascertain whether the requisite number of electors have joined in such petition; mandamus does not lie to control them in the exercise of that duty. And if they have decided the matter and refused to order the election, mandamus will not lie to compel them to make such order.

[*State* vs. *Commissioners*, 8 *Nev.*, **309.**] And it is also clear that the writ of mandamus will not be ordered to compel election officers to perform a ministerial duty before the time for its performance has arrived. The court will not anticipate a refusal of an officer to do his duty, even though he may have threatened or pre-determined not to perform it. There can be no omission, neglect or refusal to perform a duty where the time has not yet arrived for its performance. (*State* vs. *Harvey*, 3 *Kan.*, 88.]

§ 334. We have seen that mandamus does not lie to compel admission to an office, and we have also seen that it does lie to compel the proper authority to issue a commission to the person declared elected. There is no conflict between these two rules. The granting of the writ to compel admission to the office would have the effect of determining the title thereto, but this is not the effect of the writ, when granted to compel the issuance of the certificate of election. This certificate, when issued by virtue of a mandamus, has precisely the same force as if issued without such writ. In either case it is only *prima facie* evidence of title to the office, and may be attacked and overthrown by other proof. (*High on Extraordinary Remedies, Sec.* 61. *State* vs. *Gibbs*, 13 *Fla.*, 55. *People* vs. *Hilliard*, 29 *Ill.*, 419. *In re Strong*, 20 *Pick.*, 484. *People* vs. *Rivers*, 27 *Ill.*, 242. *Brower* vs. *O'Brien*, 2 *Ind.*, 423.)

§ 335. In *People* vs. *Hilliard*, (*supra*,) it was held that it is no objection to the granting of the writ to compel the issuance of a certificate of election, that the respondent has already issued certificates to other parties. The court said; "We do not propose to turn the others out of office on an application for mandamus. They are not parties to this adjudication." On the contrary, however, it was held in *Magee* vs. *Supervisors*,, (10 *Cal.*, 376,) that if the canvassers have performed their duty, and in the exercise of their discretion have declared the result of the election adversely to the claimant, he cannot have mandamus to compel the issuing of a certificate to him, his remedy being by proceedings in *quo warranto*. And this would seem the better rule since the issuing of a second certificate under the order of the court, as we have seen, does not affect in any way the question of title to the office, and it is desirable that the claimant should be put to his remedy by *quo warranto* at once, and in the first instance to the end that the case may be speedily disposed of upon the merits.

§ 336. It has also been held that mandamus is the proper remedy to compel a registering officer to register as voters the names of persons properly qualified. [*Davies* vs. *McKeely*, 5 *Nev.*, 369.)

§ 337. Where an election is held and no question is made as to the result, the inspectors of the election have no right to consider the question of the validity of such election, but must certify the result and upon their failure or refusal to do so, mandamus will lie to compel them to perform this duty. The writ of mandamus, however, even when used to place a person in possession of an office, confers no right. It merely places him in possession of the office to enable him to assert his right which in some cases he could not otherwise do. [*Brower* vs. *O'Brien*, 2 *Ind.*, 423. *Moses on Mandamus*, 90.

Kister vs. *Cameron, et. al.*, 39 *Ind.*, 488.) A few cases may be found in which the writ of mandamus has issued to the proper certifying or returning officer, commanding him to certify the election of a particular person by name, but this is believed to be an improper, or at least an unprovident use of the writ. It should be issued, if at all, simply to compel a return or certification of the result, as shown by the proper returns, but the court issuing the writ should not assume to determine, and in advance, who by such returns is entitled to the office. As we have heretofore observed, the proper use of the writ is to compel, but not control, action by the returning officers. If the person actually elected is not returned and certified to be elected, his remedy is plain, and it is desirable that all questions connected with counting the votes and declaring the result should in the first instance remain with the officers of election.

§ 338. In *Kister* vs. *Cameron, et al, supra*, it seems that no question was made as to the fact that the relator had received a majority of the votes cast. The inspectors declined to certify, on the ground that in their opinion the election was void for some reason not stated in the report of the case. Mandamus was granted on the ground that it was not the province of the inspectors to inquire as to the validity of the election, that question being for another tribunal, but simply to cast up the returns, declare the result, and issue their certificate as provided by the plain terms of the statute, and this they were required to do. We gather from all the authorities the following rules:

1. If the officers of election refuse or fail to act

mandamus will lie to compel them to discharge their duties as required by statute, but in such cases the writ will not, as a general rule, command such officers to certify that any particular person has been elected.

2. If there are two or more persons claiming the office, the writ will never issue to require such officers to declare either one elected, but only to command them to execute the duties and exercise the functions conferred upon them by law.

3. If it clearly appears that a particular person has received the majority of the votes cast, and that no question is made upon this point, perhaps mandamus may issue to compel such officers to certify the election of that person by name, although this is substantially the same thing as to order them to certify the result according to law, and therefore the latter form will always be found to be the best.

§ 339. Where the statute provides that the election of a public officer may be contested by "any candidate or elector," the person instituting such contest must aver that he is an elector, or that he was a candidate for the office in question. This must appear on the face of the record, and it is not enough that the contestant offers proof that he is an elector. The incumbent is not bound to answer or take notice of a complaint which does not contain this averment. (*Edwards vs. Knight*, 8*th Ohio*, [*Hammond*,] 375.)

§ 340. An injunction will not lie to restrain the proper officer from recording the abstract of the vote of a county, upon the question of removing the county seat, because of frauds and illegalities in conducting the election. The remedy for such wrongs is by means of a contest, as provided by law. (*Peck vs. Weddell*, 17 *Ohio St.*, 271. *Ingersall* vs. *Berry*, 14, *ib.*, 315.) (*f*)

§ 341. Notice is absolutely essential to the validity of a proceeding to oust the incumbent of an office, and proceedings instituted and carried on without notice to the incumbent, should be treated as absolutely null and void. By notice here is not meant any particular form or character of notice, but simply that some kind of notice is essential. It has accordingly been held by the court of common pleas of Philadelphia, that where a member of a municipal legislative body has been expelled without notice or hearing, a mandamus will be granted to compel such body to restore him until he has had notice and a hearing. (*Duffield's Case. Brightley's Election Cases*, 646.) It was also held in the same case, that where the council has determined after notice and hearing, that the member has incurred a disqualification by accepting a federal office, the court will not interfere, for the reason that the council has power and jurisdiction to judge of the *qualifications* of its members.

§ 342. Prior to the adoption by Congress, of any statute regulating the mode of procuring evidence

(*f*) An adequate remedy will always be found either at law or in equity, for frauds perpetrated against the purity of elections. If a result has been secured by fraud, and the statute has provided no mode of redress, it by no means follows that no redress can be had. The right of any person claiming to exercise any public function or authority under a fraudulent election, may be tested by proceedings in *quo warranto*. And doubtless if the election is to decide upon the question of levying a tax, or the adoption of a municipal charter, or the like, all proceedings under it may be enjoined upon proof of such frauds, as will render such election void.

in contested election cases, the practice was conformed as far as possible to the laws of the state, from which any case might be brought. (*Botts vs. Jones*, 1 *Bartlett*, 73.) And there is no doubt but either house of Congress should regard the laws of the states as rules of decision, upon any point not covered by congressional statute or federal constitution. (See case of *Tennessee Representatives*, 42*d Congress*.)

§ 343. The act of Congress approved 19th Feb'y, 1851, "to prescribe the mode of obtaining evidence in cases of contested elections," provides among other things that the contestant shall "within thirty days after said election, give notice in writing to the member whose seat he intends to contest and in such notice shall specify particularly, the grounds on which he relies in said contest." A good deal of discussion has arisen as to what is to be understood by the words "specify particularly the grounds on which he relies." It is evident, however, that these words are not easily defined by any others. They are as plain and clear as any terms which we might employ to explain them. Cases have arisen, and will again arise, giving rise to controversy as to whether a given allegation comes up to the requirement of this statute, and it must be for the House in each case to decide upon the case before it. It may be observed however, that this statute should receive a reasonble construction—one that will carry out, and not defeat its spirit and purpose. And perhaps the rule of construction, which will prove safest as a guide in each case is this: A notice which is sufficiently specific to put the sitting member upon a proper defense and prevent any surprise being practiced upon him, is good, but one which fails to do this is bad. (*Wright vs. Fuller*, 1 *Bartlett*, 152.)

§ 344. It seems to be settled by the decisions of the House of Representatives, that a notice is good under the law, if it specify the number of illegal votes polled, for whom polled, when and where polled, without specifying the names of the illegal voters. [*Wright vs. Fuller, supra. Vallandigham vs. Campbell*, 1 *Bartlett*, 223. *Ottero vs. Gallegos.* 1 *Bartlett*, 177.]

§ 345. On the trial of a contested election case, in the lower House of Congress, if the final return is informal or insufficient, it is proper that the committee or the House, should send for and examine the county or primary returns, and from them make an estimate of the votes, as the judges themselves might have done. [*Case of David Bard of Pennsylvania, Cl. & H., p*, 116.] It is equally true that the House in such a case may go behind *all* returns whether primary or final, and resort to any competent evidence, in order to ascertain the true state of the vote. The same point was decided in the same way in *Chapman vs. Ferguson*, 1 *Bartlett*, 267.

§ 346. In the case of *Joseph B. Varnum* of Massachusetts [*Cl. & H.*, 112,] it was held by the House of Representatives of the 4th Congress as follows:

1. That an allegation that fifty votes were given by proxy, is sufficiently certain without naming the persons in whose behalf they were cast.

2. That an allegation that "five votes were received and certified by the presiding officers, which

were given by persons not qualified by law to vote," is not sufficiently certain, because it does not give the names of such persons. But as already shown, it has been held repeatedly under the act of 1851, regulating the mode of obtaining evidence in cases of contested election, that it is not necessary to give the names of the persons by whom illegal votes are alleged to have been cast.

§ 347. In *Vallandigham vs. Campbell*, [1 *Bartlett*, 223,] the rule that a sitting member must use diligence in the preparation of his defense to a contest brought against him, was adhered to by the committee and the House. It was there held that the fact that the sitting member was a member of a previous Congress, and attended to his duties as such, during a part of the time, when by law the testimony should have been taken, furnished no ground for an extension of time in his behalf. Also, that the fact that the contestant occupied or proposed to occupy the entire sixty days after service of the answer of the sitting member, to the notice of contest, does not entitle the sitting member to an extension of time. Both parties were allowed to take testimony under the law as it then stood during the same time. And substantially the same ruling was made in the case of *Boles vs. Edwards*, [42*d Congress*.] The statute upon this subject was, however, by an act approved January 10th, 1873, amended so as to extend the whole time for taking evidence to ninety days, and so as to divide the time as follows; the first forty days to the contestant, the succeeding forty days to the sitting member, and the closing ten days, to the contestant, to be occupied in taking testimony in rebuttal only.

§348. Although the act of Congress of 1851, in relation to taking evidence in contested election cases, is not absolutely binding upon the House of Representatives, yet it is to be followed as a rule and not disregarded or departed from, except in extraordinary cases. A contestant must take his testimony under it, and in accordance with its provisions, unless he can show that it was impracticable to do so, and that injustice may be done, unless the House will order a special investigation. [*Brooks vs. Davis*, 1 *Bartlett*, 244.] The statute as it now stands after the recent amendments, affords an apportunity for investigation, so ample and complete that it is believed that it will seldom happen that the House will find it necessary to depart from its provisions in order to do the most complete and perfect justice, and it will no doubt therefore be adhered to as furnishing the best possible guide, for instituting and carrying forward inquiries of this character.

§ 349. The Houses of Congress when exercising their authority and jurisdiction to decide upon "the election returns and qualifications" of members, are not bound by the technical rules, which govern proceedings in courts of justice. Indeed the statutes to be found among the acts of Congress regulating the mode of conducting an election contest, in the House of Representatives, are directory only, and are not and cannot be made mandatory under the constitution. In practice these statutory regulations are often varied and sometimes wholly departed from. They are convenient as rules of practice, and of course will be adhered to, unless the House in its discretion shall in a given case determine that the ends of justice require a different course of action. They constitute wholesome rules not to be departed from without cause. (*Williamson vs. Sickles*, 1 *Bartlett*, 288.) It is not within the constitutional power of Congress by a legislative enactment or otherwise, to control either House in the exercise of its exclusive right to "be the judge of the elections returns and qualifications of its own members." (*Constitution*, *Art.* 1, *Sec.* 5.) The laws that have been enacted on this subject, being therefore only directory and not absolutely binding, would have been more appropriately passed as mere rules of the House of Representatives, since by their passage it may be claimed that the House conceded the right of the Senate to share with it in this duty and power conferred by the constitution. It is presumed however, that the provisions in question, were enacted in the form of a statute, rather than as a mere rule of the House in order to give them more general publicity and place such directions, as were thought proper, within the reach of whomsoever they might concern. And the constant practice on the part of the House of varying these regulations has been regarded, no doubt, as a sufficient protest against the power or right of the Senate in the premises.

§ 350. The House of Representatives of the United States, may in its discretion proceed to inquire into the validity of the election of one of its members, without any formal contest having been instituted. A contestant is not absolutely necessary. (*Reeder vs. Whitfield*, 1 *Bart.*, 189.] If circumstances arise which, in the opinion of the House, make it their duty to investigate the right of a member to a seat, the House may proceed upon its own motion. It follows of course that the death of the contestant or his withdrawal from the contest, or an attempt to compromise between the contestant and incumbent, will not make it obligatory on the House to discontinue the investigation.

§ 351. A census of population so classified as to show the number of persons in each county, possessing the qualications of voters and taken by sworn officers, under the authority of the United States, is admissible in evidence as tending to show, approximately at least, the number of voters in any given county at the time such census was taken, and of course also as showing approximately the number of voters in such county, at the time of an election, held shortly before or after the taking of such census. (*Norris vs. Handley*, 42*d Congress*. *Niblack vs. Walls*, 42*d Congress*.) But of course this is not the most reliable sort of evidence, as there is always great room for mistakes and inaccuracies, in the taking of the census. The census returns are by no means conclusive, and will be resorted to only in the absence of other satisfactory evidence, as when there is some proof of intimidation and violence, but great doubt and uncertainty as to how many legal voters were by this means deprived of the right to vote. In such a case, if it appear from the returns of a census taken about the time of the election, that the vote was an ordinarily full one, it may be fairly inferred in the absence of other evidence, that there were not a large number of persons deterred from voting at such election.

§ 352. A similiar rule to the one here stated was

adopted in the early case of *Tallaferro* vs. *Hungerford*, (*Cl. & H.*, 246,) where it was held that the land list prepared under a statute of Virginia, and required by law to give the names of all freeholders for the year prior to an election, is proper to be considered as *prima facie* evidence of the number of voters in a county, but not conclusive. And in *Blair* vs. *Barrett*, [1 *Bartlett*, 308,] it was held that the city government of St. Louis, having ordered a census to be taken with statistics of nationality and naturalization, such census, and the testimony of the census taker, were admissible in evidence.

§ 353. The House of Representatives has shown a disposition to give a liberal construction to the acts of Congress in relation to the mode of conducting cases of contested elections. They are construed with reference more to the substantial rights of the parties, than to the exact wording of the statute. And it may be expected that the House will continue so to construe these statutes, for as we have elsewhere shown, they are not absolutely binding upon the House in any case. They are adopted only as wholesome rules of practice, and of course a tribunal could hardly be expected to construe with great strictness, a statute which it may in its discretion disregard altogether. It was accordingly held in *Kline* vs. *Verree*, [1 *Bartlett*, 381,] that where the contestant failed to specify with *particularity* the grounds of his contest, he might be permitted to specify such grounds orally. This, however, should never be allowed in a case where the *substantial* rights of the sitting member might thereby be prejudiced. As for example, if the notice is so vague as not to put the sitting member upon his proper defense, and as not to inform him with reasonable certainty of the nature of the case, which he is expected to meet, it would be altogether improper to allow such notice to be amended and perfected by an oral or even by a written specification, made at the trial and after the closing of the evidence on both sides. If in such a case any amendment could be allowed, it would necessarily follow that an extension of time within which to take testimony should be ordered. To spring a *new issue* upon the sitting member, of which he has had *no notice*, and to try the same without permitting him to take testimony touching such new issue, would be a course of proceeding not to be tolerated.

§ 354. Testimony to be used in a case of contested election, in the House of Representatives, of the United States, must under the law, as it stood prior to the recent amendments, be taken within sixty days from the time the answer is served, unless further time is given by the House. Therefore a deposition taken after the sixty days has expired, and without the order of the House will be excluded. (*Knox* vs. *Blair*, 1 *Bartlett*, 521. *Todd* vs. *Jayne*, 1 *Bartlett*, 555.) In the case last named it was held that notwithstanding the requirement of the statute that notice of contest shall be served "within thirty days *after* the result has been declared," yet if the sitting member answers to a notice served before the result is declared, he should be held as waiving this objection and cannot avail himself of it on the final hearing. The true construction of the statute allows the notice to be served at any time within the thirty days, but not after the termination of that period.

§ 355. Under a statute of Virginia, requiring that all voters shall be free-holders, it was held that the land books of the county were admissible in evidence to show who were free-holders, they being regularly certified by the clerk of the county to be correct. These books were made out annually under the laws of Virginia, and were intended to contain a list of all the separate tracts of land and the owners names. (*Loyal* vs. *Newton*, *Cl. & H.*, 520.) These books were undoubtedly admissible upon the same principle that census returns are admissible in evidence, but they are only *prima facie* and proximately correct. Books and records of this character are necessarily more or less inaccurate and erroneous, and do not have the conclusive character which attaches to some other public records.

§ 356. For the purpose of showing that non-residents have voted, witnesses are often called to testify that persons whose names appear upon the roll as having voted, are not known to them as residents of the county or voting precinct, as the case may be. This kind of evidence is admissible for what it is worth, but it is manifest that its value must depend upon circumstances. If the district or territory within which the voter must reside is large, or very populous, and the witness has not an intimate and extensive acquaintance with the inhabitants, the evidence will be of little value, and standing alone will avail nothing. But on the other hand, if such district or territory is not large or populous, and if the witness shows that his acquaintance with the inhabitants is such that he could scarcely fail to know any person who may have resided therein long enough to become a voter, his evidence may be quite satisfactory, especially if it further appears that soon after the election the alleged non-resident voter could not be found in the district, within the limits of which all voters must reside. Proof of this character must at least be regarded sufficient, to shift the burden upon the party claiming that the vote of such alleged non-resident be counted, and require him to show affirmatively that he is a *bona fide* resident. It was held under the constitution of Kentucky, which only required residence in the county, that no name should be stricken from the polls as unknown, upon the testimony of one witness only, that no such person is known in the county. Also, that where a man of like name is known, residing in another county, some proof direct or circumstantial, other than finding such a name on the poll book, will be required of his having voted in the county or precinct, where the vote is assailed. (*Letcher* vs. *Moore*, *Cl. & H.*, 749.) It was further held in the same case that when the name of a particular person is found on the poll book as having voted, proof that an individual of that name resides in the county and is a minor, is not of itself sufficient to strike out the vote. Some further proof, direct or circumstantial, should be required to show that the vote was in fact cast by such minor.

§ 357. The constitution of Kentucky provided that votes "shall be personally and publicly given *viva voce*." In *Letcher* vs. *Moore* (*supra*,) it appeared that three persons had voted for Mr. Letcher who, though intelligent and able to read and write, were deaf and dumb. Of course these persons could not literally vote *viva voce,* and the question was raised whether they were legal voters under the constitution. The committee held that their votes should be received as clearly within the spirit of the constitution, although in reaching this conclusion, a previous decision of the Senate of Kentucky, in the case of *Williams* vs. *Mason* (not reported) was overruled. No doubt is entertained as to the correctness of the ruling of the committee.

§ 358. In *Follett* vs. *Delano,* (2 *Bartlett,* 113,) the committee of elections of the House of Representatives expressed the opinion, that inasmuch as there is no statute defining the mode of proving the service of notice in a contested election case in that body, such service must be proven as any other fact in the case, by the deposition of a witness, and that an affidavit is not sufficient. And the committee in the same case also expressed the opinion that inasmuch as the statute requires the contestant to "give notice in writing to the member whose seat he designs to contest," and does not define the mode of service, it must be a personal service, and that service, by leaving a copy at the residence of the sitting member is not sufficient. These points can hardly be considered as settled, by any decision of the House, since the case itself was considered upon its merits, notwithstanding the defective service, and it is the opinion of the author that it would not be safe to risk a case upon this construction of the statute, which, though perhaps technically correct, may at any time be disregarded by a majority of the House,—as it is quite likely to be in a case where the majority should consider it a construction too narrow and strict to meet the ends of substantial justice. An answer will of course operate to waive any defect in the *service* of the notice, though perhaps not in the notice itself.

§ 359. In the case just cited it was further held that the rule that a failure to answer is a confession of the allegations contained in the complaint, will not be applied to a contested election in the House of Representatives. The reason is that the inquiry is of a public nature, and not a case involving private rights alone. Upon this point the committee in the report say:

"The contestant claimed that the sitting member, by failing to answer, must be taken to have confessed the truth of the allegations in the notice. The statute requires of the sitting member, within thirty days after the service, to answer such notice, admitting or denying the facts alleged therein, and stating specifically any other grounds upon which he rests the validity of his election." If the contestant and the sitting member were the only parties interested in the representation of this district, it might not be unfair to hold that the sitting member, upon service of notice upon him according to law must answer as the law requires, or by neglect or refusal, be taken as confessing the truth of the allegations made in conformity to law against his right to his seat, and abide the judgment of the House upon such confession. But the contestant and the sitting member are by no means the only parties interested in this representation. The electors of the district, each and every one of them, have a vital interest in that question, and no one of them can be precluded, by any laches not his own, from insisting that the choice of the majority shall be regarded. No confession of the sitting member, however it might bind him personally, can place the contestant in the seat, unless he is the choice of the majority, nor deprive that majority of its rightful representation. The sitting member may well be deprived, by his neglect to answer, of reliance upon "any other grounds upon which he rests the validity of his election," for he has never given notice of any such grounds; but the committee are of opinion that the House should require proof that the sitting member has not, and that the contestant has, a majority of the legal votes before unseating the one and admitting the other, however the sitting member may have seen fit to conduct his own case in a contest."

§ 360. A similar ruling was made in the recent case of *Sheridan* vs. *Pinchback*, (43*d Congress.*) It is very clear that the usual judgment by default, such as would follow a failure to answer in the courts of the country, should not be rendered in a case of contested election in the House of Representatives. If the sitting member has not answered he may well be regarded as estopped from taking testimony or proceeding with the contest, until he shall have, with the leave of the House, filed his answer, but the House will not take the allegations of contestant as true, because they are not answered. In the case of *Sheridan* vs. *Pinchback*, the committee say, that the case of the contestant where the sitting member does not answer, is no stronger than if no one were contesting his right, and the committee had been ordered by the House to inquire whether he was elected. This distinction between contested election cases and other suits grows out of the fact that in the former the people have an interest so vital and important, as to forbid the parties to the record to conclude their full investigation and decision, by any compromise or other action of theirs.

§ 361. During the progress of the rebellion, numerous cases arose in which it was alleged that members of Congress elect, were not entitled to seats because of disloyalty and inability truthfully to take the oath prescribed by the act of Congress, of July 2d, 1862, and known as the test oath. The rule which the House adopted for the determination of these cases, is stated as follows in the Kentucky cases. (2 *Bartlett*, 368):

"While the committee entertained no doubt that it is the right and duty of the House to turn back from its very threshold every one seeking to enter who has been engaged in armed hostility to the government of the United States, or has given aid or comfort to its enemies during the late rebellion, yet we believe that in our government the right to representation is so sacred that no man who has been duly elected by the legal voters of his district, should be refused his seat upon the ground of his personal disloyalty, unless it is proven that he has been guilty of such open acts of disloyalty that he cannot honestly and truly take the oath prescribed by the act of July 2, 1862; and further, that the commission of such acts of disloyalty to the government should not be suspected merely, but should be proven by clear and satisfactory testimony, and that while mere want of active support of the government, or a passive sympathy with the rebellion, are not sufficient to exclude a person regularly elected from taking his seat in the House, yet whenever it is shown by proof that the claimant has, by act or speech, given aid or countenance to the rebellion, he should not be permitted to take the oath, and such acts or speech need not be such as to constitute treason technically, but must have been so overt and public, and must have been done or said under such circumstances, as fairly to show that they were actually designed to, and in their nature tended to, forward the cause of the rebellion."

The practice in these cases was to consider the question of the loyalty of the member elect, before allowing him to take his seat and be sworn, in all cases where charges of disloyalty and of inability truthfully to take the oath, were made to the House by a responsible party—as for example, by a member or member elect of the House.

§ 362. Record evidence is of course admissible on the trial of a case of contested election, in the House of Representatives of the United States, to the same extent and for like purposes as in Courts of Justice, and in the trial of ordinary civil actions. The question may be raised whether evidence of this character can be offered for the first time on the trial? It may be said that it should be produced before an officer taking testimony, in the presence of the opposite party, and put in evidence within the time required for completing the taking of the testimony in the case. And this is undoubtedly the correct practice, for if evidence of this character is to be used, it is but fair that the party against whom it is to be offered should have notice of it in time to offer evidence in response to it. It may therefore be laid down as the correct rule upon the subject, that a party desiring to use a record as evidence in such a case, shall at a time and place, which has been fixed for taking testimony, and of which due notice has been given, offer such record or a duly authenticated copy thereof, in evidence, and cause it to be spread upon the record. It is impossible here to designate the particular documents, papers or books, which are included in the term "record evidence," or to specify the particular mode of authenticating copies thereof, so as to make them admissible. These must depend largely upon local customs and laws. It is perhaps enough to say that any record, or certified copy, which would be admissible as evidence in the courts of justice of the country, where a similar issue is involved, may be admitted in a contested election case, in the House of Representatives.

§ 363. A statute of Ohio required tally sheets to be kept, and the board of canvassing officers were required to certify and return the vote "as shown by the tally sheets." In *Follett* vs. *Delano*, which arose under this statute, it was held that although the return might be so defective as to be unreliable, as evidence, yet if it did not appear affirmatively, that the tally sheets were also defective and unreliable, it must be presumed that they were correct. And it was, therefore, the duty of the contestant in order to make out his case, to put in evidence both the returns and tally papers, and show that neither afforded satisfactory evidence of the true result. (2 *Bartlett*, 113.) This was a correct ruling under the Ohio statute, but it must not be assumed that it is authority for any case not arising under a similar law. It was the duty of the contestant in that case, to attack the tally papers as well as the return, because the tally papers were made by statute, substantially, a part of the return. They were papers to accompany the return. They were to be certified and sent in with the return, and they were required to show the time and place of holding the election; the persons by whom it was conducted; *the number of votes cast and for whom*. It might very well happen that these papers would supply informalities and defects in the returns themselves, and as they were not produced in evidence, it was properly held that they were presumed to be correct and formal, and being so, that they did afford sufficient proof of the result in that case. But ordinarily, where the return is attacked and set aside, it is not necessary for the contestant to go further and set aside all the other election papers. The general rule is that when the return is set aside, both parties must prove their votes by other evidence. The exception to this rule is where there are papers to accompany the returns, which are in fact a part of it, and which would, if formal, cure the defect in the return. In such a case these accompanying papers must be produced. These suggestions of course apply only to cases where returns are attacked on the ground of informality. Where the attack is made upon the ground of fraud or the like, the court or tribunal having jurisdiction, will proceed with the inquiry, without reference to what appears upon the face of the returns.

§ 364. It was held by the majority of the Committee in the House of Representatives, in *Koontz* vs. *Coffroth*, (2 *Bartlett*, 23,) and also in *Fuller* vs., *Dawson*, (*Ib.*, 126,) that returns were void and should be rejected if the certificates of the oaths of the election officers were wanting. It must now, however, be regarded as settled, that if the returns are otherwise regular, they are not to be rejected because it does not appear that the officers were sworn. If the contrary does not appear it will be presumed that they were sworn, as the law directs, and even if it be shown that they were not sworn, their acts are not void for that cause alone. (*Barnes* vs. *Adams*, 2 *Bartlett*, 760,) and cases there cited.

§ 365. It is impossible to state more definitely than we have done, the general rule which should govern in determining whether a return should be set aside, and the parties on either side be required to prove their actual vote by other evidence. The rule is that the return must stand until *impeached*, *i e.* until shown to be worthless as evidence,—so worthless that the truth cannot be deduced from it. In practice it will be found necessary to apply this rule to an infinite variety of facts and circumstances. The following are examples of its application. Where it was clearly shown that the contestant received one hundred and seventy votes, and the return only gave him one hundred and forty-three votes, and there was other evidence tending to show actual tampering with the ballot box; the return was set aside. (*Washburn* vs. *Voorhies*, 2 *Bartlett*, 54.)

§ 366. In the same case, the testimony concerning another precinct, consisted wholly in a discrepancy between the number of votes actually cast for contestant, as shown by the testimony of voters, and the number returned for him. The difference was twelve votes, and in the absence of any proof of fraud, the return was not rejected, but was corrected and allowed to stand. In *Reed* vs. *Julian*, (2 *Bartlett*, 822,) the discrepancy between the vote proven, as cast for the sitting member and the vote returned for him, being very considerable, and there being other proof tending to show fraud, the return was set aside.

§ 367. Where the *place* of voting in an election precinct in the city of New York, was not designated or published until the day before the election, so that many voters were not advised of the place, and where the inspectors were in violation of law appointed from non-residents of the precinct, and where the board did not meet at the place designated by law, but selected their own place of meeting, giving no notice to electors, where they might be heard, and where the election was not held at the place designated, but "somewhere near" it, the people having great difficulty in finding the place, and where under these circumstances the vote was unusually large, and there was strong presumptive proof that a part of it was fraudulent; the return was set aside. (*Dodge* vs. *Brooks*, 2 *Bartlett*, 78.) In the report of this case will be found several examples of returns rejected, and of some attacked and not rejected for want of sufficient proof, but the details are too numerous and complicated to be inserted here with profit.

§ 368. To set aside the returns of an election is one thing; to set aside the election itself is another and very different thing. The return from a given precinct being set aside, the duty still remains to let the election stand, and to ascertain from other evidence the true state of the vote. The return is only to be set aside, as we have seen, when it is so tainted with fraud, or with the misconduct of the election officers, that the truth cannot be deduced from it. The *election* is only to be set aside when it is impossible from *any evidence* within reach, to ascertain the true result,—when neither from the returns nor from other proof, nor from all together, can the truth be determined. It is important to keep this distinction in mind.

§ 369. A statute of Alabama empowered a "board of supervisors of elections" to hear proof upon charges of fraud &c., and upon sufficient evidence, to reject illegal and fraudulent votes cast, "which rejection so made as aforesaid" the statute declared "shall be final, unless appeal be taken within ten days to the probate court." The House of Representatives of the United States in case of *Norris* vs. *Handley*, (42*d Congress*,) refused to be governed by this statute, in so far as it made the decision of the board final. Upon this point the committee's report says:

"In the opinion of the committee it is not competent for the legislature of a State to declare what shall or shall not be considered by the House of Representatives as evidence to show the actual vote cast in any district for a member of Congress, much less to declare that the decision of a board of county canvassers, rejecting a given vote, shall estop the House from further inquiry. The fact, therefore, that no appeal was taken from the decision of the board of canvassers, rejecting the vote of Girard precinct, cannot preclude the House from going behind the returns and considering the effect of the evidence presented."

§ 370. Concerning the effect which should be given to the decision of a board invested by statute with power to hear proof of fraud, and reject votes, the committee in the same report used this language:

"We have already seen that the statute of Alabama confers upon this board authority to revise the return of the vote of the several precincts, and, upon sufficient proof, to throw out such as in their judgment are illegal or fraudulent. Although this is an extraordinary, not to say a dangerous, power when placed in the hands of a board of this character, with such inadequate facilities for obtaining legal evidence and deciding upon questions of fraud, yet it is believed by the committee that the action of such a board under the statute in question, and in pursuance of the power conferred thereby, is to be regarded as *prima facie* correct, and to be allowed to stand as valid until shown by evidence to be illegal or unjust."

§ 371. In the report of the committee of elections in *Gooding* vs. *Wilson*, (42*d Congress*,) several important rules of evidence applicable to cases of contested elections were laid down, as follows:

"Evidence which might have been sufficient to put the voter to his explanation, if challenged at the polls, is not deemed sufficient to prove a vote illegal after it has been admitted. Nor has the mere statement by a witness that a voter was or was not a resident, without giving facts to justify his opinion, been considered sufficient to throw out such a vote. The testimony shows a number of instances where a witness would state positively the residence or non-residence of a voter on some theory of his own, or some mistake of fact, when other testimony would show with entire clearness that the vote was legal. After a vote has been admitted, something more is required to prove it illegal than to throw doubt upon it. There ought to be proof which, weighed by the ordinary rules of evidence, satisfies and convinces the mind that a mistake has been made, and which the House can rest upon as a safe precedent for like cases."

§ 372. Of course some weight is to be given to the decision of the judges of the election, whose province it is in the first instance to admit or exclude votes. Their action is to be presumed correct until it is shown to have been erroneous. The other rule stated above is equally sound. Whether a person is, or is not, a resident of a particular place is often a question of law as well as of fact. Unless the facts are stated, the question, in so far as it is a question of law, cannot be determined, and that question is not for the witness to decide, but for the court.

§ 373. The courts will not undertake to decide upon the right of a party to hold a seat in the legislature, where by the constitution each House is made the judge of the election and qualifications of its own members, but a court may by *mandamus*, compel the proper certifying officers to discharge their duties and arm the parties elected to such legislative body with the credentials necessary to enable them to assert their rights before the proper tribunal. And, inasmuch as canvassing and returning officers act ministerially and have no power to go behind the returns, or inquire into the legality of votes cast and returned, a court will by *mandamus* compel them to declare and certify the result *as shown by the returns*, because that is their plain duty, but the award of a certificate of election under such mandate, will not conclude the legislative body in determining the election. (*O'Farrell* vs. *Colby*, 2 *Minn.*, 180.)

§ 374. The actions provided by the statutes of most of the States to try the right to an office are in the nature of a *quo warranto* at common law. They differ in the formula of proceeding from proceedings by information, or by writ of *quo warranto*, but they are, as a general rule, in substance the same, and governed by substantially the same rules which regulated proceedings under the prior practice. Such was the ruling under the statute of New York, which is not unlike the statutes of most of the other States. (*People vs. Pease*, 30 *Barbours*, 588.)

§ 375. Where the statute creates a board for the purpose of determining election contests, and confers upon such board exclusive jurisdiction in such cases, the courts are deprived of jurisdiction to pass upon the results of any such contests. But in such a case the proper court may, by mandamus, compel such board to organize and proceed according to law to the discharge of its official duties. (*Batman* vs. *McGowan*, 1 *Met., Ky.*, 533.)

§ 376. The statute of Kentucky, under which this case arose, provided for a board to be composed of the presiding judge of the County Court, the clerk thereof, and the sheriff. It also provided as follows: "but if either is a candidate, he shall have no voice in the decision of his own case. If from any cause two of the before named persons cannot, in whole or in part, act in comparing the polls, their places shall be supplied," &c. Under this statute it was held that the board must be composed of persons entirely free from any interest, and that the sheriff and coroner, both being candidates, could not act. It would be a dangerous practice to permit two candidates to act upon such a board, for although neither one of them could vote for himself, yet they might vote for each other. They might thus have a common interest to subserve, or they might combine together to aid each other. The policy of all such legislation is to guard against improper combinations, and to secure just and impartial decisions.

§ 377. Where notice of contest is to be given within a given number of days after the determination of the result, the true rule for computing the time is to include the first and exclude the last day, or *vice versa*. Hence it was held in Kentucky that where the certificate of election was issued on the sixth day of the month, and notice of contest was served on the sixteenth day of the same month, there was not ten days notice as required by law. (*Batman* vs. *Magowan*, *supra*.)

§ 378. In the case of *Bennett, petitioner*, (32 *Maine*, 508,) it is held that under a statute which requires that "the Governor and Council shall open and compare the votes returned," &c., the act of opening and comparing such votes is an official duty to be performed by the executive department. And it was accordingly held in that case that the courts of the State could not entertain the inquiry whether that duty had been correctly or incorrectly performed, and a mandamus to compel the Governor and Council to certify the election of the petitioner to the office of County Commissioner, was refused, upon the ground that the judiciary could not control the executive department of a State, in the performance of its official functions. It is very clear that this ruling was correct, for mandamus will not lie to control the action of any board or officer, in determining the result of an election. But it does not follow that because the executive of the State and the Council are constituted the returning board,—their conclusions are final. If a board composed of the Governor and Council shall commit an error either by accident or design, or by a misconstruction of the law, in determining the result of an election, the party injured can undoubtedly have his remedy in the courts of justice, the same as if the result had been declared by a board composed of other persons.

§ 379. The fact that a person has received the certificate of election to an office, and entered upon the discharge of the duties thereof, does not oust the proper court of jurisdiction to try the title to the office. The certificate issues upon the *prima facie* case as shown by the returns, but the court may go behind the returns, and upon the merits find a different result. (*Ex parte Ellyson*, 20 *Gratt*, *Va.*, 10.)

And in Virginia the jurisdiction of the courts is held not to be limited to cases of contest between competing candidates. Under the law of that State an election may be contested, although but one person was voted for at the election. (*Ib.*)

§ 380. The rule which admits in evidence on the trial of a case of contested election, the original tally sheet, duly certified by the officer of election, as *prima facie* evidence of the election of the person, for whom it shows a majority of the ballots to have been cast, was reaffirmed in Ohio, in *State* vs. *Donnewirth*, (21 *Ohio*, 216.) We have already called attention to the provisions of the statute of Ohio, in relation to the tally sheets to be kept by the officers of the election, duly certified, and returned. And it may be observed here that the admissibility, and value of the election papers, depends somewhat upon the statutes governing the election in question. But generally, all papers required by law to be kept in connection with the conduct of an election, may be received in evidence upon being properly identified.

§ 381. While a continuance or postponement for a brief period of time may be allowed in a contested election case, where the court or tribunal trying the same, shall in its discretion believe that the ends of justice will be subserved thereby, yet the ordinary rules governing applications for continuances, in the nature of the case, cannot apply to a litigation of this kind. The proceedings must be regarded as in their nature so far summary, as to take them out of the operation of the general rule, which allows continuances from term to term, in the discretion of the court. (*Kellar* vs. *Chapman*, 34 *Cal.*, 635.)

§ 382. In a case of *quo warranto* instituted for the purpose of trying the right of an individual to hold a public office, the people are understood to be interested as a body in the investigation, and therefore the Attorney General or other officer holding a similar relation to the public, must represent the people, and is the only person whose stipulation, can be acted upon so as to affect the people. It was accordingly held in Michigan, that the court should not consider a statement of facts agreed to between the relator and the respondent, and not signed by the Attorney General. (*People* vs. *Pratt*, 15 *Mich.*, 184. *Crawford* vs. *Molitor*, 23 *Mich.*, 342.) And, as we have already seen, substantially the same rule prevails, in all cases of contested election, whether in the form of a *quo warranto*, or by statutory proceedings.

§ 383. In *Newcum* vs. *Kirtley*, (13 *B. Monroe*, 515,) it was held that the votes of two electors who according to the testimony of several witnesses, would have voted for contestant if the polls had not been closed too soon, could not be counted as if cast. It did not appear that the electors in question had presented themselves at the proper voting place, within the hours during which the law required the polls to be kept open, for the purpose of voting for contestant, and that *after doing all that was in their power* they were prevented by the fault of the election officers, from so voting. If these facts had appeared the question would have been very different from the one decided. The court seems to have placed great stress upon the fact that "their votes were not *offered* to, nor taken by the officer entrusted by law with the office of receiving and recording them," and very properly, as that was a controling fact. The true rule upon this subject has been stated in another connection and is this: In order that a ballot not actually cast, shall be counted as if cast, it must appear that the voter actually offered to cast it, and was prevented from so doing without fault on his part, or if he does not actually present his ballot to the officers of the election, that he endeavored to approach the polls for that purpose, and used due diligence in endeavoring to reach the polls, but was prevented from so doing. Doubtless a rule much more lax than this, has occasionally been adopted in legislative bodies, but every departure from this rule as here stated is, and must be, both erroneous and dangerous.

§ 384. Where a statute provided that the grounds of contest "must be verified by the affidavit of the contesting party, that the matters and things therein contained are true." It is sufficient if the ordinary form of verification is followed, viz: that the statement is true except as to matters therein set forth on information and belief, and as to those matters affiant believes it to be true. This has been held to be a substantial compliance with such a statute, and it has been well said that to require the contestant to make oath to the absolute verity of every averment of the statement or petition, would prevent the contest of an election in almost any conceivable case and would work a practical abrogation of a beneficial law. In the nature of the case, many of the facts to be averred must necessarily be derived from others and therefore must be stated upon information and belief only. (*Kirk vs. Rhoades, Supreme Court of California, Oct. Term,* 1873.)

§ 385. The mode of proceeding when a contested election case is before a legislative body, is generally prescribed by statute, or by the rules of such body. In the absence of any such statutory regulation, and in the absence of any standing rule upon the subject, the proceedings will be such as the body itself may prescribe for each particular case, and they must include due and reasonable notice to the incumbent of the office, and a fair opportunity for adducing proofs and being heard on both sides. And no notice can be considered "due and reasonable," which does not inform the incumbent with sufficient certainty to prevent any surprise upon the trial, of the grounds of the contest. The incumbent will also be required to answer, so that the issue may be understood, both by the parties themselves and by the body which is to try the case.

§ 386. In *Reed* vs. *Kneass,* (2 *Parsons,* 584. *Brightley's Election Cases,* 366,) it was insisted by counsel that a voter should not be *permitted* to testify as to the person for whom he has voted at an election. It was contended that the constitutional provision that "all elections shall be by ballot," was not simply intended as a security to the elector for the free and independent exercise of the right of suffrage, but that from considerations of public policy it should be held to prevent the voter, under any circumstances, from disclosing before a judicial or other tribunal how he voted. But this point was overruled, and it was held that while the voter has the privilege of preserving the secrecy of his ballot by refusing to testify to its contents, he is at liberty to waive that privilege. If it were otherwise it might often be impossible to bring to light the darkest frauds. It would be a strange perversion of the rule which preserves the secrecy of the ballot, for the purpose of encouraging free and independent voting, to make it serve to shield the fraud and corruption of those who would, by tampering with or changing ballots, after they are cast, altogether deprive the majority of the electors of their choice. In the case just cited two hundred and thirty witnesses were examined and testified that they had each voted at a given precinct for W. B. Read, for District Attorney, whereas, according to the official returns, he had received but one hundred and twenty votes therein. This mode of attacking and impeaching a return has been frequently recognized as proper, and this kind of evidence as competent. (*Reid* vs. *Julian*, 2 *Bartlett*, 822. *Loyal* vs. *Newton*, 1 *do*, 522.)

§ 387. It is undoubtedly the policy of the law not to throw too many obstacles in the way of investigating the correctness and *bona fides* of election returns. On this point the Court in *Reed* vs. *Kneass* (*supra*,) very justly observe.

"The true policy, to maintain and perpetuate the vote by ballot, is found in jealously guarding its purity, in placing no fine drawn metaphysical obstructions in the way of testing election returns charged as false and fraudulent, and in assuring to the people by a jealous, vigilant and determined investigation of election frauds, that there is a saving spirit in the public tribunals charged with such investigations.

ready to do them justice if their suffrages have been tampered with by fraud, or misapprehended through error."

§ 388. Concerning the admissibility of the ballots themselves, in evidence, in a case of contested election, Judge Cooley, in his Constitutional Limitations, (p. 625,) has this to say:

"But back of this *prima facie* case, (made by the certificate of election,) the Courts may go, and the determinations of the State board may be corrected by those of the district boards, and the latter by the ballots themselves, *when the ballots are still in existence, and have been kept as required by law.* If, however, the ballots have not been kept as required by law, and surrounded by such securities as the law has prescribed, with a view to their safe preservation as the best evidence of the election, it would seem that they should not be received in evidence at all, or, if received, that it should be left to the jury to determine, upon all the circumstances of the case, whether they constitute more reliable evidence than the inspectors' certificate, which is usually prepared immediately on the close of the election, and upon actual count of the ballots as then made by the officers whose duty it is to do so."

§ 389. It matters not how high and important an office may be, an election to it must be by the majority or plurality of the legal votes cast. And if any one without having received such majority or plurality intrudes himself into an office, whether with or without a certificate of election, the Courts have jurisdiction to oust him, unless some other tribunal has been clothed with this power to the exclusion of the Courts. The question arose in the case of *Governor Barstow of Wisconsin*, whether the person occupying the office of chief executive of a State can be required to appear before the Courts and defend against another claimant for that office. It was contended that the three departments of the State government were equal, co-ordinate, and independent of each other, and that each department must be the judge of the election and qualifications of its own members, subject only to impeachment and appeal to the people; that therefore the question as to who is entitled to the office of Governor, can in no case become a judicial question. But this doctrine received no countenance from the Court to which it was addressed, and it is believed to be without the support of any judicial authority. If adopted it would leave no peaceable and constitutional means for ousting a successful usurper from either of the departments of the State government. (*Cooley's Const. Lim.*, 624-5, *note* 1.)

§ 390. In *People vs. Cicote*, (16 *Mich.*, 283,) the opinion is expressed that one claiming a public office has a constitutional right to a trial by jury, and that this right cannot be taken from him by any law which shall undertake to make the decision of a canvassing board final. But see *Ewing* vs. *Filley*, 43 *Penn. State*, 384. *Commonwealth* vs. *Leech*, 44 *do*, 332.

§ 391. We have already seen that when a return is shown to be fraudulent and set aside, it proves nothing, and that other evidence must be resorted to, to show the number of votes cast and for whom cast. It is very clear that if the returns are set aside no votes not otherwise proven, can be counted. And if there are three candidates voted for at a given precinct, and the return is set aside, it is not enough to show the whole number of votes cast, and the number cast for two of the three candidates; it will not be presumed that the third candidate received the remainder. In such a case each candidate must prove, by calling the voters as witnesses or otherwise, the number of votes received by him. Thus in a recent case in New York, it appeared that at an election for Mayor of the city of Albany, seven hundred and twenty-nine votes were given according to the poll list. While the votes were being counted by gas light (having been turned from a box upon the table,) the light suddenly went out, and before the gas was relighted, some of the ballots were abstracted, so that upon completing the canvass only six hundred and fifty-two ballots for Mayor were found. Of this latter number

Geo. H. Thatcher received		460
Edmund L. Judson	"	113
Thomas McCarty	"	79

Upon the trial of a contest, growing out of this election, two of the above named candidates, Judson and McCarty, made proof of their vote, from which it appeared that Judson received two hundred and McCarty one hundred and thirty-four votes.—Thatcher made no proof of his vote, but claimed that as the whole number of votes cast was shown to have been seven hundred and twenty-nine, he was entitled to the difference between that number and the combined vote proven for the two other candidates. This position was not upheld by the Court, and was clearly untenable. It appears from the report of this case that the only question made was, as to whether Thatcher's vote should be ascertained by deducting the combined vote proven for the other candidates from the number of votes canvassed, to-wit: six hundred and fifty-two, or from the number actually cast, to-wit: seven hundred and twenty-nine. The Court below had allowed Thatcher the difference between the sum of the votes cast for the other candidates, and the whole number cast and the Supreme Court having held this to be error, went no further. From all that appears in the report of the case Thatcher did not prove any vote at all. He relied upon the return, but that should have been set aside, if, as appears, to have been the case, a gross fraud had been perpetrated in the abstraction of part of the ballots before the canvass, and in substituting others, the number abstracted, and the number substituted, being wholly uncertain. Such a return cannot be corrected by proof. It must be wholly disregarded, and the vote otherwise proved, if possible, and if other proof is not possible, the election is void. (*People ex rel, Judson* vs. *Thatcher*, 7 *Lansing*, *N. Y.*, 274.)

§ 392. It is not necessary, in order to set aside a return for fraud, that it be shown that the officers of elections participated in the fraud. If third persons unlawfully possess themselves of the ballot box during or after the close of the election, before the canvass, and destroy the ballots or a portion of them, or abstract some of the ballots and place in the box others, or in any manner so tamper with the ballots as to change or render uncertain the result; such facts being proven, will render the canvass and return void, although the canvassing officers may have had no connection with the fraud, and no knowledge of it. (*People* vs. *Cook*, 8 *N. Y.*, 86. *People ex rel Judson* vs. *Thatcher*, *supra*.)

§ 393. It has been held by the Supreme Court of Mississippi, that "evidence that one of the registrars being intoxicated, took a portion of the ballots in a handkerchief away from the other registrars, and did not return them until next morning, is not admissible without showing that some of the ballots had been lost or altered, or that the plaintiff was in some manner affected thereby." (*Pradat* vs. *Ramsay*, 47 *Miss.*, 24.) This decision was put upon the ground that the misconduct of the officer was a mere irregularity, and did not, therefore, *prima facie*, affect the result; but this was evidently a misapplication of that rule. One of the most important and imperative requirements of the law of elections is, that the ballots from the time they are cast until they are canvassed, must be safely and securely kept. Frauds upon the ballot box are very frequently perpetrated by tampering with the ballots after they are cast, and before they are counted. It is for this reason that in many of the States there are statutes requiring that the ballots be publicly canvassed, immediately upon the closing of the polls. These are most excellent statutes, and the author has found with surprise and regret, that in several of the States there are laws allowing the election officers to hold the ballot boxes a number of days before making public the canvass. If such laws had been framed for the purpose of enabling corrupt parties to perpetrate frauds, they could scarcely have been more aptly framed. (*Wallace vs. Simpson, 42d Congress.*) It is clear that where the law which requires the ballots to be safely and securely kept until canvassed, and the result announced, has been so grossly violated as to have afforded opportunity for fraud or tampering, the burden of proof should be shifted. If the ballots have been kept according to law, the presumptions are all in their favor, but if a drunken man has been allowed to carry them away and keep them in an exposed place over night, as in *Pradat vs. Ramsay, supra*, the presumption is against them, and proof should be required that they are in fact the real ballots cast. In all such cases, the evidence should go to the jury, and they should determine upon the whole case, whether the ballots counted were in fact the same ballots cast.

§ 394. The practice in cases of contested election in the House of Representatives of the United States is not, and perhaps never can be, very definitely settled, for the reason that each House is the final judge of all questions arising in such cases, and neither House is absolutely bound either by the action of any previous House, or by the statute itself. The statute, however, as we have seen, is regarded as a rule of decision, and as such is generally followed, and should never be departed from without the very strongest reasons.

In addition to what has already been said touching the practice in these cases, the following suggestions are made concerning the mode of instituting and carrying on a contest, under the statutes regulating contested elections in the House of Representatives:

1. Within thirty days after the result of the election in a district has been determined by the proper authority, the contestant must serve the returned member with notice of contest. This notice must be in writing, and must specify particularly the grounds upon which the contestant relies. (*Revised statutes, Sec.* 105.) The period of thirty days within which such notice of contest may be given, begins to run from the time when the result of the election "shall have been determined" by the proper board or officer. The statutes of the several States provide for canvassing the votes cast for Representatives in Congress, and for declaring the result, and these statutes must be consulted in each case to determine the question, when, how, and by whom the result is to be determined and declared. It is no doubt true, that for the purpose of fixing the time when the thirty days begin to run, there must be not only a decision, but a promulgation of the result, for if the result was kept secret after it was privately ascertained, and if it was in fact not communicated to the contestant, he could not be required to give notice. The promulgation need not be in any formal way, unless a formal proclamation or other publication is required by statute. It is only necessary that it be made known in some manner. (*Gunter vs. Wilshire,* 43*d Congress.*) The statute is silent as to the manner of the service of the notice; it declares that the contestant shall "give notice in writing," &c. In *Follett vs. Delano,* (2 *Bartlett,* 115,) the committee expressed the opinion

that the correct construction of the statute would require personal notice, and that service made by leaving a copy at the residence of the sitting member, would not be good. Undoubtedly the service should be made personally upon the returned member, if this is practicable ; but if by reason of his absence, or his avoidance of service, or for any other cause personal service cannot be made, then undoubtedly the notice may be served in the manner provided by the statute of the State for serving process. It is clear that the House should hold service made under these circumstances, in the manner pointed out by the local law for serving process, to be sufficient, because otherwise the incumbent might by avoiding personal service, prevent a contest altogether. Another question is, how shall the service of notice of contest be proved? Here again the act of Congress is silent. The affidavit of the person making the service has generally been taken, but in *Follett vs. Delano*, *supra*, the sufficiency of this mode of proof was denied. Where the returned member answers, he waives any informality in the service, or proof of service, but where he does not, the safe practice is for the contestant to call as a witness, the person who has made the service, and prove the fact of service, as he would prove any other fact in the case.

2. The returned member must, within thirty days from the time when he is served with the notice of contest, answer the same. The answer must be served upon the contestant. This may be done by leaving a copy with him, or if he be absent, by serving it in the same manner as required for serving

the notice of contest. The answer may deny or admit the allegations of the notice, and may state specifically, any other grounds upon which the returned member rests the validity of his election. (*Revised Statutes, Sec.* 106.) The statute makes no provision for further pleading, but the contestant may of course, if he chooses to do so, serve the returned member with a reply to any new matter in the answer. This, however, is not necessary. Inasmuch as the notice and answer are the only pleadings recognized by the statute, no further pleading can be required, and the new matter contained in the answer must be proven, to avail anything, whether it is formally denied or not.

3. The statute allows ninety days in which to take testimony in a contested election case, and requires that it be divided between the parties as follows. The contestant shall take testimony during the first forty days, the returned member during the succeeding forty days, and the contestant may take testimony in rebuttal only, during the last ten days. (*Revised Statutes, Sec.* 107.) The period of ninety days within which testimony may be taken begins with the date of the service of the answer of the returned member upon the contestant. (*See act of February,* 1875.)

4. The statute provides for taking testimony in contested election cases, either within or without the congressional district. In either case the notice provided for by Sec. 108 of the revised statutes, must be given. By Sec. 109, it is provided that testimony may be taken at two or more places at the same time. The evident purpose of the statute is to ena-

ble the parties to complete the taking of testimony within the time prescribed. The officers before whom testimony may be taken, are those named in Sec. 110 of the Revised Statutes, and the same officers are authorized to take depositions of witnesses residing out of the reach of a subpœna. (*Sec.* 117.) The party desiring to take testimony must give the notice required by Sec. 108, to his adversary, and must also apply to the officer before whom the testimony is to be taken, to issue a subpœna. The officer thus applied to, is required to issue his subpœna directed to all such witnesses as shall be named to him, requiring their attendance before him at some time and place named in the subpœna. The subpœna should follow the notice in giving names of witnesses, and fixing time and places. (*Secs.* 108, 109, 110, 111.)

5. If neither of the officers named in Sec. 110, are residing in the district, then any two justices of the peace may take testimony. (*Sec.* 113.) Depositions may be taken by consent, without notice, and before any officer authorized by law to take depositions in common law, or civil actions, or in chancery. (*Sec.* 113.) Every subpœna must be served by a copy thereof, delivered to the witness, or left at his usual place of abode at least five days before the day on which his attendance is required, and every witness must be examined within the county in which he resides, or may be served. (*Secs.* 114, 115.)

Witnesses failing to attend and testify in obedience to a subpœna duly served, unless prevented by sickness or unavoidable necessity, are liable in damages, and also to indictment and punishment for a misdemeanor. (*Sec.* 116.)

6. The statute further provides for taking the depositions of witnesses residing outside of the district and beyond the reach of a subpœna. Depositions outside of the district may be taken before any officer authorized to take testimony in contested election cases. [*Sec.* 117.]

7. The notice to take depositions of witnesses residing outside of the district and beyond the reach of a subpœna, is the same notice required to be given for taking the testimony of witnesses found within the district, and the substance of the notice, and the manner and time of its service are specified in Sec. 108.

8. When a party to a contest receives the notice provided by law of the intention of his adversary to take depositions either within or without the district, he is at liberty to name an officer [having authority to take depositions in such cases,] to officiate with the officer named in the notice, and if both officers attend, the depositions shall be taken before them both, sitting together, and be certified by both. But if only one of such officers attend, the depositions may be taken before, and certified by him alone. At the taking of testimony by deposition or otherwise, either party may appear in person or by attorney. [*Secs.* 118 and 119.]

9. As to the manner of the examination of witnesses the statute is not very clear. (*See Sec.* 120.) The language is, that "all witnesses who attend" &c., "shall be examined *by the officer*," &c. This should no doubt be construed simply as requiring the examination to be conducted *before* the officer, and not as requiring him to propound the questions to wit-

nesses. It will be seen that this section requires witnesses to be examined touching all such matters respecting the election about to be contesed as shall be proposed *by either of the parties or their agents.*" And Sec. 122 provides that the officer shall cause the testimony of the witnesses, together with the *questions proposed by the parties or their agents* to be reduced to writing," &c. From all which it seems clear that witnesses are to be examined before the proper officer, and under his direction, and that the parties or their attorneys, may appear and propound any proper questions. In the absence of the officer named in the notice, and who issued the subpœna, depositions may be taken before any other officer who is authorized to issue such subpœna, or by any officer who may be agreed upon by the parties. And this rule applies as well to testimony taken within the district as to that taken without the district. [*Sec.* 120.]

10. The testimony is to be confined to the issues joined between the parties, and the ordinary rules of evidence should be applied in determining questions of competency and relevancy. [*Sec.* 121.] Testimony must be written down, together with the questions propounded, in the presence of the officer, and in the presence of the parties or their agents, if attending, and must be attested by the witnesses. [*Sec.* 122.] Sec. 123 provides for the production of papers to be used as evidence in contested election cases. The taking of testimony may, if so stated in the notice, be adjourned from day to day. [*Sec.* 124.]

11. The notice to take depositions with the proof

or acknowledgment of service thereof, and a copy of the subpœna when one has been served, are to be attached to the depositions when completed, and a copy of the notice of contest, and the answer thereto, are to be prefixed to the same, and transmitted with them to the clerk of the House of Representatives. [*Secs.* 125 *and* 126.]

12. It is the duty of the officer who takes testimony to be used in a contested election case, without unnecssary delay to certify, carefully seal up, and forward the same to the clerk of the House of Representatives. This is to be done "when the taking of the same is completed." [*Sec.* 127.] If the testimony of a number of witnesses is taken before the same officer, he may delay the sending forward of the testimony until all have been examined—but must not delay its transmission any longer than is necessary for this purpose, and he must be careful to keep the testimony in his own possession, and securely, until it is mailed, as prescribed by the statute. Testimony of witnesses taken to be used in a contested election case, must be certified by the officer taking it, but neither the form nor the substance of the certificate is prescribed by the statute. Doubtless the form prescribed by the law of the State in which the testimony is taken, for authenticating depositions, taken under the laws of that State, should be regarded as sufficient. In cases where no form is prescribed by the local law, it will be sufficient if the officer's certificate shows that the witness came before the officer at the time and place named in the notice—that he was duly sworn and examined, that the questions propounded to him, and his answers

thereto, were written down in his presence, and in the presence of the parties or their counsel, [if they attended,] and that after being thus written out the testimony of the witnesses was duly attested by the witness, as by law required. The certificate should be signed by the officer, and attested by his seal of office, if he have a seal.

13. Testimony taken under the law and returned to the clerk of the House of Representatives, must remain in his custody unopened, until the meeting of Congress, after which it is under the control of the House, and is generally ordered to be printed and referred to the committee of elections.

CHAPTER VII.

IMPERFECT BALLOTS.

§ 395. It frequently happens that ballots are deposited in the box, which do not perfectly express the voter's intent. This is the case when the name of the person voted for is incorrectly spelled, or where the candidate's initials are not correctly given, or where the office to be filled is not clearly designated, as well as in many other similar cases.

In the case of *McKenzie vs. Braxton*, in the House of Representatives of the forty-second Congress, this subject received a very careful consideration. That was a case in which ballots were deposited for "E. M. Braxton," for "Elliott M. Braxton," for "Elliott Braxton," and for "Braxton," for Congress. The report of the committee, which was adopted by the House, presents a correct statement of the law upon this subject, and the importance of the questions discussed will justify the following quotation therefrom:

§ 396. "The proof in this case clearly shows that the sitting member is known throughout the district as well by the name of E. M. Braxton, as by that of Elliott M. Braxton; and that he is familiarly called Elliott Braxton; also, that there is no other person in the district, except the sitting member's infant son, who bears the name of Elliott M. Braxton, E. M. Braxton, or Elliott Braxton; and that the sitting member was regularly nominated for Congress by the democratic or conservative convention of the district; that his letter of acceptance was signed E. M. Braxton; that he canvassed the district and was the only person of the name of Braxton who was a candidate. These facts are not disputed by contestant; but we are asked to throw out a large number of votes, unquestionably cast in good faith for the sitting member, upon the purely technical ground that his name was printed upon the ballots E. M. Braxton, or Elliott Braxton, instead of Elliott M. Braxton. The grounds upon which the contestant makes this claim seem to be—

1. That we are not permitted to look beyond the ballot to ascertain the voter's intent; and

2. That the ballots in question cannot, upon their face, be held to have been intended for Elliott M. Braxton.

It may be, and doubtless is, sometimes necessary

to sacrifice justice in a particular case, in order to maintain an inflexible legal rule, but all just men must regret such necessity and avoid it when possible to do so. Your committee are clearly of the opinion that no such necessity exists here. So far from demanding such a sacrifice of right, the law, as well as equity, forbids it.

The contestant asks the House to apply the strict rule which has sometimes, though not always, been held to govern canvassing officers, whose duty is purely ministerial, who have no discretionary powers, and can neither receive nor consider any evidence *aliunde* the ballots themselves. It is manifest that the House, with its large powers and wide discretion, should not be confined within any such narrow limits. The House possesses all the powers of a court having jurisdiction to try the question, who was elected? It is not even limited to the powers of a court of law merely, but, under the Constitution, clearly possesses the functions of a court of equity also. If, therefore, it were conceded that the canvassers erred in counting for the sitting member the votes cast for E. M. Braxton and Elliott Braxton, it would not determine the question as to what the House should do. What, then, is the true rule for the government of the House in determining what votes to count for the sitting member? Your committee are clearly of the opinion that where the ballots give the true initials of the candidate's name, that is sufficient, and we, therefore, without hesitation, hold that the ballots given for E. M. Braxton must be counted for the sitting member.

Another objection, urged with much more zeal by

contestant's counsel, is, to the votes cast for Elliott Braxton, two hundred and thirty-five in number. These, it is urged, cannot be counted for Elliott M. Braxton, the sitting member. Even if we were not permitted to look beyond the ballots themselves, we could have little doubt as to our duty; but, under some circumstances, and for certain purposes, evidence outside of the ballots themselves is admissible. It is true that no evidence *aliunde* can be received to *contradict* the ballot, nor to give it a meaning when it expresses no meaning of itself, but, if it be ambiguous or of doubtful import, the circumstances surrounding the election may be given in evidence to explain it, and to enable the House to get at the voter's intent. We see no reason why a ballot, ambiguous on its face, may not be construed in the light of surrounding circumstances, in the same manner and to the same extent as a written contract. The true rule, which should govern upon the subject of the admissibility of extrinsic evidence to explain such a ballot, is thus laid down in *Cooley on the Constitutional Limitations, page* 611:

We think evidence of such facts as may be called the circumstances surrounding the election, such as who were the candidates brought forward by the nominating conventions; whether other persons of the same name resided in the district from which the officer was to be chosen; and if so, whether they were eligible or had been named for the office; if the ballot was printed imperfectly, how it came to be so printed, and the like, is admissible for the purpose of showing that an imperfect ballot was meant for a particular candidate, unless the name is so different that to thus apply it would be to contradict the ballot itself; or unless the ballot is so defective that it fails to show any intention whatever, in which case it is not admissible."

To the same effect are the following decisions: *Attorney General vs. Ely*, (4 *Wis.*, 430.) *People vs. Ferguson*, (8 *Cowen*, 102.) *People vs. Cook*, (14 *Barbour*, 259.) *People vs. Pease*, (27 *N. Y.*, 64.)

In *People vs. Ferguson*, *supra*, it was held that, on the trial of a contested election case before a jury, ballots cast for H. F. Yates should be counted for Henry F. Yates, if, under the circumstances, the jury were of the opinion that they were intended for him; and that to arrive at that intention it was competent to prove that he generally signed his name H. F. Yates; that he had before held the same office for which these votes were cast, and was then a candidate again; that the people generally would apply the abbreviation to him, and that no other person was known in the county to whom it would apply. This ruling was followed in *People vs. Seaman*, (5 *Denio*, 402,) and in *People vs. Cook*, 8 *N. Y.*, 67. In *Attorney General vs. Ely*, the court went so far as to hold that ballots cast for "D. M. Carpenter," "M. D. Carpenter," "M. T. Carpenter," and "Carpenter," might be counted for Mathew H. Carpenter, upon proof, made to the satisfaction of the jury, that they were intended for him.

In an early case in Michigan (*People vs. Tisdale*, 1 *Doug.*, 65,) it was held that no extrinsic evidence was admissible in explanation or support of the ballot, and this ruling has been followed in that State in several later cases. The Supreme Court of that

State, however, in its latest decision on the subject, (*People vs. Cicotte*, 16 *Mich.*, 283,) through a majority of the judges, expresses the opinion that the doctrine laid down in *People vs. Tisdale*, is erroneous, and it is adhered to upon the sole ground that it has been too long the law of that State to be overthrown, except by the legislature. The chief justice, in a masterly dissenting opinion, advocates the entire overthrow by the Court of the erroneous and pernicious doctrine of the earlier cases. We quote from this dissenting opinion, as follows :

'All rules of law which are applied to the expression, in constitutional form, of the popular will, should aim to give effect to the intention of the electors; and any arbitrary rule which is to have any other effect, without corresponding benefit, is a wrong, both to the parties who chance to be affected by it, and to the public at large. The first are deprived of their offices, and the second of their choice of public servants.

The chief argument in favor of the rule of *People vs. Tisdale*, is, that ballots cast for parties by their initials only, are so uncertain that they cannot be applied without resort to extrinsic and doubtful evidence to ascertain the voter's intention, and therefore should be rejected. But nothing can be more fallacious. It frequently happens that a man is better known by the initials of his baptismal name than by the name fully expressed ; simply because he is not in the habit of writing his name in full, or of being thus addressed in business transactions. I think it highly probable that that is the case with each of the parties before us.

In political conventions, or legislative bodies, no one deems it important to write the full name of a candidate for whom he is voting, and no one ever thinks of challenging the vote for uncertainty. Under the application of this rule to the present case, the curious spectacle will be exhibited of votes cast for E. V. Cicott and G. O. Williams, being rejected because the courts cannot determine for whom they were intended, while not a single person in the county of Wayne has the slightest doubt that they were cast for Edward V. Cicott and Gurdon O. Williams, the opposing candidates at this election. Thus the courts are required to close their eyes to what everybody else can see distinctly. The fallacy of the rule consists in its assuming that a certain form of ballot clearly expresses the voter's intention, while another form is so uncertain that it is dangerous to attempt to arrive at the meaning by evidence. But, in fact, no ballot can identify with positive certainty the persons for whom it is cast; and notice must be taken of extrinsic circumstances in order to apply it. It is always possible that other persons may reside in the election district, having the same names, with some of the candidates; but neither the canvassers nor the courts ever assume that there is any difficulty in these cases, but they count the votes for the persons who have been put forward for the respective offices. And in some cases, where an element of uncertainty is introduced into the ballot unnecessarily, as by the addition of an erroneous designation, the courts resolve the difficulty by rejecting the erroneous addition, and counting the ballot for the person for whom it was evidently designed.'

There is, then, no room for doubt that the rule laid down by Judge Cooley, and quoted above, is the true rule, having for its support both authority and reason. To reject it, and establish the doctrine contended for by contestant, would be to defeat, in every such case as the one before us, the undoubted will of the majority. And this injustice would not be compensated by the establishment of a rule which is in itself either salutary or important. The cases are numerous where an imperfect ballot, by the aid of extrinsic evidence, can be made clear and perfect. No harm can result from admitting such extrinsic evidence so long as it is only admitted to cure or explain such imperfections and ambiguities as could be cured if they occurred in the most solemn written instruments, and to this extent, and no further, would we carry it. Thus guarded and qualified, the rule is most salutary and most just."

§ 397. The doctrine of this report will be found fully sustained by the decisions of the House of Representatives in the case of *Chapman vs. Ferguson*, (1 *Bartlett*, 267,) where votes for "Judge Ferguson" were counted for the sitting member, Fenner Ferguson, and in which also ballots which read "Bird B. Chapman for Congress," instead of "for Congress, Bird B. Chapman," were held good, and counted for contestant. And see also *Gunter vs. Willshire*, (43*d Congress*,) where votes returned for "T. M. Gunter," "T. Ross Gunter," "Thomas N. Gunter," and "Gunter," were, upon proof of the intention of the voters, allowed to be counted for Thomas M. Gunter. In this case, however, the committee found that the original ballots were correct, and the error was in the returns.

§ 398. In *Commonwealth vs. Ely*, (4 *Wis.*, 420, *Brightley's Election Cases*, 258,) it was held that if a ballot contains the names of two persons for the same office, when but one is to be chosen, it is bad as to both, but this does not vitiate it as to candidates for other offices, upon the same ticket. It often happens that an elector, without any evil intent, casts a ballot, through inadvertence or mistake, which contains the names of two persons for one and the same office. Tickets are often printed in this way, with a view to giving the voter a choice, which can be indicated by striking off one of the names. It would be a very rigorous and unjust rule to say such a ballot is bad as to all other names on it, because bad as to the two names indicated for the same office.

§ 399. It is well settled that where a limited number of persons are to be chosen to fill a given office—as, for instance, where the law provides for the election by the same constituency of two Representatives in the State Legislature,—a ballot containing the names of a greater number for that office is void. It was accordingly held in *People vs. Loomis*, (8*th Wendell*, 396,) that where the number of constables to be chosen was limited to four, ballots containing the names of five persons designated as voted for that office, cannot be canvassed, but must be rejected. "If," says Nelson, J., "one elector can cast a ballot containing *five* names, he may, one of *eight*, and thus vote (if he chooses to insert the names,) for both tickets. It would be impossible for the presiding officers to select the four according to the intention of the voter, and four only should be counted."

§ 400. In many of the States there are statutory provisions prohibiting the marking of ballots, or the placing upon the exterior thereof any character or figure. The purpose of these statutes is, of course, to protect the secrecy of the ballot, and public policy demands their enforcement. Cases will arise, however, in which it will be found very difficult, if not impossible, to carry out strictly all provisions of this character. We have shown in another connection, that, although the law forbids the numbering of ballots, yet, if under a misapprehension of their duty, the judges of election number all the ballots to correspond with a number opposite to the name of the voter on the poll list, and if no one is injured thereby, the ballots thus marked should not be rejected. [*McKenzie vs. Braxton*, 42*d Congress*.]

§ 401. And it has also been held that where the statute provided that all ballots should be written or printed upon white paper without any marks or figures thereon, to distinguish one from another, ballots upon paper tinged with blue, and which had ruled lines, were legal ballots within the meaning of the act. (*People vs. Kilduff*, 15 *Ill.*, 492.) This ruling, however, went upon the ground that the ruled paper was not used with any intent to violate the statute, and it is quite clear that where the statute distinctly declares that ballots having distinguishing marks upon them shall not be received, or shall be rejected, it should be construed as mandatory, and not simply directory. And so it was held by the Supreme Court of Pennsylvania, under a statute of this character, that ballots having an eagle printed thereon were in violation of the law, and should be rejected.

(*Commonwealth vs. Wallper*, 3 *S. & R.*, 29. *Luzerne County Election*, 3 *Penn., L. J.*, 155. *Clinton County Election*, *ibid*, 160.)

§ 402. Where a statute prohibits the marking of ballots so that they may be distinguished by others than the voter, and declares such ballots void, there is good reason for construing such statute as mandatory. Such marks destroy the secrecy of the ballot, and it is well known that the plan of voting by ballot, instead of *viva voce*, was adopted for the very purpose of securing to every voter absolute secrecy if he desires it, and protecting him therein, and this was thought necessary in order to place the poor and dependent voter in a situation where he may act according to his own judgment, and without intimidation from the rich or powerful. In *Commonwealth vs. Wallper*, (*supra*,) the Supreme Court of Pennsylvania said:

"The engraving [on the ticket,] might have several ill effects. In the first place it might be perceived by the inspectors, even when the ticket was folded. This knowledge might possibly influence them in receiving or rejecting the vote. But in the next place it deprived those persons who did not vote the German tickets, [which had an eagle on them,] of that secrecy which the election by ballot was intended to secure. A man who gave in a ticket *without an eagle*, was set down as anti-German, and exposed to the animosity of that party. Another objection is that these symbols of party increase that heat which it is desirable to assuage."

§ 403. The Supreme Court of California has very recently had occasion to consider the force and effect of a statute regulating the size and form of ballots, the kind of paper to be used, the kind of type to be used in printing them, &c. The Court held, and we think upon the soundest reason, that as to those things over which the voter has control, the law is mandatory, and that as to such things as are not under his control, it should be held to be directory only. [*Kerr vs. Rhoades, Supreme Court of Cal., October Term,* 1873.] The conclusion of the Court was that the purpose and object of the statute was to secure the freedom and purity of elections, and to place the elector above and beyond the reach of improper influences or restraint in casting his ballot, and that it should have such a reasonable construction as would tend to secure these important results. And so construing the statute the Court conclude that a ballot cast by an elector in good faith, should not be rejected for failure to comply with the law in matters over which the elector had no control; such as the exact size of the ticket, the precise kind of paper, or the particular character of type or heading used. But if the elector wilfully neglects to comply with requirements over which he has control, such as seeing that the ballot, when delivered to the election officers, is not so marked that it may be identified, the ballot should be rejected.

§ 404. A statute of Indiana provided that all ballots should "be printed on plain white paper, without any distinguishing marks or other embellishment thereon, except the names of candidates and the offices to be voted for," and that "inspectors of election shall refuse all ballots offered of any other description." Under this statute it has been repeatedly held by the Supreme Court of that State that a ballot may be headed with the words "Republican ticket," or "Democratic ticket," printed on the same side with the names of the candidates. These are not "distinguishing marks or embellishments," within the meaning of the statute. The law was framed to forbid any marks or characters on the exterior of the ballot to distinguish it, and thus destroy its secrecy. [*Druliner vs. State*, 29 *Ind.*, 308. *Napier vs. Mayhew*, 35 *Ind.*, 275.] And this ruling was followed by the lower House of the forty-third Congress, in the case of *Neff vs. Shanks.*

§ 405. There are also in some of the States laws requiring that the voter shall endorse on the outside of his ballot the name of the office voted for. These statutes are generally held to be directory only. Thus in *People vs. McManus*, 34 *Barb.*, 620, it was held that a ballot endorsed "for trustees of *public* schools," instead of *common* schools, was sufficient. The intention of the voter must control, and therefore, if that intention is clearly manifested, it is enough. (*People vs. Matteson*, 17 *Ill.*, 167.) And it was held in Wisconsin, that where the description or designation of the office on a ballot is applicable to two or more offices, parol evidence is admissible to show which of them was intended by the voter. [*State vs. Goldthwait*, 16 *Wis.*, 146, and see *State vs. Elwood*, 12 *Wis.*, 552.] If a ballot contains the names of more persons than are to be voted for, for a specified office, it is void as to that office, and must be rejected, [6 *Philadelphia*, 437, 2 *Pars.*, 534. *State vs. Tierney*, 23 *Wis.*, 430,] but is good as to the other offices named on it.

§ 406. But where a ballot contains the name of the person voted for, and the office for which he is designated, several times repeated, it is not for that reason void, but is to be counted as one ballot. (*People vs. Holden*, 28 *Cal.*, 124. *Ashfield's Case, Cush. Election Cases*, 583.) There seems to be no reason why a ballot containing a less number of names for a given office, than the number to be chosen, should not be counted for those who are designated. If three Representatives in the legislature are to be chosen by the voters of a given county or district, an elector may vote for one, or for two only, if he choose to do so.

§ 407. While it is true that evidence *aliunde* may be received to explain an imperfect or ambiguous ballot, it does not by any means follow that such evidence may be received to give to a ballot a meaning or effect hostile to what it expresses on its face. The intention of the voter cannot be proven to contradict the ballot, or when it is opposed to the paper ballot which he has deposited in the ballot box. Thus where a ballot is cast which has upon it the names of two persons for the same office, proof offered to show that the voter intended to vote for the one or the other of them, and not for both, must be rejected. (*The People vs. Seaman*, 8 *Cowan*, 409.) Such a ballot may be void, but it is not ambiguous, and therefore cannot be helped by parol proof.

§ 408. It very often happens that a printed ticket is changed by the voter, by erasing some part of it, or by writing on the face of it, or by both, to make it conform to his wishes. A ballot is to be construed in the same way as any other written or printed document, and the construction must be such as to give effect to the voter's intent if that can be ascertained from the face of the ballot, or in some cases, as we have seen from the ballot as explained by evidence *aliunde*. If, therefore, a voter has *written* upon his ballot the name of a particular person in connection with the title of an office, and omits to strike out the name of another person *printed* upon it in connection with the same office, the writing must prevail, and the vote must be counted for the person whose name is written. This is upon the ground that the writing is the highest evidence of the voter's intention.

§ 409. In such a case the voter's intention can be clearly ascertained from the face of the ballot; there is no ambiguity, and therefore, evidence *aliunde* is not admissible to explain it, and the Court must, in such a case, find, as matter of law, that the writing on the face of the ballot prevails over the printing. (*The People vs. Saxton*, 22 *N. Y.*, 8 *Smith*, 309.)

§ 410. In New York, since the decision in *People vs. Sexton*, and *People vs. Cook*, *supra*, it has been considered as settled that upon the trial of a case where the question as to who was elected to a particular office, and what was the intention of certain ballots, is investigated before a jury, the Court and jury are not confined to the narrow limits which control boards of canvassers who have no power to take evidence *aliunde* the ballot itself. Such boards cannot, but courts and juries can, hear and consider evidence for the purpose of elucidating any apparent ambiguity on the face of a ballot or any apparent incongruity between it and the surrounding circumstances. And it has accordingly been held that the placing of a "paster" containing one name over another name, on a ticket, indicates an intention to substitute one name for another. If it be placed over another name which is under the title of an office, it indicates an intention to substitute for that office the name upon the paster. If it be done in such a manner as to afford any ground for doubt, whether the voter intended to designate two persons for the same office, that doubt may be safely left to be solved by a jury, in view of all the facts, the appearance of the ballot and the surrounding circumstances. And in cases where there is doubt as to the intention of the voter, because of some apparent ambiguity on the face of the ballot, it is error for the Court to reject proper evidence offered to explain the ambiguity, and to instruct the jury as matter of law, that such ballot cannot be counted. (*The People vs Love*, 63 *Barbour*, 535.)

§ 411. Where a pen or pencil mark is drawn over a name which has been printed on a ballot, it will be presumed that an erasure of the name was intended, although it be still legible, unless the contrary is shown. It is not necessary to obliterate the name entirely. And where the inspectors have rejected such a ballot, on the ground that the name was erased, and where the ballot itself is not in evidence, the correctness of the decision of the inspectors will be presumed. (*Adams vs. Wilson*, *Cl. & H.*, 373.)

§ 412. Where the constitution declares that all ballots shall be "fairly written," a *printed* ballot is good. (*Temple vs. Mead*, 4 *Vt.*, 541. *Henshaw vs. Foster*, 9 *Pick.*, 312.) The term "written" is held to include what is printed, following the definition of that term, as given by the best lexicographers, viz: "to express by means of letters." No doubt to the common understanding the term "written" conveys the idea of forming letters into words with a pen or pencil; but to give it this meaning in this connection would be to sacrifice the spirit for the sake of the letter. "The letter killeth, but the spirit maketh alive," is the forcible expression of scripture.

§ 413. The constitution of Indiana provides that "all elections by the people shall be by ballot." A statute of that State, passed in 1869, provides that "it shall be the duty of the inspector of any election, &c., on receiving the ballot of any voter, to have the same numbered with figures on the outside or back thereof, to correspond with the number placed opposite the name of such voter on the poll list, kept by the clerk of said election." The question of the validity of this statute came before the Supreme Court of Indiana, in the case of *Williams vs. Stein*, (38 *Ind.*, 89.) The case presented squarely the question whether under a constitution guaranteeing to every voter the right to vote at all elections by the people, by *ballot*, it is competent for the legislature to provide for numbering the ballots in such manner as to destroy their secrecy. The court held the statute to be unconstitutional and void. Upon an elaborate review of the authorities, the conclusion is reached, upon what seems to be good ground, that in this country the ballot implies absolute and inviolable secrecy, and that this doctrine is founded in the highest considerations of public policy. That the term ballot implies secrecy, and that this mode of voting was adopted mainly to enable each voter to keep secret his vote, is clear. (*Cushing on Leg. Asssmblies, Sec.* 103. *May's Constitutional History of England, Vol.* 1, *p* 353. *People vs. Pease,* 27 *N. Y.*, 45. *Cooley's Const. Lim.*, 604. *Temple vs. Mead,* 4 *Vt.*, 535.)

§ 414. A statute of Indiana provided, that in an election to determine the question whether a county subscription should be made to aid in constructing a railroad, the form of an affirmative ballot should be "for the railroad appropriation." At an election held under this statute, ballots were cast which had printed or written upon them only the words "for the railroad." This was held to be an irregularity which would not affect the election. (*R. R. Co. vs. Bearss, et al,* 39 *Ind.*, 39.)

§ 415. Where a statute authorizes an election to be held by a county, city, or township, for the purpose of determining a given question—as for example, whether such municipality shall subscribe to the stock of a railroad company—and where such statute points out no mode for conducting such election, it has been held that it should be conducted in the manner prescribed by law for other elections by the same body. For example, if an election in a township is held for such a purpose under a statute silent as to the manner of proceeding, it should be held in the manner township elections are required to be held, in the election of their town officers, and not under the general election laws of the State. (*People vs. Dutcher,* 56 *Ill.*, 144.) The doctrine of this case is that where the legislature authorizes a township or other corporate body to hold an election, and has prescribed no mode, it is to be presumed that it was designed to authorize it to be conducted in the manner usually adopted and authorized by the laws governing the action of the body.

CHAPTER VIII.

VIOLENCE AND INTIMIDATION.

§ 416. If it clearly appear that the fairness, purity or freedom of an election has been materially interfered with by acts of violence, intimidation, or armed interference, such election should be set aside. Slight disturbances frequently occur, and are often sufficient to alarm a few of the more timid, without materially affecting the result or the freedom of the election. The true rule is this. The violence or intimidation should be shown to have been sufficient either to change the result, or that by reason of it the true result cannot be ascertained with certainty from the returns. To vacate an election on this ground, if the election were not in fact arrested, it must clearly appear that there was such a display of force as ought to have intimidated men of ordinary firmness. (*Harrison vs. Davis*, 1 *Bartlett*, 341. *Bruce vs. Loan*, *Ibid*, 482.)

§ 417. In *Harrison vs. Davis*, the committee say in their report: "It (the specification,) nowhere makes the formal allegation that the law requires, either that the election was arrested and broken up in every ward, or that so many individuals were excluded by violence and intimidation as would, if allowed to vote, have given the contestant the majority. Either of these grounds, if stated and proved, would have been in law decisive of the case, but neither is stated in the specification, and neither is proved by the evidence."

The case of *Bruce vs. Loan* arose in Missouri in the early part of the war of the rebellion, (1862,) and the allegation was that the election in many places was controlled, and large numbers of voters overawed by the "enrolled militia," a State military organization which had been raised and armed for military service. There was much dispute about the facts, but both the majority and minority of the committee appear to have conceded the correctness of the general rule of law laid down in *Harrison vs. Davis.*

§ 418. There can, however, be no doubt but that the law looks with great disfavor upon anything like an interference by the military with the freedom of an election. An armed force in the neighborhood of the polls is almost of necessity a menace to the voters, and an interference with their freedom and independence, and if such armed force be in the hands of, or under the control of the partisan friends of any particular candidate, or set of candidates, the probability of improper influence becomes still stronger. And although the fact that an armed force was stationed at or near the polls will not, of itself, vitiate an election in the absence of proof that it did in fact deter from voting a portion of the electors sufficiently large to change or render doubtful the result, yet, in such a case, it would not be necessary to show that the electors who declined to vote would have been in actual danger if they had attempted to do so. If it be made to appear that there was an armed force at the polls, and that a number of voters sufficiently numerous to affect the result, or render it doubtful, considered the presence of such force so menacing to them as to render it unsafe for them to vote, and that they had reasonable cause so to think, and if for this reason they declined to go to the polls, the election ought to be set aside.

§ 419. In *Giddings vs. Clark*, a contested election case tried by the U. S. House of Representatives of the forty-second Congress, the following facts were shown in relation to the election in the county of Limestone.

"The colored voters generally failed to vote, so that only twenty-eight votes were cast for Clark, to one thousand, one hundred and fifty-three for Giddings. That a state of excitement and fear existed in this county about the time of the election, is clear. A collision occurred between some colored policemen and certain white men, which resulted in the death of one of the latter, and the wounding of one of the former. This produced great excitement, and was followed by a general uprising and arming of both whites and blacks. On the day of election, the town where the election was held was occupied by an armed force under command of one Captain Richardson. Pickets were stationed on all the roads leading into town, and persons coming in to vote were obliged to obtain a pass from the military authorities. Although the witnesses say that all voters were permitted to come and go in peace, and that the freedmen were urged to vote, yet it is clear that they abstained from doing so for reasons which most men would consider good and sufficient."

The committee were of the opinion that this was not a free and fair election, and so reported to the House. The correctness of this decision cannot be doubted. Where the polls are surrounded by a military force, and voters required to pass pickets, and procure permission of military authorities, in order to approach them, there can be no free election. It is no answer to this, to say that the military are stationed around the polls to *preserve* the peace, and secure freedom to all voters.

§ 420. A case may perhaps arise where it will not be improper to station troops in the *vicinity* of the election, at a place where they can be called upon in case of emergency to suppress riot or prevent bloodshed, but in all such cases the troops should be removed from the actual presence of the voters, and should not be permitted in any manner to interfere with persons going to or returning from the polls. We have inherited from our British ancestors a strong aversion to interference by the military power with the conduct of elections, and this feeling has been heightened by the long enjoyment in this country of the larger liberty of American citizenship. As early as 1741 an attempt was made to interfere with an election held for the city of Westminster, by stationing a body of armed soldiers near the poll. On this being shown to the House of

Commons, it was by that body resolved "that the presence of a regular body of armed soldiers at an election of members to serve in parliament, is a high infringement of the liberties of the subject, a manifest violation of the freedom of elections, and an open defiance of the laws and constitution of this kingdom." In some of the States there are statutes prohibiting the employment of troops or their presence at any place of election during the time of such election. Such a statute was enacted in Pennsylvania as early as 1803. (4 *Smith's Laws*, 101.) (*g.*)

§ 421. In the early case of *Trigg vs. Preston*, in the House of Representatives of the third Congress (1793,) the question arose whether the presence of a part of the military force of the United States at the polls, and certain disorderly and improper conduct of theirs was sufficient to vitiate the election. The facts were as follows: A brother of the sitting member was the commander of a company of federal troops, which was quartered near the voting place. On the day of the election the said troops were marched, in a body, twice or three times around the court house, where the election was held, and paraded in front of and close to the door thereof. The troops were allowed to vote and voted generally in favor of the sitting member, but their votes were thrown out by the returning officers. Some of them threatened to beat any person who should vote in favor of the contestant. One of the soldiers struck and knocked down a magistrate who was attending

(*g.*) And the bringing of armed troops to a place of election, except to repel the armed enemies of the United States, or to keep the peace, is prohibited by act of Congress. (*Revised statutes U. S., Sec. 2002.*)

at said election. Three soldiers stood at the door of the court house, and refused to admit a voter because he declared he would vote for contestant. There were altercations between the soldiers and the people, which terminated *after the poll was closed* in a violent affray. Upon these facts the committee found and reported that the conduct of the soldiers as well as that of their commander, "was inconsistent with that freedom and fairness which ought to prevail at elections; and that, although it does not appear, from any other than hearsay testimony, that any voter was actually prevented from voting, yet there is every reasonable ground to believe that some were, and that the election was unduly and unfairly biassed by the turbulent and menacing conduct of the military." (*Cl. & H.*, 78.) The report of the committee was lost in the House. It may be conceded that the facts in that particular case did not constitute such violence and intimidation as should have vitiated the poll, and still the rule we have stated remains well settled. If this case did not fall within the rule it was because it did not appear that the presence and conduct of the soldiery actually deterred from voting, a number of legal voters, sufficiently numerous to change or render uncertain the result.

§ 422. We conclude—

1. That an armed force should never be stationed immediately at the polls.

2. That in cases where riot and bloodshed are apprehended troops may be stationed in the neighborhood, if so ordered by competent authority, with a view to keep the peace, and suppress such violence

as is beyond the power of the local peace officers or courts to control.

3. That in all cases where it is alleged that armed soldiers have interfered with the freedom of an election, either by their presence or their conduct, or both, all the facts are to be considered and the question is, whether by reason of the action of such armed soldiers, legal voters have, for sufficient cause, felt themselves obliged to abstain from voting in numbers so large that if they had voted it would have changed the result or rendered it uncertain.

§ 423. In the case of *Biddle & Richard* vs. *Wing*, (*Cl. & H.* 506-7,) the committee of elections of the House of Representatives expressed the opinion that it was not the duty of the House "to inquire into the causes which may have prevented any candidate from getting a sufficient number of votes to entitle him to the seat." They considered that the duty of the House was to inquire, and if possible, ascertain "who had the greatest number of legal votes actually given at the election." And accordingly the committee held that they could not inquire into the truth of the allegation of one of the contestants, who did not claim to have received the greatest number of votes actually cast, but alleged that "he would have received the greatest number of votes had not his friends, at the election holden in the city of Detroit, *been intimidated from voting*," &c. This report was never acted upon by the House, and therefore is without its sanction, and depends for its force as a precedent solely upon the committee's recommendation.

It can hardly be said to state the doctrine upon

the subject with completeness or accuracy. Intimidation of voters may always be shown, and allegations and proof upon this subject should always be heard. It must, however, in the nature of things, be a rare case in which the votes of persons prevented from voting by violence or intimidation can be counted for one or the other candidate, as if actually cast. In order that a vote not cast, shall be counted as if cast, it must appear that a legal voter offered to vote a particular ballot, and that he was prevented from doing so by fraud, violence, or an erroneous ruling of the election officers. Just what is to be understood by offering to vote is not perhaps perfectly well settled. If a voter approaches or attempts to approach the polls, for the purpose of depositing his ballot, and is driven away, or by violence, intimidation or threats, prevented from the actual presentation of his ballot to the proper officer, and if he used proper diligençe in endeavoring to reach the polls and deposit his ballot, and was not intimidated without sufficient reason, the better opinion seems to be that his vote may be counted. But of course voters who do not present themselves at the polls, and offer their ballots, or who do not attempt to go to the polls at all, or attempting, fail, without reasonable cause, cannot in any case ask that their votes be counted. (*Newcum vs. Kirtley*, 13 *B. Monroe*, 515.)

§ 424. But there is another ground upon which it is, in such a case, proper to offer proof of intimidation and violence, and that is to the end that the House may determine whether there has been a free and fair election. For, if, by this means legal voters

21

have been deprived of their right to vote in numbers sufficient to change the result, the election may be set aside. In the report just referred to, the committee concede that there may be a case in which "fraud and corruption should appear sufficient to destroy all confidence in the purity and fairness of the whole proceeding." And it is very clear, that, if in the course of an investigation it should become apparent, that there was intimidation and violence sufficient to destroy the election, it would be the duty of the House to declare it void, even though no party to the contest has formally alleged that it was so. If the allegation be as in the case of Biddle and Richard vs. Wing, *supra*, that enough of the friends of a contestant were deterred from voting by violence and imtimidation to have elected him, if they had been allowed to vote, as was their right, yet, if the evidence shows that the election should be set aside, the House will not stop short of its duty for want of an allegation that the election was fraudulent and void. A court of justice might be so hampered by the rules of pleading as to be unable to grant any relief beyond that prayed for, but the House of Representatives is not.

§ 425. In saying that upon sufficient proof of violence and intimidation an election may be set aside, we mean, of course, that the particular poll or polls, where such violence occurs, shall be thrown out of the count. Whether in a case where a number of counties or precincts vote for the same officer, and a portion of them are rejected for this cause, the entire election is to be held void, is often a question of difficulty. It is very clear that if the violence has prevented a large proportion of the electors in the whole district from participating, the election is void, and it is also clear, that if only a small part of the district was disturbed by it so that the great body of the electors have had a fair opportunity to vote, then the election must stand, unless it can be shown that but for the violence the result would have been different. The difficulty arises in cases where the infected part of the district is neither so large as to make it clear that the election is void, nor so small as to make it clear that the election is not void. Each case of this character must be determined by the circumstances surrounding it, and with a view to promote the ends of justice. Much will, of course, depend upon the relative vote of the several candidates outside of the infected districts, because if any one has a very large majority in the peaceable localities, and the vote of the infected precincts is not large, there will be less probability that the result has been achieved because of the violence; while on the other hand, if the vote of the peaceable precincts is very close, the rejection of a small district for violence might be regarded as fatal to the election. In a word, if it is apparent that to accept the result as shown by the peaceable precincts, would be to allow the minority to choose the officer, then the election is to be held void.

§ 426. It was laid down by the committee of elections of the forty-first Congress, in several cases, that violence and intimidation in some of the precincts does not invalidate the election in those which are peaceable. (*Hunt vs. Sheldon*, 2 *Bartlett*, 530-703. *Sypher vs. St. Martin*, *do*, 699. *Wallace vs. Simpson*, *do*, 731. *Darrall vs. Bailey*, *do*, 754.)

But thus broadly stated this is not a sound rule. This will be apparent upon a moment's reflection. Suppose there are ten counties in a congressional district, and there is in nine of them such violence at the polls, as to destroy the fairness and freedom of the election; can it be claimed that the one peaceable county should choose a representative for the ten? Clearly not. The true principle is, that if the great body of the electors are prevented, without their fault, from participating in an election, it is not a valid election. Where the majority *voluntarily* remain away from the polls, the minority, however small, who do vote, may elect, but not so where the majority are kept from the polls by violence and intimidation.

§ 427. The rule laid down, in the cases just cited, cannot be said to have received the unqualified sanction of the House of Representatives, though in some of the cases the recommendations of the committee were adopted. The House soon found that under the operation of the rule, persons were likely to be seated in that body, who were not the choice of the majority. In the case of *Sypher*, *supra*, the report of the committee, which was based upon this rule entirely, was overruled, and the election declared to be null and void, for the reason, as we learn from the debate, that the parishes rejected for violence, contained a majority of the voters of the district. The case of *Hunt vs. Sheldon*, *supra*, is regarded as the leading case favoring the rule, but it was claimed by some, at least, of the members who voted for that report, that notwithstanding the violence, there was a peaceable election in the larger and more populous portions of the district. In the course of the debate in Sypher's case, Mr. Garfield, of Ohio, explained his vote in Sheldon's case, as follows:

" Mr. Garfield, of Ohio. When the case of *Hunt vs. Sheldon*, was before the House, I stated the ground on which I acted. It was that in nine hundred and ninety-nine parts, out of one thousand of the territory embraced by the district, there was no disturbance, and among the majority of the population, as exhibited by the census report, there was no disturbance. I considered, therefore, that a very large proportion of the territory, and a majority of the population of the district, had a peaceable election, and that, therefore, we should not throw the election out."

And it is manifest, not only from the debate, but from the action of the House, in voting down the report in Sypher's case, that the decision in Sheldon's case was not intended as an endorsement of the doctrine that the peaceable precincts may elect, without regard to their number or population.

§ 428. It was claimed by those who sustained the rule, as it was laid down by the committee in Sheldon's case, that it was necessary for the protection of the freedmen of the South, who were, as it was claimed, "peculiarly exposed to violence and intimidation by the former master class, prone by habit and inclination to domineer over their former slaves." It may be hoped that the very anomalous condition of things which existed in that region at the time of the elections, which gave rise to the reports under consideration, was transient, and has already or will soon pass away forever. At all events, it is by no means safe to establish a rule applicable to all cases and for all time, and capable of incalculable mischief in its general and universal application, in order to provide for a few exceptional and extraordinary cases. Nor can it be conceded that this rule was necessary, even for the protection of the freedmen. The best protection against violence is the enactment and enforcement of laws for its punishment. Beyond this, it is enough that the community in which it occurs to such an extent as to prevent the holding of free and fair elections, should go unrepresented, and if need be, suffer the rigors of military rule until they decide to obey the laws and appreciate the blessings of freedom for themselves and for all others.

§ 429. It would seem, therefore, that the following rules, if administered in the light of the general principles, which have now been stated, will afford a safe guide:

1. If the violence and intimidation has been so extensive and general as to render it certain that there has been no fair and free expression by the great body of the electors, then the election must be set aside, notwithstanding the fact that in some of the precincts or counties there was a peaceable and fair election.

2. Where there has been an election, embracing a number of counties or precincts, in which there has been violence and intimidation, enough to exclude from the count one or more precincts, or voting places, but not enough to destroy the freedom and fairness of the election, as a whole, such violence

will not invalidate the election, nor affect the result of it, unless it be shown affirmatively, that but for it, the result would have been different.

3. The question in each case must be, has the great body of the electors had an opportunity to express their choice, through the medium of the ballot, and according to law, and this question must be decided in the light of all the facts and circumstances shown in the evidence. If some of the precincts or voting places are necessarily thrown out of the count, because of unlawful disturbances or violence, it will be necessary to determine from the evidence, whether their exclusion necessarily destroys the fairness and freedom of the election, as a whole.

§ 430. It was held in *State vs. Mason*, (14 *La. An.*, 505,) that a petition which demanded that an election be set aside, because of violence and intimidation at the polls, must allege that a sufficient number of voters were prevented from voting, to have varied the result of the election. The Court observes: "It is evident there would be no reason to contest an election, if the result could not be changed, and such would be the event, unless a number of voters had been prevented from voting, sufficient to have varied the result. And to the same purport is *Augustin vs. Eggleston*, (12 *La. An.*, 367.)

§ 431. Where it is alleged that a large number of persons have been deterred from voting, by violence and intimidation, the testimony of those persons, or some of them, should be produced. The opinions and impressions of others is not sufficient. Upon this point the report in *Norris vs. Handley*, *42d Congress*, has this language:

"It would seem that if over two thousand electors were deterred from voting, by violence, threats, or intimidation, some of these electors could be found to come forward and swear to the fact. Your committee think that it would establish a most dangerous precedent, to allow a fact of this character, so easily established by the direct and positive testimony of so many witnesses, to be proven solely by hearsay and general reputation. We have not forgotten nor overlooked the fact that the same state of things which would make men afraid to vote for a particular party might also make it difficult to secure testimony in behalf of that party. But in many parts of the district where testimony was taken there is no pretense that witnesses were intimidated; and, beside, if the contestant had shown, to the satisfaction of the House, that witnesses needed the protection of the Federal Government in order to be safe in testifying fully and freely, that protection would have been afforded at any cost."

§ 432. The freedom of elections is of the utmost importance. The law justly regards all attempts to interfere with the electors in the peaceable and quiet exercise of their rights, or to improperly influence them against their judgment or desire, as a crime, and in addition to the ordinary punishment of the crime of bribery of an elector, it is provided by the constitution of many of the States that whoever shall be convicted of that crime shall forfeit the right to any office of profit or trust under the State. (See the *Constitutions of Maryland, Missouri, New Jersey, West Virginia, Oregon, California, Kansas, Texas, Arkansas, Rhode Island, Alabama, Florida,*

New York, Massachusetts, Vermont, Nevada, Tennessee, Connecticut, Louisiana, Mississippi, Ohio and Wisconsin.)

§ 433. In some of the States it is provided by statute that the militia shall not be called out for exercise or drill on the day of election, and it has been held in New York that a defendant, sued under an act of this character, cannot plead in justification that he acted under the orders of his superior officer. Nor is it any defense that defendant was ignorant of the existence of the law. (*Hyde vs. Malone*, 11 *Johnson* 520.)

§ 434. It is clear that fraud, violence or intimidation committed against the purity or freedom of an election for representative or delegate in Congress may be prohibited and punished by act of Congress. And it is competent for Congress to provide by law for the punishment of persons who at such an election violate a State law, regulating either such election, or the registration of voters preceding it. Congress may, under the constitution, declare fraudulent registration, for the purpose of voting for a representative or delegate in Congress, or fraudulent voting for such delegate or representative, to be a crime against the United States. (*The U. S.* vs. *Quinn, Brightley's Election Cases*, 592. *Ante*, § 309.)

§ 435. The act of Congress of 31st May, 1870, Sec. 19, provides, among other things, for the punishment of any person or persons who "by violence or any unlawful means hinders, delays, prevents or obstructs any citizen from doing any act required to be done to qualify him to vote, or from voting at any election," &c. It has been held that an indictment under this act can be sustained by proof; that the defendant and others attacked a number of voters waiting in line for their turn to cast their ballots, and expelled them from the room, though they afterwards returned and actually voted. The offense was complete by the expulsion of the voters from the polls. [*United States* vs. *Louders*, 2 *Abbot, U. S. Rep.*, 456.] It is not necessary that the attempt to deprive a voter of his rights, by violent or unlawful means, shall have been successful; the offence is complete if the attempt be made with an unlawful or criminal intent.

CHAPTER IX.

FRAUD AND ILLEGAL VOTING.

§ 436. Although the return of the vote of a given precinct, made in due form, and signed by the proper officers, is the best evidence as to the state of the vote, yet it may be impeached, on the ground of fraud or misconduct on the part of the officers of the election themselves, or on the part of others. In election cases, however, before a return can be set aside, there must be proof that the proceedings in the conduct of the election, or in the return of the vote, were so tainted with fraud, that the truth cannot be deduced from the returns. The rule is thus stated in *Howard* vs. *Cooper*, (1 *Bartlett, p.* 275.)

"When the result in any precinct has been shown to be so tainted with fraud that the truth cannot be deducible therefrom, then it should never be permitted to form a part of the canvass. The precedents, as well as the evident requirements of truth, not only sanction, but call for, the rejection of the entire poll, when stamped with the characteristics here shown."

§ 437. The rule just stated needs the following explanation, in order that it may be correctly understood. The committee, no doubt, meant to say that if the result, *as shown by the returns*, is tainted with fraud, the returns are to be rejected as false, and worthless. But, as we have elsewhere seen, the question whether the entire vote of the precinct shall be rejected for fraud, depends upon another question, viz: Whether from any evidence it is possible to ascertain the true result. The returns may be rejected as fraudulent, and yet the true vote may, in some cases, be ascertained, and where it can be ascertained, independently of the rejected returns, the law requires that it be respected and enforced. Where the true vote cannot be ascertained either from the returns, or from evidence *aliunde*, the vote of the precinct is to be rejected.

§ 438. The return must stand until such facts are proven as to clearly show that it is not true. When shown to be fraudulent or false, it must fall to the ground. This ruling is well settled by numerous authorities, including the following. (*Blair vs. Barrett*, 1 *Bartlett*, 308. *Knox vs. Blair*, 1 *Bartlett*, 520. *Howard vs. Cooper*, *supra*. *Washburn vs. Voorhies*, 2 *Bartlett*, 54.) The following remarks concerning the dangers which may attend the application of this rule, are here quoted with emphatic approval, from the report of the committee of elections, in the House of Representatives, in *Washburn vs. Voorkies*, (*supra.*)

"In adopting this rule the committee do not lose sight, however, of the danger which may attend its application. Wholesome and salutary, not less than necessary, in its proper use, it is extremely liable to abuse. Heated partisanship, and blind prejudice, as well as indifferent investigation, may, under its cover, work great injustice. It is not to be adopted if it can be avoided. No investigation should be spared that would reach the truth without a resort to it. But it is not to be forgotten or omitted, if the case calls for its application. If the fraud be clearly shown to exist to such an extent as to satisfy the mind that the return does not show the truth, and no evidence is furnished by either party to a contest, and no investigation of the committee enable them to deduce the truth therefrom, then no alternative is left but to reject such a return. To use it under such a state of facts, is to use as true what is shown to be false."

§ 439. Where the return showed that Geo. W. Julian, had received at a given precinct, only one hundred and forty-three votes, parol proof was admitted to prove that the return was false, and that in fact he had received a larger number of votes than said return allowed him. (*Reid vs. Julian*, 2 *Bartlett*, 822.) In this case one hundred and seventy legal voters of the precinct were called, and were permitted to testify that they had each voted for Mr. Julian. It was objected that the proof was not competent because the ballots were the best evidence; but this objection was very properly overruled. The allegation was, that the ballots had been tampered with; that a fraud had been committed, by which a number of ballots legally cast had not been fairly deposited in the box and honestly counted out and returned. Of course in such a case the ballot might sustain the fraud. The ballots are the best evidence, when it is shown or conceded that they are the identical ballots and all the ballots deposited by legal voters; but when the question is whether fraudulent ballots have been deposited, or honest ballots abstracted, the ballots in the box are by no means the best evidence. Fraud of this character may, therefore, always be proven by parol. (And see also *Washburn vs. Voorhies*, 2 *Bartlett*, 54.)

§ 440. But of course the parol evidence offered to set aside a return upon the ground of fraud, must be such as to establish the fraud or mistake in the reception and deposit, or in the count or return of the votes. The official acts of sworn officers are presumed to be honest and correct until the contrary is made to appear. It has accordingly been held that a return cannot be set aside upon proof that a recount made by unauthorized persons sometime after the official count has been made, showed a different result from the official count. This was upon the ground that the count made by sworn officers immediately upon the closing of the polls, was better evidence of the true result than a count made by interested parties not sworn, at a subsequent period, and after the result of the official count had been made known, such evidence comes far short of establishing either fraud or mistake in the official count. (*Gooding vs. Wilson*, 42*d Congress.*)

§ 441. Fraud, in the conduct of an election, may be committed by one or more of the officers thereof, or by other persons. If committed by persons not officers, it may be either with or without the knowledge or connivance of such officers. There is a difference between a fraud committed by officers or with their knowledge and connivance, and a fraud committed by other persons, in this: the former is ordinarily fatal to the return, while the latter is not fatal, unless it appear that it has changed or rendered doubtful the result. If an officer of the election is detected in a wilful and deliberate fraud upon the ballot box, the better opinion is that this will destroy the integrity of his official acts, even though the fraud discovered is not, of itself, sufficient to affect the result. (*Ante*, § 184. *Judkins vs. Hill*, 50 *N, H.*, 104.) The reason of this rule is, that an officer who betrays his trust in one instance, is shown to be capable of the infamy of defrauding the electors, and his certificate is, therefore, good for nothing. If, for example, an election officer, having charge of a ballot box, prior to or during the canvass, is caught in the act of abstracting certain ballots, and substituting others, although the number shown to have been abstracted, be not sufficient to affect the result, yet no confidence can be placed in the contents of a ballot box, which has been in his custody. We repeat, therefore, the opinion expressed in a former chapter, that a wilful and deliberate fraud on the part of such an officer, being clearly proven, should destroy all confidence in his official acts, irrespective of the question whether the fraud discovered is of itself sufficient to change the result. The party taking anything by an election conducted by such an officer, must prove his vote, by evidence other than the return.

§ 442. Fraud, in the conduct of an election, may be shown by circumstantial evidence. It is sometimes a difficult matter to decide whether misconduct on the part of election officers, is to be regarded as constituting fraud, or as only the result of carelessness, ignorance, or negligence. If, however, such misconduct has the effect to destroy the integrity of the returns, and avoid the *prima facie* character, which they ought to bear, such returns will be rejected, and other proof demanded of each vote relied on. And this is the rule concerning such misconduct, whether it be shown to have been fraudulent, that is to say, prompted by a corrupt purpose, or whether it arise from a reckless disregard of the law, or from ignorance of its requirements. In either case the effect may be to destroy the integrity of the returns. For example, in *Covode vs. Foster*, (2 *Bartlett*, 600,) a return was rejected, upon proof that a hat and a cigar box were used, instead of the regular ballet boxes; that they were placed in or near the window, through which the votes were received; that persons other than members of the board were permitted in the room where the votes were received, and were near the boxes, and were passing in and out at pleasure during the day; that there was great noise and confusion in the room; that whisky was kept in the room, and members of the board drank to intoxication; that challenges were disregarded; and when the votes were counted, there were six ballots in the box over and above the number of names on the tally list. These facts, together with the further fact, that one Speers acted as clerk without authority, and without being sworn, were regarded by the committee, and by the House, as furnishing good ground for rejecting the return.

§ 443. The fact that persons, other than members of the board of election officers, are allowed to be in the room with such officers when votes are being received and deposited, will not of itself and in the absence of any proof of misconduct on their part, be sufficient to invalidate the return; but the admission of such persons is decidedly improper, especially if the persons admitted be the partisans of any particular candidate or ticket, and the fact of their presence and misconduct may be shown as circumstances tending to invalidate the return. (*Thompson vs. Ewing*, 1 *Brewster*, 111. *Covode vs. Foster*, *supra*.)

§ 444. It is not a valid objection to an election, that illegal votes were received, if they did not change the majority. If, therefore, a number of legal voters withdraw from an election and decline to vote upon the ground that illegal votes are being received, they do so at their peril, and take their chances of being able afterwards to show that the number of such illegal votes was large enough to change the result. (*First Parish &c. vs. Stearns*, 21*st. Pick*, 148. *Trustees &c. vs. Gibbs*, 2 *Cush.* 39.)

§ 445. If an election is held according to law and a fair opportunity is afforded for all legal voters to participate, those who do not vote, are bound by the result, (*ib.*) It has been held that if the majority expressly dissent, and do not vote, the election of the minority is good. (*Oldknow* vs. *Wainwright*, 1 *Wm. Bl.*, 229.) And see *Commonwealth* vs. *Read*, 2 *Ashmead*, 261. *Brightley's Election Cases* 126.

§ 446. Votes must be cast in the manner provided by law. Under a statute requiring that the manner of voting shall be by ballot; votes given *viva voce* cannot be counted, and in the case of an election by a board of county commissioners, of a county Treasurer, it was held in *Commonwealth* vs. *Read*, *supra*, that the only lawful mode of voting under the statute of Pennsylvania, governing the election, was by ballot and that, inasmuch as the majority voted *viva voce*, the minority voting by ballot would elect, even if that minority consisted of but one member of the board. It seems, however, that in case of an election by a corporation, or a board composed of a definite and fixed number of persons, a quorum should vote. Where the elective body consists of an indefinite number of persons, the principal of *Commonwealth* vs. *Read* can be applied. Accordingly in *State* vs. *Burder*, (38 *Mo.*, 450,) it was held that in the absence of any evidence to the contrary, it will be presumed that the voters voting at an election, were all the legal voters of the city, or that those who did not see fit to vote acquiesced in the action of those who did vote, and consequently are equally bound and concluded by the result.

§ 447. This doctrine, however, must be taken with some qualifications. If, for example, the election is held under such circumstances as to preclude the possibility that a majority of the persons entitled to vote could have had the opportunity to do so, it is void, although held at the time and place provided by law. It was accordingly held, in a number of cases, arising in the southern States during the rebellion, that where the larger part of the district was at the time of the election, in the armed occupation of rebel forces, an election attempted to be held in a portion of the district not so occupied was void.

(*Case of Upton*, 1 *Bartlett*, 368.
" *Beach*, *do* 391.
" *Segar*, *do* 414.
" *Segar*, *do* 426.
" *Segar*, *do* 577.
" *Cloud & Wing*, 1 *Bartlett*, 455.
" *McKenzie*, *do* 460.
" *Grafton*, *do* 464.
" *McKenzie vs. Kitchen do* 468.
" *Chandler*, *do* 520.

§ 448. The true rule is this; if the opportunity to vote is given to all alike, and if those who abstain from voting do so, of their own fault or negligence, then those who do attend and vote, have the right to decide the result, but in a case where those who fail to vote constitute a large proportion of the voting population, and where they did not have the opportunity to vote, there can be no valid election. Elections in the south during the progress of the rebellion were accordingly held valid, where there was an opportunity for the great body of the electors to participate. (*Flanders & Huhn*, 1 *Bartlett*, 438. *Case of Clements*, *do*, 366.)

§ 449. Every circumstance which tends to show

that an election was fraudulent, may be proven, and the Court must determine, from all the evidence, whether fraud has been shown. As, for example, if the aggregate vote cast is largely in excess of the number of legal voters, resident in the precinct, or if the vote cast at the election in question is largely in excess of the vote cast at any previous or subsequent election, and this fact is not explained, or if a large number of persons, unknown to the oldest residents of the precinct, were present at the election, and were seen voting, or if the list of voters contains the names of a large number of persons who are unknown to those inhabitants best acquainted with the people residing within the limits of the precinct, such facts as these, if unexplained, will often establish the fact that frauds have been perpetrated, and illegal votes cast, and make it necessary to throw out the poll altogether, unless it can be sifted and purged. (*Knox* vs. *Blair*, 1 *Bartlett*, 521.)

§ 450. Where the law required a consolidated return of the vote of a county to be prepared by the election officers, who officiated at the county seat, or a majority of them, and at least one officer from each of the other precincts, it was held that a consolidated return made up by a person not an officer, and who had no legal connection whatever with the election, and who had no right to handle any of the papers, was fraudulent and void. (*Sloan* vs. *Rawls*, 43*d Congress*.)

§ 451. As we have already had occasion to remark, it is an unsettled question, whether Congress has power under the recent amendments to the constitution, to provide for the punishment of fraud, violence and intimidation of voters generally, or only for such violence, fraud or intimidation as is committed against a voter, or class of voters, on account of race, color, or previous condition of servitude. (*Ante Secs.* 12 *to* 16.) Thus in *United States* vs. *Cruikshank*, (13 *Am. Law Register, N. S.*, 630,) Mr. Justice Bradley, sitting as Circuit Judge, laid down the doctrine, that the act of Congress of May 31, 1870, commonly called the enforcement act, so far as it assumes to regulate the right to vote, is beyond the scope of the fifteenth amendment, and void. Also that an indictment, under said act, for conspiracy to hinder certain citizens of African descent, in the exercise of their right to vote, cannot be sustained in a United States Court, without an allegation that the conspiracy was to hinder, &c., by reason of their race, color, or previous condition of servitude.

§ 452. The opinion of Mr. Justice Bradley, in the case last cited, is elaborate and able. The substance of it is thus set forth in the syllabus:

"Where rights of individual citizens are not derived originally from the constitution, but are part of the political inheritance from the mother country, the power of Congress does not extend to the enactment of positive laws for the protection of such rights, but only to the prevention of the States from violation of them. But where a right is derived from the constitution, and affirmative legislation is necessary to secure it to the citizen, then Congress may pass positive laws for the enforcement of the right, and for the punishment of individuals who interfere with it.

"These principles apply to the fourteenth amendment equally with the rest of the constitution, and there can be no constitutional legislation under that amendment, for directly enforcing the privileges, and immunities of citizens of the United States, by original proceedings in the federal courts, where the only constitutional guaranty of such privileges is that no State shall pass any law to abridge them, and where the State has in fact passed no such laws.

"The thirteenth amendment gave Congress power to pass positive laws for doing away with slavery, but it did not give power to pass laws for the punishment of ordinary crimes, against the colored race any more than against any other race. That power remains to the States.

"To constitute an offense, of which Congress and the federal courts can take cognizance under this amendment, there must be a design to injure a person, or deprive him of his right, by reason of his race, color, or previous condition of servitude.

"The fifteenth amendment confers no right to vote. That is the exclusive prerogative of the States. It does confer a right not to be excluded from voting by reason of race, color, or previous condition of servitude, and this is all the right that Congress can enforce.

"*Semble*, Congress may pass laws to protect this right, under the fifteenth amendment, from individual violation, although the laws of the States are not repugnant to the amendment. But offences against the right to vote are not cognizable under the power of Congress, unless they have, as a motive, the race color, or previous condition of servitude, of the party whose right is assailed.

"The *war of races*, whether it assumes the dimensions of civil strife and domestic violence, or is limited to private outrage, is subject to the jurisdiction of the United States, but outrage, or violence, whether against colored people or white people, which lacks this motive, and springs from the ordinary impulse of crime, is within the sole jurisdiction of the individual State, unless the latter, by its laws, denies to any race the full equality of protection.

An indictment for conspiracy to interfere with the right, peaceably to assemble, &c., or with the right to bear arms, or "to deprive certain citizens of African descent of their lives and liberties, without any due process of law," where the State has not passed any law interfering with such rights, or denying equal protection to all its citizens, is not sustainable in a United States Court, under any law that Congress had power to pass.

An indictment for conspiracy to deprive certain citizens of African descent, of the free exercise and enjoyment of the right to the full and equal benefit of all laws and proceedings, for the security of persons and property which is enjoyed by white citizens, does not, in the absence of a specific allegation of a design to deprive the injured persons of their rights on account of their race, color, or previous condition of servitude, charge any offence cognizable in a United States Court."

§ 453. The doctrine of *United States vs. Cruikshank*, was endorsed by Hughes, District Judge in U. S. Circuit Court, District of Virginia, but the opposite view was taken by Bond, Circuit Judge in the same Court. (*The U. S. vs. Petersburg Judges of*

Elections, et al, 14 *Am. Law Reg., N. S.*, 105. *Same vs. same, Ibid*, 238.) In the course of his opinion in this case in support of the constitutionality of the enforcement act of May 31st, 1870, Judge Bond says:

"There is a citizenship of the States, and a citizenship of the United States.

What the States may do by reason of this relationship, the United States may do. To give any other construction to the clauses of the fourteenth amendment we have been considering, would be to say, that everybody born or naturalized in the United States, had a right to call himself citizen, and that the amendment drew the relation of citizenship no closer than before its adoption; and that in view of the great contest just over, the people adopted an amendment, declaring every one born or naturalized in the United States, a citizen, and that Congress might enforce that nominal relation, and the empty claim to be called such by appropriate legislation.

To overrule this demurrer it is necessary to claim only that the sovereignty of the United States is equal in its sphere for the protection of the rights and privileges of citizens, to that claimed by the States in the protection of their own. Nor does this construction of the amendment interfere with the rulings of the Supreme Court in what is known as the Slaughter-house case. The right to slaughter animals within the limits of the city of New Orleans was not a right appertaining to citizenship at all; aliens might do it; but in this case the right to vote is given to all citizens of the United States as such, and no one else can exercise it. It is an immunity, a defense, a privilege peculiar to that relation, and is not shared in common with all persons whatsoever. It was not personal to a man by reason of his manhood at common law. It is the endowment of the State, peculiar to citizenship. Before the State was, men had certain rights which belonged to them, because they were men. As our declaration of independence declares, men are born with certain inalienable rights. These rights we do not contend the fourteenth amendment empowers the United States to protect. It is only such rights, privileges and immunities as the State or United States confers upon them, because of their citizenship to the United States, that the laws of the United States can insure. The fear that this construction will draw into the United States Courts all cases of offences against the person and property of individuals is groundless. The rights which are inalienable and belong to men as men, and not as citizens, are life, liberty, and the pursuit of happiness. The right to be secure in one's person or property is not peculiar to citizenship. Citizens share that with aliens. Offences against the person as well as those against property are cognizable in the State Courts, except where the controversy arises between citizens of different States, a choice of forum is given, but all such privileges as are peculiar to citizenship, this fourteenth amendment, it seems to me, was adopted to enforce.

And all that the Supreme Court decided in the slaughter-house cases was, that the United States by force of the fourteenth amendment, was not clothed with authority to enforce the rights, common to all men, but those only peculiar to citizenship. The right to vote is not the common right of all persons resident in Virginia. It is not the right of all citizens of Virginia *per se*, because a person might be a citizen of Virginia who is not a citizen of the United States, and the constitution of the State confers the right to vote, upon citizens of the United States solely. The demurrer insists upon it, that as the State has passed no law abridging the right of citizens in any particular, the indictment is bad. This view leaves out of consideration the final clause of the fourteenth amendment, which empowers Congress to enforce its provisions by appropriate legislation. The mischief to be prevented by the fourteenth amendment, was the obstruction of the citizens in the exercise of the rights of citizenship, whatever they, from time to time, might be. There is no way, as yet, pointed out by which a State can be punished, and the mischief sought to be prevented, might be flagrant in violation of State law, or without any color of authority under it.

The white people in Virginia might, without law or in spite of it determine that no colored man should vote, and the colored people in South Carolina might, in the same unlawful manner, unite to violently obstruct their white fellow citizens from exercising the elective franchise. The mischief to be prevented would be flagrant, and yet if this demurrer be good, no remedy could be found. Now, Congress, in this view of the case, has thought it appropriate legislation to punish the individuals who commit the wrong, whether under color of State authority, or without pretending to any authority at all. Who can say this is not appropriate legislation? It remedies the existing evil and a law which accomplishes or tends to accomplish, a purpose required by the constitution to be effected, cannot be said by a judicial tribunal to be inappropriate. (*Fugitive Slave Law Act, Sept.* 18*th*, 1850.)

In answer to the objection that these indictments do not allege that the obstruction had, was done on account of race, color, or previous condition of servitude, it is sufficient to say that the statute under which the indictments are drawn, uses no such language, and it is most generally sufficient in setting out in pleading a statutory offence, to use the words of the statute creating it. But if it be contended that the only power Congress had to pass the statute, was that granted by the fifteenth amendment which prevented discrimination among voters, on account of race, color, or previous condition, &c., and authorizes appropriate legislation to prevent such discrimination, there is answer to it in this: that it is impossible to prove, though the fact may be so, if a body of colored men in South Carolina assault and beat fifty white people at the polls, and prevent their voting, and at the same time knock two colored people down, that this was done on account of race or color. Congress thought to cut the thing up by the roots, and enacted what is really and practically the only appropriate legislation, as any person who has seen the efforts to enforce this section must know, that no person shall disturb another at an election, to prevent his exercise of the franchise, and as the greater includes the less, if he can do so from no motive, he cannot do it, because of race color, or previous condition, &c. And from these considerations we have drawn the following conclusions:

1. That by the fourteenth amendment to the constitution the people have provided a citizenship to the United States direct, positive, paramount, springing from birth within its jurisdiction, or by statutory naturalization.

2. That what the States have claimed to do by virtue of their sovereign power, over their citizens, the United States may do over its citizens by virtue of its sovereign power, and the direct relationship thus established.

3. That while the fourteenth amendment in furtherance of this view declares that no State shall make nor enforce any law contrary to this provision, it likewise declares that Congress shall enforce the amendment by appropriate legislation. And that as Congress cannot punish a State *qua* State, it is appropriate legislation within the meaning of the statute, to attain its end, *i. e.*, the protection of the citizen in his right to vote, by punishing the individuals who obstruct him in its exercise. And that even under the fifteenth amendment, where experience has shown the obstruction of voters on account of race and color, cannot be, in the judgment of Congress, otherwise prevented, it is appropriate legislation to provide by statute that no such obstruction shall take place at all. And that this construction of the fourteenth and fifteenth amendments does not affect the right of the States to define the rights of citizenship, nor does it draw into the jurisdiction of the United States Courts, the question of the inva-

sion of the rights of persons or property as such. It concerns only the rights which distinguish persons as citizens, and which they hold in that character."

§ 454. These conflicting decisions leave the question of the true construction of the recent constitutional amendments still open. It is expected that these important and interesting questions will receive the consideration of the Supreme Court of the United States, at an early day, and the country will await the authoritative exposition of that august tribunal, and accept it when it comes as final and conclusive.

§ 455. It would be difficult, if not impossible, to specify in detail the various acts of election officers, which will constitute fraud. Without attempting such specification, it will be sufficient here to say that *any* act on the part of such an officer, by which a legal voter has been designedly and wrongfully deprived of his vote; or by which an illegal vote has been purposely and unjustly received; or by which a false estimate has been imposed upon the public as a genuine canvass, is fraudulent. Fraud, however, cannot be predicated of a mere emotion of the mind disconnected from an act occasioning an injury to some one. There must be a fraudulent transaction, and a party injured thereby. (*People vs. Cook*, 8 *N. Y.*, 67.)

§ 456. In *Littlefield vs. Green*, (*Brightley's Election Cases*, 493,) it appeared that in a precinct containing only about four hundred and fifty legal voters, there was actually cast, counted and returned, two thousand, eight hundred and twenty ballots. It also appeared that a large number of names on the poll list were recorded in *alphabetical order*. It was a clear case of fraud, and the only question considered was, whether there was any proof upon which the poll could be purged, and the legal votes separated from the illegal. The Court refused to allow any of the votes cast at the precinct in question to be counted, on the ground that there was no sufficient proof of any legal vote whatever. It was shown that there were over four hundred persons in the precinct who were entitled to vote, but there was no proof outside of the return, that any of these voted, or as to how they voted. The Court properly rejected the return as utterly unreliable and unworthy of credit. The return was, therefore, not admissible in evidence for any purpose, and it was the duty of respondent to have shown the legal vote by other evidence. There was no proof upon which the Court could purge the return and separate the good votes from the bad, and therefore the whole poll was necessarily thrown out.

§ 457. Naturalization certificates fraudulently issued by the clerk of a Court, without the order of the Court itself, are void, and although regular on their face, confer no right upon the holders, and their fraudulent character may, on the trial of a contested election case, be shown by parol. (*Ante* § 21.) But an election officer cannot go behind the certificate of naturalization. (*Ante* § 35.) Such an officer may, however, act upon the voter's admission of facts, which, if true, avoid his certificate. (*Ante* § 95.) As to punishment of fraudulent registration for the purpose of voting for a member of Congress, see *ante* § 309. As to effect of a fraud committed by election officers, which does not, of itself, affect the result, see *ante* § 184, § 185. As to remedy for fraud, see *ante* § 340, note (f.) As to what frauds will vitiate a return, see *ante* § 365, 366, 386, 387, 391, 392, 393.

§ 458. The remedy for frauds committed in the conduct of an election, is not always by a contest in a proceeding at law. The rule is, that if the statute or the common law will afford adequate relief, equity will not interfere. Where the election is for the choice of one or more public officers, there is always a remedy at law, and a court of equity will not take jurisdiction. Cases may, however, arise which do not present the question which of two persons is entitled to an office, and which are in their nature unlike an ordinary contest. For example, a vote of the people of a county may be taken upon the question of the location or removal of a county seat; or upon the question of subscribing to the capital stock of a railroad company; or upon subscribing or appropriating money to aid any work of internal improvement; or by the people of a city or town, upon the question of adopting a charter. And it may happen that the modes of proceeding provided by statute, or by the common law, for contesting elections, or trying the title to an office, are altogether inapplicable to the determination of questions of fraud, accident or mistake, in the conduct of such elections as these. In all such cases equity will afford relief. Whether the proper remedy is by a bill to enjoin the canvassing of the vote cast at such an election, on the ground of fraud, or by bill filed after the result is declared to set it aside, and enjoin all proceedings under it, has been made a question, but the better opinion is, that the latter is the proper remedy. The canvassing of the vote concludes nothing. The validity of the election, and of every vote cast, remains an open question, which may be subsequently tried by any Court of competent authority. Besides, the result cannot be legally known until the vote has been canvassed. Proceedings, therefore, to test the validity and *bona fides* of an election, should be instituted after the canvass is made, and the result announced, and this rule applies as well to such cases as must, for the reasons stated above, be brought in equity, as to those in which the remedy is at law. As to remedy in equity, see *People vs. Wiant*, 48 *Ill.*, 263. *Boren vs. Smith*, 47 *Ill.*, 485.

CHAPTER X.

PROSECUTIONS FOR VIOLATION OF ELECTION LAWS.

§ 459. Upon an indictment under the statute of Massachusetts, for giving false answers to the selectmen who presided at a meeting for the election of officers, or for wilfully voting at such meeting without being qualified, it is not necessary to prove that the selectmen were legally chosen and qualified; it is sufficient if it be proved that they were acting as selectmen. (*Commonwealth vs. Shaw*, 7 *Metcalfe*, (*Mass.*,) 52.)

§ 460. It is no cause for arresting judgment, on an indictment for giving false answers to selectmen, and for voting wilfully without being qualified, for Governor, Lieutenant Governor, and Senators, for the district of M., that it is not alleged that the district of M. is in the commonwealth. (*Ib.*)

§ 461. An allegation in an indictment for illegal voting, that a meeting of the inhabitants of the town of A. was duly holden, is proved by evidence that a meeting of the inhabitants of the town of A., who were qualified to vote, was duly holden. (*Ib.*)

§ 462. An indictment charged that the defendant gave certain false answers to the selectmen, and that such answers were given by defendant with the fraudulent intent to procure his name to be placed on the list of voters, *and* to obtain permission to vote. The evidence was that the defendant's name was on the list of voters when he gave the false answers. *Held*, that there was a material variance between the allegation and the proof. (*Ib.*)

§ 463. It has been held, that if a party indicted under the statute of Massachusetts for wilfully giving in a vote at an election, knowing himself not to be a qualified voter, admits on his trial that he voted at the election, it is equivalent to an admission that he voted wilfully. (*Commonwealth vs. Bradford*, 9*th Metcalfe*, 268.) But this could hardly be true, if the term wilfully was here used in the ordinary sense as implying a corrupt or unlawful purpose. Such a purpose could not be inferred from the mere fact of voting. It was not, however, in this sense, that the term was used by the Court, but as the judge delivering the opinion declares, it was employed as meaning only "designedly, purposely, with an intent, to claim and exercise the right of suffrage."

§ 464. On the trial of a party indicted for wilfully giving in a vote at an election, knowing himself not to be a qualified voter, when the only question is whether he had resided in the town where he voted, six months next preceding the election, evidence that he had resided in another town until within seven months of the election, does not put upon him the burden of showing that he had changed his residence, but the burden of proof to support the indictment remains on the commonwealth. (*Ib.*)

§ 465. Evidence that a party consulted counsel as to his right to vote, and submitted to them the facts of his case, and was advised by them that he had the right, is admissible in his favor, on the trial of an indictment against him for wilfully voting, knowing himself not to be a qualified voter, but is not conclusive that he had not such knowledge. (*Ib.*)

§ 466. In an indictment, under the statute of Pennsylvania, providing for the punishment of any officer of election who shall "knowingly reject the vote of a qualified citizen," it was held that the officer could not be held criminally liable for a mere mistake of judgment, but only for a wilful disregard of duty. It was also held that the presumptions are in favor of the officer, the law presuming that he has acted conscientiously, and not corruptly, until the contrary appears. (*Commonwealth vs. Lee*, 1 *Brewster*, 273. *Cushing's Election Cases*, 98.)

§ 467. In considering whether an officer of election has acted wilfully and corruptly in rejecting a vote which is offered, it is proper to look at the character of the question he was called upon to decide, and the manner in which he conducted himself in hearing and disposing of it. If the question be a plain one to the common understanding, one about which men of ordinary intelligence would be likely to agree, and if it be decided without deliberation, and against the right, a strong presumption of wilfulness and corruption will arise. But if it be a question of doubt, or of difficulty, one about which men of ordinary intelligence might honestly differ, and if the judge acts with deliberation, and with an apparent desire to decide rightly, and errs in his judgment, it is fair to presume that it is a case of honest error. (*Ib.*)

§ 468. In *Commonwealth vs. Samuel Silsbee*, (9 *Mass.*, 416,) the indictment charged that the defendant, a legal voter, at the town meeting held on the eleventh day of March, 1811, at Salem, for the choice of town officers, " did then and there wilfully &c., give in more than one vote for the choice of selectmen for said town of Salem, at one time of balloting."

This was not made an offense by the express provisions of any statute, but the Court held it to be an offense at common law.

"There cannot be a doubt," says the court, " that the offense described is a misdemeanor at common law. It is a general principle that where a statute gives a privilege, and one wilfully violates such privilege, the common law will punish such violation. In town meetings every qualified voter has equal rights, and is entitled to give one vote for every officer to be elected. The person who gives more, infringes and violates the rights of the other voters, and for this offense the common law gives the indictment."

§ 469. The better opinion seems to be that double voting or any other wilful and corrupt attempt to defeat a fair expression of the legal voters through the ballot box is, in the absence of statute, an offense which may, as a general rule, be punished by indictment under the common law. This rule, however, is not universal. For example, in Ohio it has been decided "that the common law, though in force in this State in all civil cases, could not be resorted to for the punishment of crimes and misdemeanors." (*Key vs. Vattier*, 1 *Ohio*, 132. *Van Valkenburg vs. The State*, 11 *Ohio*, 404.) And in some of the States there are statutes expressly providing that all crimes and misdemeanors shall be defined and punished by statute. (*Bishop on Crim. Law, Secs.* 44-45.)

§ 470. Under a statute providing that any person who shall vote "without being duly qualified," shall be punished, &c., and also providing that no person is entitled to vote elsewhere than in the township of his residence, it was held that a person who was a resident of and qualified voter in, one township, and who voted in another, was liable upon an indictment under such statute. The same statute required the voter if challenged to swear to his residence in the township, and it was held that he was liable to indictment, both for perjury and for illegal voting. (*The State vs. Minnick*, 15 *Iowa*, 123.)

§ 471. In the same case it was held that it is not necessary in an indictment to state what officers were to be chosen at the election at which the illegal vote was given. The Court will take judicial notice of the statutory provisions which provide for the election of certain officers on a given day. Nor is it necessary that in such an indictment there should be an averment that the defendant voted for or against any particular person. It being shown that defendant voted, the presumption that he voted for some person, necessarily arises.

§ 472. Where the defendant, an unmarried man, left his father's home, in D. township, and went to F. township, on the Sunday before the election, remained there chopping wood until the evening of or the next morning after the election, and (having, while there, voted,) quit his work and returned home, it was held that the verdict of guilty was fully warranted by the facts. (*Ibid.*)

Such circumstances as these are not only admissible to prove a wilful and corrupt violation of the election law, but, if unexplained, they are well nigh conclusive upon the question.

§ 473. On the trial of an indictment under a statute for "wilfully voting when not a citizen of the United States," evidence that the defendant consulted "friends" as to his right to vote, "and was advised by them that such right existed," was held admissible. A person who votes illegally cannot be excused on the ground that he has taken counsel of those no better informed than himself. If he had consulted persons learned in the law, and being advised by them with full knowledge of all the facts that he was a legal voter, this fact might have been shown as tending to disprove a criminal intent, but such evidence would not be conclusive. [*State vs. Shelley*, 15*th Iowa*, 404.]

§ 474. If an indictment against a party for voting illegally, charges that the election was held on the day fixed by law, what officers were then to be elected, and that such election was authorized by law, it is not necessary to aver further that the election was held by the proper officers. As we have seen it is not necessary even to state what officers were to be chosen at the election, because the law fixes that, and the Courts must take judicial notice of it. An averment that the defendant voted illegally at an election held upon a specified day, and authorized by law, includes the idea that the election was held by the proper officers. Such an averment clearly and necessarily implies not only that the election held that day throughout the State was authorized, but also that the polls at which the defendant voted, were opened, and the election conducted by the properly constituted officers. (*The State vs. Douglass*, 7*th Iowa*, 413.)

§ 475. It is a disputed question whether under an indictment for illegal voting it is necessary, in order to convict, to show that the defendant had knowledge of his disqualification. In *Commonwealth* vs. *Aglar*, (*Thacher's Criminal Cases*, 412. *Brightley's Election Cases*, 695,) the municipal court of the city of Boston held that a person is not liable criminally for illegal voting, unless he knew at the time that he was not a qualified voter, and that he was doing or attempting to do, an illegal act; and that if he honestly believed that he had a right to vote, it is not a wilful act punishable by indictment. The same doctrine prevails in Rhode Island, where the courts hold that to sustain an indictment for illegal voting, the ballot must be *fraudulently* cast, that is, with knowledge by the voter of his disqualification. (*State vs. Macowber*, 7 *Rhode Island*, 349.) It has also been held that whether the offense was wilfully committed, is a question for the jury. (*Commonwealth vs. Wallace, Thach. Cr. Cases*, 592.)

In Tennessee it is held, that ignorance of the law will not excuse illegal voting, but that in order to convict, it must appear that the voter knew a state of facts which would, in point of law, disqualify him. (*McGuire vs. State*, 7 *Humph.*, 54.) And so in North Carolina. (*State vs. Hart*, 6 *Jones*, [*Law*,] 389. *State vs. Boyett*, 10 *Ired*, 336.)

In California the courts have avoided both extremes, and planted themselves upon a sort of middle ground, by adopting the following rule: Where an unlawful act is proved to have been done by the accused, the law in the first instance presumes it to have been intended, and the proof of justification or excuse lies on the defendant. (*People vs. Harris*, 29 *Cal.*, 578.)

§ 476. It is held in Indiana that on the trial of an indictment for illegal voting, the defendant's statements made at the polls on being challenged, are not admissible evidence in his favor, nor is the decision of the election officers in favor of his right to vote any defense. (*Morris vs. State*, 7 *Black f.*, 607.)

§ 477. The question when the act of voting is to be considered as complete, is also a disputed question. Thus, in Alabama it was held that it is not complete until the ballot is put into the box, and the name of the voter registered by the clerks, and that a defendant cannot, therefore, be convicted of illegal voting, if the act is not thus consummated. [*Blackwell vs. Thompson*, 2d *Stew. & Port*, 348.] But in Tennessee it is held that when a voter presents himself before the judges, hands his ticket to the officer, and his name is announced and registered, the act of voting is complete, without the actual placing of the ballot in the box. [*Steinwehr vs. State*, 5 *Sneed*, 856.]

§ 478. In Iowa it has been held that where a statute provided that where any person knowing himself not to be qualified, shall vote at any election authorized by law, he shall be punished, &c., it is sufficient if the indictment follow the language of the statute, and it need not state in what the disqualification consisted. [*State vs. Douglass*, 7 *Iowa*, 413.] But this is not the uniform doctrine of the courts of this country. The weight of authority, as well as of reason, probably is, that the defendant is entitled to be advised by the indictment more definitely as to the nature of the charge against him, *e. g.*, if he is charged with voting without being qualified, the indictment ought to state wherein he is disqualified.

§ 479. A statute of New Jersey provided for the punishment of "any person who shall vote or fraudulently offer to vote," knowing that he is not duly qualified, &c. It was held by the Supreme Court of that State, that in charging a defendant with the offense of voting illegally under this statute, it was not necessary to allege that the illegal vote was *fraudulently* given, but in charging such defendant with offering to vote illegally, it must be charged that he fraudulently offered to vote, knowing that he was not duly qualified, &c. It was also held in the same case that an indictment which failed to specify the particular disability which is relied on as a disqualification of the defendant as a voter, is fatally defective. [*State vs. Moore*, 3 *Dutch.*, 105.] And see also *State vs. Tweed*, 3 *Dutch.*, 111.

§ 480. And in Tennessee it is held that an indictment charging the defendant with having "unlawfully and knowingly voted, not being a qualified voter, is bad," though in the words of the statute. There are various disqualifications, and the indictment must show which one is wanting. [*Pearce vs. State*, 1 *Sneed*, 937.] These cases are in conflict with *State vs. Douglass*, *supra*, and the doctrine of the latter case is sustained by *The United States vs. Quin*, 12 *Int. Rev. Rec.*, 151, and *U. S. vs. Bullard*, 13 *do* 195.

The ground upon which the courts proceed in holding that it is necessary to specify the disqualification, is this. There are numerous disqualifications, such as want of age, non-residence, having once voted, having been convicted of felony, non-payment of taxes, want of registration, and the like; it is, therefore, but fair that the defendant should be advised by the indictment, which of these disqualifications he is charged with, in order that he may intelligently prepare his defense. And this reasoning seems entirely sound.

§ 481. Nor is it always sufficient to charge an offense in the words of a statute. Whether this is sufficient or not will depend upon the question whether to do so will make the indictment as specific as, according to the well known rules of criminal pleading, it ought to be. Thus, where the statute provided that "if any inspector, judge, or clerk, shall be convicted of any wilful fraud in the discharge of his duties, he shall undergo an imprisonment," &c. It was held that an indictment charging that these officers "did commit wilful fraud in the discharge of their duties," without stating the particular acts constituting the fraud, was fatally defective. [*Commonwealth* vs. *Miller*, 2 *Parsons*, 480. *Brightley's Election Cases*, 711.] It was further held in the same case, that the inspectors, judges, and clerks, cannot be joined in one indictment as defendants, their offices being distinct and their duties distinct and separate. And in *Commonwealth* vs. *Gray*, [3 *Duvall*, 373,] a similar ruling will be found. In that case the indictment was against one of the judges, and charged him with knowingly and unlawfully receiving the vote of an unqualified person. This was held sufficient, without showing whether the other judges of the election were opposed to, or in favor of allowing the illegal vote, to be cast. And see also *Commonwealth* vs. *Ayer*, [*Cush. Elect. Cases*,, 674.]

§ 482. And it has been held in Indiana, that an indictment which charges that the defendant voted at an election "not having the legal qualifications of a voter," is bad for not specifying what qualifications the voter lacked—for alleging, not a fact, but a conclusion of law. [*Quinn vs. The State*, 35 *Ind.*, 485.] Under such an indictment, if held good, the State might prove the want of any one of the many qualifications required to be possessed by a voter, and the defendant could not learn from the indictment, precisely what he is expected to meet. This was, therefore, held to be one of the cases in which it is not sufficient to charge the offense in the words of the statute.

§ 483. Mere irregularities in the manner of holding or conducting an election, constitutes no defense to an indictment for illegal voting. If there was an election held in pursuance of law, at the proper time and place, it is sufficient. (*State* vs. *Cohoon*, 12 *Ired*, 178.) But if the election is an illegal one, the indictment cannot be maintained. [*State* vs. *Williams*, 25 *Maine*, 561.]

§ 484. Inasmuch as illegal voting is a local offense, it is necessary that an indictment therefor should state with precision, where the illegal vote was cast. [*State* vs. *Fitzpatrick*, 4 *Rhode Island*, 269.]

§ 485. In Maine it has been held that an indictment against a person for voting twice at one balloting, for the choice of a selectman at a town meeting, cannot be sustained unless such meeting was warned and notified in the manner prescribed by the statute. [*State* vs. *Williams*, 25 *Maine*, 561.] But this ruling, to be sustained, must be based upon the fact, that under the statute of that State no valid town meeting for the choice of selectmen, could be held, without such warning and notice. The true rule governing indictments for illegal voting is that the election at which the illegal vote was cast, was a lawful and valid election. An informality or irregularity which does not go to the validity of the election itself, cannot be pleaded as a defense to such an indictment.

§ 486. On the trial of an indictment under a statute prohibiting a person from voting at any election, who has been convicted of any infamous crime, unless he shall have been pardoned and restored to all the rights of citizenship,—the fact that the defendant was a minor when convicted of the felony, and also when discharged from prison, is no defense. [*Hamilton* vs. *People*, 57 *Barb.*, *N. Y.*, 625.]

§ 487. The statute of Michigan, of 1851, provided that "if any person offering to vote shall be challenged as unqualified, &c., the chairman of the board of inspectors shall declare to the person so challenged, the constitutional qualifications of an elector," after which, if he insists upon his right to vote, the inspectors are required to tender him the statutory oath. Subsequently, in 1859, the legislature of the same State passed a registry law, which, among other things, provided "that the vote of no person shall be received whose name is not registered." Under these two statutes it was held that the inspectors were not bound to administer the oath to an unregistered voter, though he demanded it. [*Wattles* vs. *The People*, 13 *Mich.*, 446.]

§ 488. It is no defense to a prosecution for voting a second time at an election, to show that the first vote was illegal and not entitled to be counted. [*State* vs. *Perkins*, 42 *Vt.*, 399.]

§ 489. A person charged with a public offense is entitled, before he can be required to answer, to demand a specific averment of the *facts* which constitute the offense charged. It is, therefore, not sufficient to charge in general, in an indictment, that the officers of an election did commit wilful fraud in the discharge of their duties ; there must be some specific averment of a fact which constitutes the fraud charged. It is not sufficient to lay the offense in the words of the statute, unless those words serve to allege the fact with all the necessary additions, and without any uncertainty or ambiguity. (2 *Parson's Select Cases*, 480.)

§ 490. The statute of Rhode Island provided for the punishment of any person who at "any election shall *fraudulently* vote, not being qualified." Under this statute it was held, that to warrant a conviction it must be shown that the vote was fraudulently cast, that is, with knowledge by the voter that he was not qualified to vote; and that an honest mistake by a voter, as to his right, and an assertion of it by voting, will not render him liable under the statute, even though he is cognizant of the *facts* which constitute the defect in his right. [*State* vs. *Macowber*, 7 *R. I.*, 349.] In this case it is said that "the distinction between acts done honestly, under a mistaken sense of right, and acts done fraudulently, with a consciousness of wrong, is familiar to every one who has had occasion to trace the boundary line between trespass and larceny." And see also *State* vs. *McDonald*, 4 *Harrington*, 555. *State* vs. *Porter*, *do*, 556.

§ 491. Substantially the same doctrine was laid down in *State* vs. *Smith, et al*, [18 *N. H.*, 91.] This was an indictment charging defendants, as selectmen, with erasing from the list of voters of the town of Boscamen, the name of Timothy Kelley, alleged to have been a legal voter of that town. It was, under the statute, the duty of the selectmen to hear all applications for the insertion of the name of any person upon the list, or for the erasure of any name therefrom, and to hear proof, and decide all such applications. And the statute provided that "if any selectman at any session holden for the correction of any list of voters, shall * * * * *knowingly* erase from or omit to insert the name of any legal voter, he shall be punished," &c. It was held that the selectman could not be punished for an erroneous decision merely, but only for corruption.

§ 492. And it was observed by the Court, that notwithstanding the effort to distinguish by law clearly and plainly the persons who are entitled to vote, "there are still cases of no little difficulty constantly arising under those laws, some of which might well tax the acumen of persons more accustomed to investigate such questions than many of those persons are, who are required in every town to decide and to settle them. They are questions, in short, in the decision of which errors are not unlikely to occur, and it is certainly an anomaly in the law if those, who are charged with the duty of deciding them, are liable to be charged criminally for forming an opinion that the court may, upon inquiry, pronounce to be erroneous."

§ 493. And in Wisconsin the same doctrine was very clearly and forcibly stated in *Byrne et al*, vs. *The State*, [12 *Wis.*, 519.] It was there very clearly shown that the rule that ignorance of the law excuses no man, has no application to acts which are in their nature official, and done in the exercise of a discretionary power conferred by law. That maxim applies to acts which are voluntary, and will estop such officers from setting up their ignorance of the penalties inflicted by a statute, as an excuse for their wilful violation of the duties which it imposes upon them. Where the officer is obliged by law to act and to decide, the most that reason or justice can require of him, is a *bona fide* effort to discharge his duties according to the best of his knowledge and ability.

CHAPTER XI.

CIVIL LIABILITY OF ELECTION OFFICERS FOR MISCONDUCT IN OFFICE.

§ 494. The general rule is that an officer of election, or of registration, who shall wilfully and corruptly refuse to any citizen who is duly qualified, the right to vote, or to register, is liable in damages to the person injured. In several of the States, as we shall presently see, it is regarded as sufficient to show that the plaintiff has been unlawfully deprived of his right, without proof of a malicious or corrupt purpose on the part of the officer, but the general doctrine is as above stated. In Massachusetts, where it is not necessary to show malice, it has been held that the officer is not liable, if he acted under a mistake, into which he was led by the conduct of plaintiff. (*Humphrey* vs. *Kingman*, 5 *Metcalfe*, 162.)

§ 495. In England, and in most of the States of the Union, the rule above stated is regarded as well settled, and no action is held to be maintainable against an officer of election for rejecting the vote of a citizen, without proof that such rejection was wilful and malicious. In Massachusetts, by a series of decisions, the law is settled otherwise. (*Killiam* vs. *Ward*, 2 *Mass.*, 236. *Lincoln* vs. *Hapgood*, 11 *Mass.*, 350. *Henshaw* vs. *Foster*, 9 *Pick.*, 312. *Capen* vs. *Foster*, 12 *Pick.*, 485. *Blanchard* vs. *Stearns*, 5 *Metcalfe*, 298.) But in the latter case it was held that in order to recover, the plaintiff in such an action must allege and prove that he furnished defendants with sufficient evidence of his having the legal qualifications of a voter, before defendants refused to receive his vote. This decision comes almost up to the rule as it exists in most of the other States, because if the voter furnished sufficient evidence of his right, that fact would go far to prove wilfulness on the part of the officer, who, in the face of such evidence, refuses him the privilege of voting.

§ 496. The rule laid down in the Massachusetts cases has been followed in Ohio, (*Jeffries* vs. *Ankeney*, 11 *Ohio*, 373. *Anderson* vs. *Milliken*, 9 *Ohio State R.*, 568,) and also in Wisconsin, (*Gillespie* vs. *Palmer*, 544.) But the weight of authority is decidedly the other way. (*Jenkins* vs. *Waldron*, 11 *Johnson*, [*N. Y.*,] 114. *Weckerly* vs. *Guyer*, 11 *S. & R.*, 35. *Moran* vs. *Rennaud*, 3 *Brewster*, 601. *Commonwealth* vs. *Sheriff*, 1 *Brewster*, 183. *State* vs. *Smith*, 18 *N. H.*, 91. *State* vs. *Daniels*, 44 *N. H.*, 383. *State* vs. *McDonald*, 4 *Harrington*, [*Del.*] 555. *State* vs. *Porter*, *ibid*, 556. *Carter* vs. *Harrison*, 5 *Black f.*, 138. *State* vs. *Robb*, 17 *Ind.*, 536. *Peaney* vs. *Robins*, 3 *Jones*, [*Law*,] 339. *Caulfield* vs. *Bullock*, 18 *B. Mon.*, 494. *Morgan* vs. *Dudley*, *ibid*, 693. *Miller* vs. *Rucker*, 1 *Bush.*, 135. *Rail* vs. *Potts*, 8 *Humph.*, [*Tenn.*,] 225. *Bevard* vs. *Hoffman*, 18 *Ind.*, 479. *Anderson* vs. *Baker*, 23*d Md.*, 531.) Even in those States where the Massachusetts rule prevails, it is believed that no more than nominal damages is ever allowed, in the absence of proof of a corrupt purpose.

The action in those States is regarded rather as one for the determination and settlement of the plaintiff's right to vote, than as a suit to recover damages. (*Brightley's Election Cases*, 194.) In *Jeffries* vs. *Ankeney*, *supra*, the Supreme Court of Ohio said:

"It is generally true that no suit lies against an officer for a mistake in the exercise of his judicial discretion; but when we reflect how highly the privilege of voting is generally valued, and that the legislature has provided, and the forms of law admit, no other remedy than this action, we unite in the opinion that a necessity exists for entertaining this remedy. In the absence of malice, where the suit is brought merely to assert the right, the damages will be nominal and small."

§ 497. And the Supreme Court of Mass., while maintaining the rule that election officers are liable for rejecting a legal vote without proof of malice, seems to have endeavored to so administer the law under that rule as to take away much of its severity. Thus in *Lincoln* vs. *Hapgood*, [11 *Mass.*, 357,] the Court said:

"But, notwithstanding we deem it necessary that this action should be supported as the only mode of ascertaining and enforcing a right which has been disputed, we do not think it ought to be a source of speculation to those who may be ready to take advantage of any injury, and turn it to their profit, to the vexation and distress of men who have unfortunately been obliged to decide on a question sometimes intricate and complicated, but who have discovered no disposition to abuse their power for private purposes. And we, therefore, think that juries should always, in estimating the damages, have regard to the disposition and temper of mind discoverable in the act complained of, and probably the Court would determine that a sum, comparatively not large, would be excessive damages, in a case where no fault but ignorance or mistake was imputable to the selectmen." And in *Henshaw* vs. *Foster*, [9 *Pick.*, 312,] the same Court assessed a fine of only one dollar against an election officer who had rejected a legal vote, but who had done so in the honest discharge of his supposed duty.

§ 498. The Supreme Court of Pennsylvania, in *Weckerly vs. Geyer*, laid down as the law of that State the rule that malice must be shown to sustain an action on the case against an officer of an election for refusing the plaintiff's vote, and enforced it as follows:

"We have no doubt that malice is an ingredient without which the action cannot be supported. By malice, I mean the refusal of a vote from improper motives and contrary to the inspector's own opinion. It is not necessary that this should be expressly proved; the jury may infer it from circumstances; direct and positive proof in a case of this kind is hardly to be expected. But a man who is placed in public station as an officer of the commonwealth, or of a corporation, in which, though not strictly a judicial office, he must necessarily exercise his judgment, (such as inspector or judge of an election) is not liable to an action, provided, he act with purity and good faith; but, that he is responsible if he act wilfully and maliciously, was decided in the English House of Lords in the case of *Ashby vs. White*, 1 *Bro, P. C.* 49, and has been held for law ever since."

§ 499. It has been held that registering officers are not responsible, in damages, for refusing to register an elector however erroneous their refusal may be, if produced by an honest mistake or error of judgment, but if they act corruptly or maliciously, they are liable to the person injured. [*Pike* vs. *Magoun*, 44 *Mo.*, 492.]

§ 500. In this latter case the doctrine is laid down that a judicial officer is in no case to be held liable in damages for an error of judgment, and where there is no malice, and this doctrine is supported by the citation of numerous authorities. The Court further inquires whether the officers of registration, under the statute of Missouri, were judicial officers, and upon this point the Court say:

"Their duties were partly ministerial and partly judicial; that is, they were required to exercise a discretion and judgment when determining the qualifications of those presenting themselves for registration," and while holding that these officers were not in a strict sense, judicial officers, the Court yet held that they were, like judges of election, clothed with discretionary power, and acted *quasi* judicially, and that it was therefore necessary to allege and prove that their official action was knowingly wrongful, malicious or corrupt, in order to hold them liable in damages therefor.

§ 501. The duties of election officers are generally clearly defined by statute, particularly as to the manner of conducting the election and of determining disputed questions as to the right of individuals to vote. In some of the States if the voter will make an affidavit, the form or substance of which is prescribed, his vote is to be received without further evidence or inquiry. Such is the law of Illinois.—[*Spragins vs. Houghton*, 3 *Ill.*, 377, *Brightley's Election cases*, 162.] And in New York, [*People vs. Pease*, 30 *Barbour*, 588.]

It is the policy of the law upon this subject to leave as little as possible to the discretion of election officers. In the statutes of most, if not of all of the States, there are numerous and minute provisions framed for the purpose of anticipating questions, which may arise at the polls, and the manner of their determination. These statutes are wisely so framed, as to prevent uncertainty and debate as to the proper decision of questions arising amid the confusion and excitement of an election. For example, the statute of Illinois, under which the case of *Spragins* vs. *Houghton* arose, prescribed the form of the oath to be taken by a voter when challenged and provided that "if the person so offering his vote shall take such oath or affirmation, his vote shall be received, unless it shall be proved by evidence, satisfactory to a majority of the judges, that such oath or affirmation is false." And it was held that under this statute the judges had no discretion;

they were bound to receive the vote of a person who took the oath, unless proof was offered to show that the oath was false. And this construction of the Illinois statute was doubtless correct in its application to the case decided, for it is beyond question that if the officer obeys such a statute he cannot incur any of its penalties. But a case may arise where the officer knows, or has reason to believe, that notwithstanding the oath taken by a person offering to vote, he is not a legal voter, where in fact the officer knows, or has reason to believe, that the oath is false. May not the officer reject such a vote notwithstanding the person offering it takes the oath, and justify his act by proving that the oath was false? In such a case, of course, the officer takes upon himself the burden and the risk of proving the oath of the alleged voter to be false.

Thus in *State* vs. *Robb*, [17 *Indiana*, 536,] it was held that the election board, whose duty it was to decide upon the qualifications of voters, may refuse the vote of a person who takes or offers to take the oath prescribed by law as to his qualifications, but they do so at the peril of being able to show that he was not a legal voter, upon a prosecution for refusing the vote. It was further held, however, that when the person offering to vote takes the prescribed oath, the board are justified in receiving the vote, unless it can be shown that they acted corruptly, and were cognizant of the fact that he was not a legal voter. The doctrine of this case seems to be that if the board know that the voter swears, or offers to swear falsely, and that he is not entitled to vote, it is not only their right, but their duty to refuse the vote, notwithstanding such offer to swear. The statute of Indiana, under which this case arose, unlike that of Illinois, *supra*, was intended to, and did preclude the election board from taking testimony relative to the right of any person to vote who might offer to take the oath therein prescribed. The plaintiff offered his vote, and offered to take the oath prescribed, but the defendant, who was an inspector of the election, refused to administer said oath, or to permit him to vote, and he was permitted to prove as his justification, that the plaintiff was not a legal voter, and that if he had taken the oath, he would have sworn falsely.

§ 502. Subject to the qualification above stated, the general rule is that a statute prescribing the form of oath to be taken by a person offering to vote, and requiring the vote to be received if the oath be taken, leaves no discretion in the judges of election, and takes from them all power to decide upon the qualifications of a voter. Thus in New York it is held that, except in certain special cases, (as where the party has been convicted of a crime, or has made a bet on the election,) the voter is made the judge of his own qualifications and his conscience, for the occasion, takes the place of every other tribunal. If there is any doubt as to the voter's qualifications, the inspectors are required to examine him on oath, touching the same, and if, in their opinion, he be not duly qualified, they are to admonish him as to the points in which they consider him deficient, nevertheless, if after this he persists in his claim to vote, they are compelled to administer to him the general oath in which he affirms the posssession in himself of all the legal qualifications, and if he take the oath, his vote must be received; the inspectors have no discretion in the matter; they can only reject the vote, if he refuses to answer the interrogatories put to him touching his qualifications, or to take the general oath. (*People vs. Pease*, 30 *Barb.*, 588. 27 *N. Y.*, 45.)

§ 503. In *Bacon vs. Benchley, et al*, (2 *Cush.*, 100,) which was an action to recover damages against selectmen, for refusing to place the plaintiff's name on the list of voters, it appeared that the plaintiff was duly qualified, that he applied to the selectmen to place his name on the list, and that they refused the application. It further appeared, however, that afterward, and before the close of their session, the selectmen re-considered their refusal, and did place plaintiff's name on the list, but of this he was not informed. *Held*, that plaintiff could not recover, and that it was his duty to ascertain after the close of the "list," that his name was not on it, before he could hold the selectmen liable. This, for this reason, that the selectmen had the right to alter or correct the list, and to insert a name on it, up to the close of the session for revising. The Court was of opinion that the defendants did seasonably place the plaintiff's name on the list.

§ 504. We have already seen, that according to the decisions in Massachusetts, it is incumbent upon a person offering to vote to furnish to the selectmen sufficient evidence of his having the legal qualifications of a voter. It seems that where a voter before offering his vote, makes statements not under oath, to the selectmen, relating to his residence, in an action against such selectmen for refusing his vote, the plaintiff may prove that he made such statements, and what they were. (*Lombard* vs. *Oliver and others*, 7 *Allen*, 155.) But it would doubtless be otherwise if the plaintiff had been requested by the selectmen to make his statement under oath, and had not done so. In determining the question of a party's right to vote, the statements of such party concerning his residence, cannot be overlooked or disregarded, but the party must, if required, make oath to his statement.

§ 505. If a registered voter tenders his vote at an election, and the judges wilfully, corruptly and fraudulently refuse to receive it, he is entitled to recover in an action against them, such exemplary damages as the jury may consider proper under the circumstances. (*Elbin* vs. *Wilson*, 33 *Md.*) But in no case can a party recover exemplary damages unless wilful and corrupt action on the part of the officer charged, is proven, and indeed, (as we have already seen,) in most of the States, the officers of election are not liable at all—not even for actual damages—unless a corrupt purpose is shown. It was also held in the same case, that where the defendant claimed to have rejected plaintiff's vote upon the ground of his disloyal sentiments, it was proper for plaintiff to show that defendant, as register, had permitted another person, known to hold the same disloyal sentiments, to be registered as a voter. This was admittted as tending to show malice as against the plaintiff.

§ 506. And it was held in the same case, that in an action for damages against judges for corruptly refusing the vote of the plaintiff, the fact that the defendants knew that plaintiff differed from them in his political sentiments is admissible as an element of proof to be considered by the jury together with other facts, to determine how far they were influenced by bias, prejudice, or corrupt motives in rejecting his vote. This ruling was probably correct, and yet such proof should have little or no weight, unless it appears from the acts, declarations, or conduct of the defendants, that they were not disposed to treat fairly and honestly the claims of a political opponent. The fact that the defendants and the plaintiff differed in politics standing alone, should be held as a fact of no moment. If it were otherwise the judges of an election would not be safe in deciding against the right of a political opponent to vote, except in the clearest case. It would destroy that independence that is requisite to judicial fairness.

§ 507. Where an officer of election has decided a difficult and doubtful question, against the right of a person claiming a vote, he will be deemed, until the contrary appears, to have acted without malice, even though his decision may have been erroneous. Thus, in New York, the inspectors refused the vote of a registered citizen, who had been challenged on the ground that he was a deserter from the U. S. military service, it appearing that by the act of Congress, deserters were rendered incapable of exercising the rights of citizens. In a suit against these inspectors for rufusing this vote, it was held that they were not liable without proof of malice notwithstanding the fact that the act of Congress was afterward construed to refer only to deserters who had been properly convicted as such. (*Goechens* vs. *Matthewson*, 5 *Laws*, *N. Y.*, 214.)

CHAPTER XII.

OF THE ORGANIZATION AND POWERS OF LEGISLATIVE BODIES.

§ 508. Inasmuch as the failure of the legislative department of a government, (whether national, State, or municipal,) to organize and proceed regularly in the discharge of its duties, may prove a most grave and serious evil, it is important that the rules governing the organization of such bodies be defined as clearly as possible, and be adhered to and enforced with great strictness. It will be our purpose in this chapter, in the first place, to lay down at least the more important of these rules, and secondly, to speak briefly of the power of a legislative body over its members, and over other persons.

§ 509. It is to be observed in the outset that when a number of persons come together, each claiming to be a member of a legislative body, those persons who hold the usual credentials of membership, are alone entitled to participate in the organization. For it is, as we have had occasion several times to repeat, a well settled rule, that where there has been an authorized election for an office, the certificate of election, which is sanctioned by law or usage, is the *prima facie* written title to the office. (*Kerr* vs. *Trego*, 47 *Pa. State Rep.*, 292.)

§ 510. Of course the first organization must be temporary, and if the law does not designate the person who shall preside over such temporary organization, the persons assembled and claiming to be members may select one of their number for that purpose. The next step is to ascertain in some convenient way the names of the persons who are, by reason of holding the proper credentials, *prima facie* entitled to seats, and therefore entitled to take part in the permanent organization of the body. In the absence of any statutory or other regulation upon this subject, a committee on credentials is usually appointed, to whom all credentials are referred, and who report to the body a roll of the names of those who are shown by such credentials to be entitled to seats. This report being adopted, the body is prepared to proceed to the election of permanent officers, by such mode as the rules of the body may prescribe.

§ 511. There are, however, in this country numerous statutes, prescribing the mode of organizing legislative bodies. Thus, it is prescribed by an act of Congress that in the organization of the House of Representatives of the United States, the clerk of the preceding House shall preside and shall make up a roll of members. He is required to place upon such roll the names of all persons claiming seats as representatives, from States which were represented in the next preceeding Congress, and whose credentials show that they were regularly elected in accordance with the laws of their States respectively—or the laws of the United States. In case of a vacancy in the office of clerk or of his absence or inability to act, the duties imposed upon him relative to the preparation of the roll or the organization of the House devolve upon the sergeant at arms, and in case of vacancy in both of said offices, or the absence or inability of both to act, the said duties are to be performed by the door-keeper of the House. (For this statute in full, see appendix to this volume.) And by the laws of most of the States, similar statutory regulations are provided. Thus, in many of the States the Lieutenant Governor is *ex officio* president of the State Senate, and presides over the organization of the new Senate which commences with the expiration of his term of office. In most of the States, (and perhaps in all of them,) the lower House of the General Assembly is required to be called to order by the clerk of the preceding House, and to be organized by proceedings similar to those above described, in the organization of the lower House of Congress.

§ 512. Of course no business other than that which pertains to the organization of the body, can be properly transacted until after the members have been sworn according to law. In the absence of any law designating the person by whom the oath of office shall be administered, it is usual to require the services of a judge of one of the higher Courts, and the chief justice of the Supreme Court of the State is apt to be called upon to discharge this duty, though it is presumed that in the absence of any established rule upon the subject, the oath may be administered by any person having authority to administer oaths generally. Immediately upon the election of a permanent presiding officer, and upon his being sworn, it is proper to proceed to call the roll of members, to the end, that each member as his name is called, may advance and take the oath of office. In the House of Representatives of the United States, the oath of office is administered to the speaker by a member of the House, (usually by that one who has been longest a member,) and the other members are sworn in by the speaker.

§ 513. Notwithstanding the fact that these rules and regulations governing the organization of legislative bodies, are well settled, and generally understood, it will sometimes occur that an organization may not be effected without great delay and difficulty, and it has sometimes happened that two bodies have organized and elected officers, being nearly equal in point of numbers, and each claiming to be the lawful organization. Nor has the lower House of Congress always been able to organize without delay or difficulty. In the twenty-sixth Congress, the Clerk of the House undertook to omit from the roll both the claimants for each of several contested seats, and by this action the organization was delayed for some ten days. In this he was clearly wrong, for it was his duty to place upon the roll the names of the persons holding proper certificates of election, without regard to the question whether the seats of any such persons were to be contested. In the thirty-first, thirty-fourth, and thirty-sixth Congresses, the organization of the House was delayed by reason of the failure of a majority of the members to vote for any candidate for speaker, thus preventing an election. Delay from this cause may frequently occur, and cannot be prevented, so long as the votes of a majority of members are required to elect a speaker. It was found necessary, in the 31st and 34th Congresses, to adopt the plurality rule in the election of a speaker, for the reason that the majority seemed altogether unable to agree upon any person for that office. This was effected by a resolution of the House, authorizing an election of speaker by a plurality, and afterwards by the passage of a confirmatory resolution, declaring him "duly elected." (*Barclay's Dig.*, 126.)

§ 514. In case of a division of a legislative body, that ought to be a unit, it becomes important to determine which is the legal, and which the illegal assembly. In such a case the true test is this ; that is the legal organization which has "maintained the regular forms of organization, according to the laws and usages of the body, or in the absence of these, according to the laws, customs and usages of similar bodies in like cases, or in analogy to them." *Kerr* vs. *Trego, supra.*) This rule affords the best possible test of legitimate organization.

In all cases where part of a legislative body remains, and where the body is to be completed by the reception of new members, the old members who hold over remain as an organized nucleus, which receives the new members, when the whole body proceeds to the exercise of all its functions. The new members, though they be in the majority, must meet with the old at the time and place fixed by law, and proceed regularly with the organization of the body, and they cannot assemble elsewhere and organize the body. They must join themselves to the existing body, for the members holding over, though they may be in the minority, and not sufficiently numerous to constitute a quorum, are yet the body, for the purposes of receiving the new members and acting as the organs of re-organizing the body. And this principle applies, and often becomes very important, in those cases where but a single officer of the preceding body holds over, and is authorized to take charge of the organization of the new body. Thus, as we have seen, the Clerk of the previous House of Representatives of the United States, is authorized, by law, to preside at the organization of the new House, and he is, therefore, (unless he be absent, or incapacitated, or the office be vacant, in which cases the law provides a substitute,) the only person who can take charge of the organization. Even if a quorum of the House should refuse to recognize him, and should choose another to preside over the organization, that action would be null and void.

It is apparent that this rule will, if adhered to, ensure a legal organization, and prevent a schism of the body, in every case, though the process of organization may, in some cases, be tardy. It may be urged that this rule puts too much power in the hands of the person or persons who are empowered to prepare a roll of members, and take charge of the organization, but the answer is, that whatever of inconvenience or hardships may result from this rule, cannot be compared to the advantages of securing a regular and legal organization, and avoiding the possibility of division, disorganization, and conflict. Besides, the majority can always, by legal and orderly means, correct errors and redress wrongs, if any are attempted upon their rights.

§ 515. In the event that a municipal or legislative body which ought to be a unit, divides into two separate bodies, each claiming to be the legitimate and legal organization, what is the remedy by which the authority of the lawful body may be maintained, and the unlawful body be restrained from assuming and attempting to exercise functions which do not belong to it? In considering this question, we must keep in view the fact that there are two classes of legislative bodies, to-wit: those which are supreme, and those which are subordinate. To the former class belong the Congress of the United States, and the legislatures of the several States. These represent the supreme legislative power of the nation and of the State. To the latter class belong the common councils of cities and towns, and other similar municipal legislative bodies. These are *under law*, and subordinate to the judgments and orders of the courts of justice.

For a failure to organize a supreme legislature, there is no remedy which courts of justice can administer, and this fact makes it all the more important that the rules which have been established to prevent such failure, and avoid the anarchy, confusion, and possible bloodshed, which might ensue, should be adhered to. As to subordinate legislatures, such as are not supreme, but subject to the jurisdiction of the judiciary, it has been held that an illegal body may be restrained by injunction, from acting. In the case of *Kerr vs. Trego, supra,* the Supreme Court of Pennsylvania discussed the question of the remedy for these evils, as follows:

"Have the Courts authority to redress this wrong?

We think they have. All bodies, except the supreme legislature, are *under law*, and therefore, for all transgressions of law are subject to the autnority of the judicial power established by the constitution. The corporation itself is subject to this authority, so far as its acts are directed by law, though it is not, and can not be so, in so far as it is itself a law making power; in so far as its judgment and direction are uncontrolled by the law of the land, it is free from the control of the courts, but in so far as its acts are directed by law, it is subject to the judicial authority; much more then are its officers subject to this authority, and especially those that pretend to act as its officers, without right, and as there cannot be two common councils, one of these bodies must be a mere pretender to the right to act as such. May the wrongful party be restrained from acting by the means of the equitable remedy of injunction? We think it may; this remedy extends to all acts that are contrary to law, and prejudicial to the interests of the community, and for which there is no adequate remedy at law; and we can hardly imagine any act that more clearly falls within this description than one that casts so deep a shade of doubt and confusion on the public affairs of a city as this does. In such a case no remedy is adequate that is not prompt and speedy as this one. If a private partnership or corporation were to fall into similar confusion affecting all its members, and all its creditors, we can think of no better remedy than this for staying the confusion that would be caused by two opposite parties pretending to act as the society. It is the very remedy usually adopted when churches divide into parties, and we have applied it in three such cases in the last year; therein we decided directly on rights of *property*, because that became the aim of dispute; here we must decide on the right to public *functions*, because that is here the purpose of the dispute. The main question in all such cases is regularity of organization, and the right to functions and property is a mere consequence of this. May one of the conflicting bodies, or the members of it, maintain this action against the other? We think they may; this could not be doubted in relation to private corporations and partnerships; but it is argued that in relation to public corporations the attorney general alone can file such a bill; we do not think so; it is a right for those to whom public functions are entrusted, to see that they are not usurped by others. Either of these bodies has the right to demand of the courts that it, and all the interests of the public alleged to be committed to it, shall be protected against the usurpation of the other. We decided a similar principle in *Mott vs. The Railroad*, 30 *Penn., St. R.*, 9, and we need say no more about it now. This case is, therefore, regularly before us, and we proceed to the consideration of it, premising that there is no material fact in dispute, and that we have no authority to decide directly upon the validity of the election of any one of the claiming members."

§ 516. Inasmuch as Senators of the United States are chosen in each State by the legislature thereof, it is manifest that the Senate may sometimes find it necessary to inquire and determine whether a body claiming to be the legislature of a State is in fact such. If two bodies have organized, each claiming to be the legislature, and each has elected a Senator, of course the Senate, in order to decide between them, must inquire and determine which was the legislature. Such a case arose in *Sykes vs. Spencer*, in the Senate of the United States, (forty-third Congress, first session, report number two hundred and ninety-one.) And in determining that case the Senate of the United States laid down a rule which may at first appear to be, but which is not in reality, in conflict with the doctrine we have been considering in the preceding sections of this chapter. The contest between the two legislatures in this case depended upon this: In one body were eight or nine members who had received regular certificates of election, but who were conceded not to have been elected, while in the other was found an equal number of persons duly elected, but without certificates of election. To make a quorum of the former body, it was necessary to count the persons holding certificates, but not elected, and to make a quorum of the latter, it was necessary to count the members duly elected, but without certificates. The former body was called the State house legislature, while the latter was called the court house legislature. The Senate held that the body having a quorum of members in fact duly elected, should be regarded as the legislature of the State, for the purpose of electing the Senator in Congress, and the grounds of this decision are thus stated in the committees' report, submitted by Senator Carpenter of Wisconsin:

"The matter, then, comes to this: The State house legislature was the legislature in form, and the court house legislature was the legislature in fact. While these two pretended legislatures were in existence, each claiming to possess the legislative power of the State, Spencer was elected to the Senate by the court house legislature, and Sykes was elected by the State house legislature. Spencer was first elected, and on the day of his election the court house legislature was recognized by the governor as the legal legislature of the State. Therefore, in determining as to the right of Spencer or Sykes to this seat, the Senate is compelled to choose between the body in fact elected, organized, acting, and recognized by the executive department as the legislature, and another body, organized in form, but without the election and without a recognition on the part of the executive of the State at the time they pretended to elect Sykes. When we consider that all the forms prescribed by law for canvassing and certifying an election, and for the organization of the two houses, are designed to secure to the persons actually elected the right to act in the offices to which in fact they have been elected, it would be sacrificing the end to the means, were the Senate to adhere to the mere form, and thus defeat the end which the forms were intended to secure.

The persons in the two bodies claiming to be the Senate and House of Representatives who voted for Spencer, constituted a quorum of both Houses of the members actually elected; the persons in the State House legislature who voted for Sykes did not constitute a quorum of the two Houses duly elected, but a quorum of persons certified to have been elected to the two Houses. Were the Senate to hold Sykes' election to be valid, it would follow that erroneous certificates, delivered to men conceded not to be elected, had enabled persons who in fact ought not to vote for a Senator to elect a Senator to misrepresent the State for six years. On the other hand, if we treat the court house legislature as the legal legislature of the State, it is conceded that we give effect to the will of the people as evidenced by the election. So that, to state the proposition in other words, we are called upon to choose between the form and the substance, the fiction and the fact; and, considering the importance of the election of a Senator, in the opinion of your committee the Senate would not be justified in overriding the will of the people, as expressed by the ballot-box, out of deference to certificates issued erroneously to persons who were not elected.

In the opinion of your committee it is not competent for the Senate to inquire as to the right of individual members to sit in a legislature which is conceded to have a quorum in both houses of legally elected members. But, undoubtedly, the Senate must always inquire whether the body which pretended to elect a Senator was the legislature of the State or not; because a Senator can only be elected by the legislature of a State. In this case, Spencer having been seated by the Senate, and being *prima facie* entitled to hold the seat, the Senate cannot oust him without going into an inquiry in regard to the right of the individual persons who claim to constitute the quorum in these respective bodies at the Court House and at the State House. We cannot oust Spencer from his seat without inquiring and determining that the eight or nine individuals who were elected were not entitled to sit in the legislature of the State, because they lacked the certificates. But if the Senate can inquire into this question at all, it must certainly inquire for the fact rather than the evidence of the fact. It cannot be maintained that when the Senate has been compelled to enter upon such an examination it is estopped by mere *prima facie* evidence of the fact, and the certificate is conceded to be nothing more than *prima facie* evidence. But the Senate must go back of that to the fact itself, and determine whether the persons claiming to hold seats were in fact elected. When we do this we come to the conceded fact that these persons, lacking the certificate, had in fact been elected, and that the persons who claimed to be a quorum of the two houses were in fact the persons who, in virtue of the election, were entitled to constitute the quorum of both houses."

§ 517. The case here decided was without an exact precedent in the history of contested seats in the United States Senate. It was, of course, insisted in opposition to the doctrine of the report that the Senate was bound to recognize as the legislature of Alabama, that body which consisted of a quorum of members holding the usual *prima facie* evidence of election thereto. But the answer to this was that the Senate may in such a case as this, inquire into the question who *in fact* composed the legislature, and shall not be concluded by the *prima facie* evidence by which a legislative body *in organizing itself,* ought to be bound. There was an important fact in the case, of which we are speaking, which must not be overlooked. The two bodies did not remain separated, but came together, and after uniting and forming a legislature, about the legality of which there was no question, they adjudicated the question concerning the several contested seats in favor of the persons who sat in the court house body, which elected Mr. Spencer. So that the legislature of Alabama itself having adjudicated this question, it become in the Senate of the United States simply a question whether effect should be given to the votes of persons who had in fact no right to vote. This precedent should not be extended beyond the case decided, and therefore all the facts should be kept in view. It is believed that the case was well decided upon the following rule, which may be safely followed as a precedent, to-wit:

Where a State legislature, which ought to be a unit, is divided into two bodies, one of which is composed of a majority of the members elected, but not of a majority of the members returned, if this body assumes to be the legislature, and as such elects a Senator in Congress, and if afterwards the two bodies unite, the validity of such election of Senator will depend, not upon the question whether the persons composing that body were *prima facie* entitled to the office, but upon the question whether they were *in fact* so entitled. Whether this rule would apply where the two bodies remained permanently separated, was not decided, for the question did not arise. That it should apply to a case like the one under consideration, is manifest from the consideration that to adopt the opposite rule would be in effect to say that a minority of the members elected, the consolidated legislature being itself the judge as to who was and who was not elected, shall be held to have composed the legislature.

This would be to put the *form* above the *substance*, and to sacrifice the real merits out of regard to the first appearances, and regardless of the fact that the *prima facie* evidence of title to seats, upon which alone such a decision could be based, has been set aside and overcome by subsequent proof.

But it may be said that the six persons holding certificates, but not elected, should have been regarded as members of the legislature *de facto*, and their acts as such held valid until they were unseated by a contest. Here again is a misapplication of a well settled rule.

The election of a Senator in Congress is not in the nature of an ordinary legislative act; it is an *election*, and not the enactment of a law. Of the validity and *bona fides* of such an election the Senate of the United States is the sole and exclusive judge.

The cases in which the official acts or votes of members of a legislative body who are such *de facto* only, and not *de jure*, have been held valid, *are all cases in which there was no question as to the legality of the body in which they sat.* They are cases in which the body admitting such persons was, in doing so, acting within its admitted jurisdiction, and in such cases the courts will not inquire into the title of such members to their seats. The courts, in such cases, will go no further than to inquire as to the legal *status* and authority of the body as a whole, but where there are two bodies, each claiming to be the legislature, then the Court, whose duty it is to respect and execute the acts of such legislature, must of necessity decide which is the legislature.

§ 518. From these considerations it is apparent that the case of *Sykes* vs. *Spencer*, is not in conflict with the rule that in the organization of legislative bodies, persons holding the usual credentials are alone authorized to act; nor is it in conflict with the general doctrine that the acts of a member of a legislative body who is such *defacto* only, are valid. It goes no further than to hold that the particular election in question, though perhaps irregular, was not void; that it was by the action of the consolidated and legal legislature, shown to have been an election by the quorum of members duly elected to the legislature; and that the Senate of the United States acting as sole judge of said election, might with propriety admit to a seat the person chosen at said election.

§ 519. A legislative body has power to preserve order and decorum, enforce its rules, and prevent or punish any breach of decorum or of the privileges of the body or of any of its members. Mr. Cushing in his manual of parliamentary practice, in speaking of the rights and duties of members of a deliberative assembly says: "The only punishments which can be inflicted upon its members by a deliberative assembly of the kind now under consideration consist of reprimanding, exclusion from the assembly, a prohibition to speak or vote for a specified time, and expulsion; to which are to be added such other forms of punishment as by apology, begging pardon, &c., as the assembly may see fit to impose, and to require the offender to submit on pain of expulsion." (*Cushing's Manual, chap.* 3.)

§ 520. A member may be accused or complained of by any other member, or by the presiding officer, and it is the duty of the latter to make such complaint to the House, in case any member is guilty of irregular and disorderly deportment in the course of the sessions of the body. When a complaint of this kind is made, the offender is named, that is the announcement is made to the assembly, that such a member, calling him by name, is guilty of certain irregular and improper conduct. The accused member may be heard in his defense, and after being heard, must withdraw, while the body deliberates upon the case, unless the assembly resolve to allow him to remain. He must not, however, in any case, be allowed to vote on his own case, "it being," says Mr. Cushing, " contrary not only to the laws of decency, but to the fundamental principles of the social compact, that a man should sit and act as a judge in his own case."

§ 521. The power of the two Houses of Congress over their members is derived from Art. 1, Sec. 5, of the constitution, which provides: "Each House may determine the rules of its proceedings; punish its members for disorderly behavior, and with the concurrence of two-thirds, expel a member." The question has been much discussed, whether a member may be punished or expelled for an act or acts done prior to his election. The question seems first to have arisen in the case of Senator Marshall, of Kentucky. (1804.) The Senate in that case refused to take jurisdiction, for the reason, among others, that the alleged offense had been committed prior to the Senators election, and was matter cognizable by the criminal courts of Kentucky. But the doctrine of this case was antagonized by the report submitted to the Senate by John Quincy Adams, in December, 1807, in the case of Senator John Smith, of Ohio, who, after his election, but not during the session of the Senate, had been, as was alleged, involved in the treasonable conspiracy of Aaron Burr. In this latter case it was held that the power to expel should be used as a means of relieving the body of the presence of corrupt or infamous persons. The report says:

"The power of expelling a member for misconduct results, on the principles of common sense, from the interests of the nation that the high trusts of legislation shall be invested in pure hands. When the trust is elective, it is not to be presumed that the constituent body will commit the deposit to the keeping of worthless characters. But when a man whom his fellow citizens have honored with their confidence on a pledge of a spotless reputation, has degraded himself by the commission of infamous crimes, which become suddenly and unexpectedly revealed to the world, defective indeed would be that institution which should be impotent to discard from its bosom the contagion of such a member; which should have no remedy of amputation to apply until the poison had reached the heart."

§ 522. The question was again raised in the case of *Matteson in the 35th Congress*. The charges against Mr. Matteson had been preferred in the previous Congress, and a committee of investigation had reported against him, recommending his expulsion. Pending these resolutions he had resigned, having, however, at the time of his resignation been re-elected. When he took his seat in the new Congress by virtue of such re-election, the charges were renewed. A majority of the committee reported adversely to the jurisdiction of the House. In the Report, as well as in the debate, the want of jurisdiction was based upon various grounds, and among them, upon the ground that the offense was committed prior to the election of the accused member. After a long debate the whole subject was laid upon the table, so that it cannot be said that the question was authoritatively determined, one way or the other. Thus the question stood, when the whole controversy came up anew upon the report of the special committee to investigate the alleged Credit Mobilier bribery. This investigation took place in the forty-second Congress, and related chiefly to transactions of members of the fortieth Congress. The report of this case discussed the question at length, and concludes that the power to expel is not limited to those cases where the accused has been guilty of misconduct as a member, and subsequent to his election. From this report we quote as follows:

"It is universally conceded, we believe, that the House has ample jurisdiction to punish or expel a member for an offense committed during his term as a member, though committed during a vacation of Congress and in no way connected with his duties as a member. Upon what principle is it that such a jurisdiction can be maintained? It must be upon one or both of the following: that the offense shows him to be an unworthy and improper man to be a member, or that his conduct brings odium and reproach upon the body. But suppose the offense has been committed prior to his election, but comes to light afterward, is the effect upon his own character, or the reproach and disgrace upon the body, if they allow him to remain a member, any the less? We can see no difference in principal in the two cases, and to attempt any would be to create a purely technical and arbitrary distinction, having no just foundation. In our judgment, the time is not at all material, except it be coupled with the further fact that he was re-elected with a knowledge on the part of his constituents of what he had been guilty, and in such event we have given our views of the effect.

"It seems to us absurd to say that an election has given a man political absolution for an offense which was unknown to his constituents. If it be urged again, as it has sometimes been, that this view of the power of the House, and the true ground of its proper exercise, may be laid hold of and used improperly, it may be answered that no rule, however narrow and limited, that may be adopted, can prevent it. If two-thirds of the House shall see fit to expel a man because they do not like his political or religious principles, or without any reason at all, they have the power, and there is no remedy except by appeal to the people. Such exercise of the power would be wrongful, and violative of the principles of the Constitution, but we see no encouragement of such wrong in the views we hold.

"It is the duty of each House to exercise its rightful functions upon appropriate occasions, and to trust that those who come after them will be no less faithful to duty, and no less jealous for the rights of free popular representation than themselves. It will be quite time enough to square other cases with right reason and principle, when they arise. Perhaps the best way to prevent them, will be to maintain strictly public integrity and public honor in all cases as they present themselves. Nor do we imagine that the people of the United States will charge their servants with invading their privileges, when they confine themselves to the preservation of a standard of official integrity which the common instincts of humanity recognize as essential to all social order and good government."

§ 523. Precisely the opposite doctrine was, however, maintained in a report made to the House, from the committee on the judiciary, by Mr. Butler, of Mass., and which was submitted within a few days after that of the Credit Mobilier investigating committee just quoted from. (*Cong. Globe, Third Session, 42d. Congress, part* 3, *page* 1651.) The question now under consideration, entered very largely into the debate upon the report of the Credit Mobilier investigating committee, and at the close of that debate Mr. Sargeant of California offered a substitute for the pending resolutions, which substitute proposed to change the punishment of the accused members from expulsion, to condemnation and censure. This substitute consisted of two resolutions, and the following preamble:

"Whereas, by the report of the special committee herein, it appears that the acts charged as offenses against members of this House, in connection with the Credit Mobilier of America, occurred more than five years ago, and long before the election of such persons to this Congress, two elections by the people having intervened, and whereas grave doubts exist as to the rightful exercise by this House of its power to expel a member for offenses committed by such member long before his election thereto, and not connected with such election. Therefore," &c. The resolutions of condemnation and censure, following this preamble, were first voted upon and were adopted by the House. A separate vote was then taken on the adoption of the preamble, and it was lost by a vote of ninety-eight yeas to one hundred and thirteen nays. (See *Globe, third session, 42d Congress, pages* 1830 *to* 1835.) Thus the House decided to sustain the doctrine contended for by the special committee, and against the doctrine laid down in the above mentioned report from the committee on the judiciary. It may, therefore, be said that the House has fairly decided the question, and has held that a member may be expelled or punished for offenses committed prior to his election, especially if those offenses were unknown to his constituents at the time of his election. It will of course occur to every one that this is a power which should be exercised with great circumspection, and moderation, and with a due regard to the rights both of constituencies and of individual members of Congress.

§ 524. It is very clear that either House of Congress possesses the power to punish for contempt of its authority. In this respect and for this purpose each House is a court, and exercises judicial functions. The power to punish for contempt of course includes the power to hold in confinement a person summoned as a witness in the course of an investigation before either House, or before a committee thereof, and who refuses to answer proper questions put to him, by the House or by the committee under the order of the House. This latter is not strictly punishment for the contempt, because in such a case the recusant witness may release himself from confinement by answering, but it is a necessary and proper exercise of the authority of the House to compel the disclosure of all facts within the knowledge of any witness which affect the order, the dignity, or the purity of its legislation. These general rules are well settled by the authorities. (*Cooley on Constitutional Limitations*, 133. *Anderson vs. Dunn*, 6 *Wheat*, 14 *East*, 1. *Stockdale vs. Hansard*, 9. *Adolphus and Ellis*, 231. *Burnham vs. Morrisey*, 14 *Gray*, 226. *State vs. Mathews*, 37 *N. H.*, 450. Case of *Irwin*, 43*d Congress*. Case of *Walcott*, 35*th Congress*.)

§ 525. An examination of these and other authorities upon the subject, will show that not alone the two Houses of Congress, but our legislative bodies generally, possess the power to protect themselves by punishing for contempt, and by expulsion of a member. This is a power inherent in every legislative body. The power to punish contempts of its authority which belongs to legislative bodies in general, is not limited to the punishment of members, but reaches other persons, and it belongs to each House of our State legislatures, whether expressly conferred by constitutional provision or not. Where, however, imprisonment is imposed by a legislative body as a punishment for contempt, or as a means of compelling disclosures by a witness, it must terminate with the final adjournment of the House, and if the prisoner be not then discharged by its order, he may be released on habeas corpus. (*Jefferson's Manuel*, § 18. *Cooley on Constitutional Limitations*, 134.)

§ 526. An act of Congress of 24th January, 1857, provides for the punishment by fine, and the imprisonment of any person who having been summoned as a witness by the authority of either House of Congress, shall wilfully make default or who having appeared shall refuse to answer any question pertinent to the question under inquiry. The said act further provides in the last section thereof as follows:

"That when a witness shall fail to testify as provided in the previous sections of this act, and the fact shall be reported to the House, it shall be the duty of the Speaker of the House or the President of the Senate to certify the fact, under the seal of the House or Senate, to the district attorney for the District of Columbia, whose duty it shall be to bring the matter before the grand jury for their action." (*Revised Statutes, U. S., page* 17.)

Under this statute it has been claimed that the Houses of Congress are deprived of the power to punish for contempt and that they have authority only to report a case of contempt to the proper district attorney to be laid before the grand jury. But this is an erroneous view of the effect of the statute. Because a contempt of the authority of the House is made by statute a misdemeanor, it does not thereby cease to be a contempt. The power of the House or Senate to punish ceases with its final adjournment, and the punishment which it may inflict is therefore often very inadequate. If the offense is committed near the close of a Congress, the utmost that either House can do, may be to confine the offender for a few days or possibly only for a few hours. It was for this reason, doubtless, that Congress provided by the statute above named a more effective remedy by indictment. This view of the statute was sustained by the criminal court of the District of Columbia in the case of R. B. Irwin, decided by judge McArthur, January, 1875. The House of Representatives having committed Irwin to the common jail of the District of Columbia for comtempt, in refusing to answer proper questions put to him in the course of an investigation, he applied to said court for release upon habeas corpus, and his counsel urged, as one ground for his discharge from imprisonment, that under the statute above mentioned, the House had no power to commit him, its authority over him having been exhausted by a certification of the facts to the district attorney. The court overruled this point and in the course of his opinion the judge used this language:

"It is said that in as much as Congress has created the act of a witness refusing to answer a misdemeanor, they have abolished it as to contempt. I can not so regard it. It appears to me that the punishment provided in the statute for this as an offense does not merge the contempt, and does not abolish the power of the House. It appears to me that it has not been so understood from the time of the enactment of the statute; and I believe this is the first time that that aspect of the case has ever been presented for judicial examination. There is nothing clearer than that the same act may be both a misdemeanor and a contempt. If one member should strike another while the House was in session, and in its presence, it would be a contempt of the House, and a misdemeanor under the law, for which he could be punished. It would be no answer to the proceedings in the House for contempt to say that he was liable under the general law of the land, to be punished for the misdemeanor."

§ 527. The power to punish persons not members of the body for contempt, is not conferred upon the Houses of Congress by any express provision of the constitution, but in *Anderson vs. Dunn, supra,* in which the whole subject is exhaustively discussed, it is held that the Houses respectively possess this power, and that it is conferred by necessary implication, under the constitution, growing out of the power to legislate, and to make and enforce rules. It was there declared to be a power essential to enable the Houses of Congress to discharge the duties, and exercise the powers which the people have entrusted to them.

§ 528. The power given to each House of Congress to "judge of the election returns and qualifications of its own members," does not authorize an inquiry into the moral character of a person elected and returned as a member. Such an inquiry can only be made, if at all, in the prosecution of proceedings for expulsion. The term "qualifications," as used in the constitution, means the constitutional qualifications, to-wit: that the person elected shall have attained the age of twenty-five years, been seven years a citizen of the U. S., and shall be an inhabitant of the State in which he shall be chosen. (*Maxwell vs. Cannon, 43d Congress.*)

APPENDIX.

LAWS OF THE UNITED STATES

IN RELATION TO

THE ELECTIVE FRANCHISE.

ELECTION OF SENATORS.

ELECTION OF REPRESENTATIVES.

ORGANIZATION OF MEETINGS OF CONGRESS.

CONTESTED ELECTIONS.

PRESIDENTIAL ELECTIONS.

ALSO—A DISCUSSION OF THE QUESTION OF RESIDENCE AS A QUALIFICATION FOR VOTING, BEING PART OF REPORT OF THE COMMITTEE OF ELECTIONS IN THE HOUSE OF REPRESENTATIVES, U. S., IN CASE OF CESSNA *vs.* MYERS.

THE ELECTIVE FRANCHISE.

(FROM THE REVISED STATUTES.)

SEC. 2002. No military or naval officer, or other person engaged in the civil, military, or naval service of the United States, shall order, bring, keep, or have under his authority or control, any troops or armed men at the place where any general or special election is held in any State, unless it be necessary to repel the armed enemies of the United States, or to keep the peace at the polls.

SEC. 2003. No officer of the Army or Navy of the United States shall prescribe or fix, or attempt to prescribe or fix, by proclamation, order, or otherwise, the qualifications of voters in any State, or in any manner interfere with the freedom of any election in any State, or with the exercise of the free right of suffrage in any State.

SEC. 2004. All citizens of the United States who are otherwise qualified by law to vote at any election by the people in any State, Territory, district, county, city, parish, township, school district, municipality, or other territorial subdivision, shall be entitled and allowed to vote at all such elections, without distinction of race, color, or previous condition of servitude ; any constitution, law, custom, usage, or regulation of any State or territory, or by or under its authority, to the contrary notwithstanding.

SEC. 2005. When, under the authority of the constitution or laws of any State, or the laws of any Territory, any act is required to be done as a prerequisite or qualification for voting, and by such constitution or laws persons or officers are charged with the duty of furnishing to citizens an opportunity to perform such prerequisite, or to become qualified to vote, every such person and officer shall give to all citizens of the United States the same and equal opportunity to perform such prerequisite, and to become qualified to vote.

SEC. 2006. Every person or officer charged with the duty specified in the preceding section, who refuses or knowingly omits to give full effect to that section, shall forfeit the sum of five hundred dollars to the party aggrieved by such refusal or omission, to be recovered by an action on the case, with costs, and such allowance for counsel fees as the court may deem just.

SEC. 2007. Whenever under the authority of the constitution or laws of any State, or the laws of any Territory, any act is required to be done by a citizen as a prerequisite to qualify or entitle him to vote, the offer of such citizen to perform the act required to be done shall, if it fail to be carried into execution by reason of the wrongful act or omission of the person or officer charged with the duty of receiving or permitting such performance or offer to perform, or acting thereon, be deemed and held as a performance in law of such act; and the person so offering and failing to vote, and being otherwise qualified, shall be entitled to vote in the same manner and to the same extent as if he had in fact performed such act.

SEC. 2008. Every judge, inspector, or other officer of election whose duty it is to receive, count, certify, register, report, or give effect to the vote of such citizen, who wrongfully refuses or omits to receive, count, certify, register, report, or give effect to the vote of such citizen upon the presentation by him of his affidavit, stating such offer and the time and place thereof, and the name of the officer or person whose duty it was to act thereon, and that he was wrongfully prevented by such person or officer from performing such act, shall forfeit the sum of five hundred dollars to the party aggrieved by such refusal or omission, to be recovered by an action on the case, with costs, and such allowance for counsel fees as the court may deem just.

SEC. 2009. Every officer or other person, having powers or duties of an official character to discharge under any of the provisions of this Title, who by threats, or any unlawful means, hinders, delays, prevents, or obstructs, or combines and confederates with others to hinder, delay, prevent, or obstruct any citizen from doing any act required to be done to qualify him to vote, or from voting at any election in any State, Territory, district, county, city, parish, township, school district, municipality, or other territorial, subdivision, shall forfeit the sum of five hundred dollars to the person aggrieved thereby, to be recovered by an action on the case, with costs, and such allowance for counsel fees as the court may deem just.

SEC. 2010. Whenever any person is defeated or deprived of his election to any office, except elector of President or Vice-President, Representative or Delegate in Congress, or a member of a State legislature, by reason of the denial to any citizen who may offer to vote, of the right to vote, on account of race, color, or previous condition of servitude, his right to hold and enjoy such office, and the emoluments thereof, shall not be impaired bysuch denial; and the person so defeated or deprived may bring any appropriate suit or proceeding to recover possession of such office, and in cases where it appears that the sole question touching the title to such office arises out of the denial of the right to vote to citizens who so offered to vote, on account of race, color, or previous condition of servitude, such suit or proceeding may be instituted in the circuit or district court of the U. S. of the circuit or district in which such person resides. And the circuit or district court shall have, concurrently with the State courts, jurisdiction thereof, so far as to determine the rights of the parties to such office by reason of the denial of the right guaranteed by the fifteenth article of the amendment to the Constitution of the United States, and secured herein.

SEC. 2011. Whenever, in any city or town, having upward of twenty thousand inhabitants, there are two citizens thereof, or whenever, in any county or parish, in any congressional district, there are ten citizens thereof, of good standing, who, prior to any registration of voters for an election for Representative or Delegate in the Congress of the United States, or prior to any election at which a Representative or Delegate in Congress is to be voted for, may make known, in writing, to the judge of the circuit court of the United States, for the circuit wherein such city or town, county or parish, is situated, their desire to have such registration, or such election, or both, guarded and scrutinized, the judge, within not less than ten days prior to the registration, if one there be, or, if no registration be required, within not less than ten days prior to the election, shall open the circuit court at the most convenient point in the circuit.

SEC. 2012. The court, when so opened by the judge, shall proceed to appoint and commission, from day to day, and from time to time, and under the hand of the judge, and under the seal of the court, for each election district or voting precinct in such city or town, or for such election district or voting precinct in the congressional district, as may have applied in the manner hereinbefore prescribed, and to revoke, change, or renew such appointment from time to time, two citizens, residents of the city or town, or of the election district or voting precinct in the county or parish, who shall be of different political parties, and able to read and write the English language, and who shall be known and designated as supervisors of election.

SEC. 2013. The circuit court, when opened by the judge as required in the two preceding sections, shall therefrom and thereafter, and up to and including the day following the day of election, be always open for the transaction of business under this Title, and the powers and jurisdiction hereby granted and conferred shall be exercised as well in vacation as in term time ; and a judge sitting at chambers shall have the same powers and jurisdiction, including the power of keeping order and of punishing any contempt of his authority, as when sitting in court.

SEC. 2014. Whenever, from any cause, the judge of the circuit court in any judicial circuit is unable to perform and discharge the duties herein imposed, he is required to select and assign to the performance thereof, in his place, such one of the judges of the district courts within his circuit as he may deem best; and upon such selection and assignment being made, the district judge so designated shall perform and discharge, in the place of the circuit judge, all the duties, powers, and obligations imposed and conferred upon the circuit judge, by the provisions hereof.

SEC. 2015. The preceding section shall be construed to authorize each of the judges of the circuit courts of the United States to designate one or more of the judges of the district courts within his circuit to discharge the duties arising under this Title.

SEC. 2016. The supervisors of election, so appointed, are authorized and required to attend at all times and places fixed for the registration of voters, who, being registered, would be entitled to vote for a Representative or Delegate in Congress, and to challenge any person offering to register; to attend at all times and places when the names of registered voters may be marked for challenge, and to cause such names registered as they may deem proper to be so marked; to make, when required, the lists, or either of them, provided for in section two thousand and twenty-six, and verify the same; and upon any occasion, and at any time when in attendance upon the duty herein prescribed, to personally inspect and scrutinize such registry, and for purposes of identification to affix their signature to each page of the original list, and of each copy of any such list of registered voters, at such times, upon each day when any name may be received, entered, or registered, and in such manner as will, in their judgment, detect and expose the improper or wrongful removal therefrom, or addition thereto, of any name.

SEC. 2017. The supervisors of election are authorized and required to attend at all times and places for holding elections of Representatives or Delegates in Congress, and for counting the votes cast at such elections; to challenge any vote offered by any person whose legal qualifications the supervisors, or either of them, may doubt; to be and remain where the ballot-boxes are kept at all times after the polls are open until every vote cast at such time and place has been counted, the canvass of all votes polled wholly completed, and the proper and requisite certificates or returns made, whether the certificates or returns be required under any law of the United States, or any State, territorial, or municipal law, and to personally inspect and scrutinize, from time to time, and at all times, on the day of election, the manner in which the voting is done, and the way and method in which the poll-books, registry-lists, and tallies or check-books, whether the same are required by any law of the United States, or any State, territorial, or municipal law, are kept.

SEC. 2018. To the end that each candidate for the office of Representative or Delegate in Congress may obtain the benefit of every vote for him cast, the supervisors of election are, and each of them is, required to personally scrutinize, count, and canvass each ballot in their election district or voting precinct cast, whatever may be the indorsement on the ballot, or in whatever box it may have been placed or be found; to make and forward to the officer who, in accordance with the provisions of section two thousand and twenty-five, has been designated as the chief supervisor of the judicial district in which the city or town, wherein they may serve, acts, such certificates and returns of all such ballots as such officer may direct and require, and to attach to the registry list, and any and all copies thereof, and to any certificate, statement, or return, whether the same, or any part or portion thereof, be required by any law of the United States, or of any State, territorial, or municipal law, any statement touching the truth or accuracy of the registry, or the truth or fairness of the election and canvass, which the supervisors of the election, or either of them, may desire to make or attach, or which should properly and honestly be made or attached, in order that the facts may become known.

SEC. 2019. The better to enable the supervisors of elections to discharge their duties, they are authorized and directed, in their respective election districts or voting precincts, on the day of registration, on the day when registered voters may be marked to be challenged, and on the day of election, to take, occupy, and remain in such position, from time to time, whether before or behind the ballot-boxes, as will, in their judgment, best enable them to see each person offering himself for registration or offering to vote, and, as will best conduce to their scrutinizing the manner in which the registration or voting is being conducted; and at the closing of the polls for the reception of votes, they are required to place themselves in such position, in relation to the ballot-boxes, for the purpose of engaging in the work of canvassing the ballots, as will enable them to fully perform the duties in respect to such canvass provided herein, and shall there remain until every duty in respect to such canvass, certificates, returns, and statements has been wholly completed.

SEC. 2020. When in any election district or voting precinct in any city or town, for which there have been appointed supervisors of election for any election at which a Representative or Delegate in Congress is voted for, the supervisors of election are not allowed to exercise and discharge, fully and freely, and without bribery, solicitation, interference, hinderance, molestation, violence, or threats thereof, on the part of any person, all the duties, obligations, and powers conferred upon them by law, the supervisors of election shall make prompt report, under oath, within ten days after the day of election to the officer who, in accordance with the provisions of section two thousand and twenty-five, has been designated as the chief supervisor of the judicial district in which the city or town wherein they served, acts, of the manner and means by which they were not so allowed to fully and freely exercise and discharge the duties and obligations required and imposed herein. And upon receiving any such report, the chief supervisor, acting both in such capacity and officially as a commissioner of the circuit court, shall forthwith examine into all the facts; and he shall have power to subpœna and compel the attendance before him of any witness, and to administer oaths and take testimony in respect to the charges made; and, prior to the assembling of the Congress for which any such Representative or Delegate was voted for, he shall file with the Clerk of the House of Representatives, all the evidence by him taken, all information by him obtained, and all reports to him made.

SEC. 2021. Whenever an election at which Representatives or Delegates in Congress are to be chosen is held in any city or town of twenty thousand inhabitants or upward, the marshal for the district in which the city or town is situated shall, on the application, in writing, of at least two citizens residing in such city or town, appoint deputy special marshals, whose duty it shall be, when required thereto, to aid and assist the supervisors of election in the verification of any list of persons who may have registered or voted; to attend in each election district or voting precinct at the time and places fixed for the registration of voters, and at all times and places when and where the registration may by law be scrutinized, and the names of registered voters be marked for challenge; and also to attend, at all times for holding elections, the polls in such district or precinct.

SEC. 2022. The marshal and his general deputies, and such special deputies, shall keep the peace, and support and protect the supervisors of election in the discharge of their duties, preserve order at such places of registration and at such polls, prevent fraudulent registration and fraudulent voting thereat, or fraudulent conduct on the part of any officer of election, and immediately, either at the place of registration or polling place, or elsewhere, and either before or after registering or voting, to arrest and take into custody, with or without process, any person who commits, or attempts or offers to commit, any of the acts or offenses prohibited herein, or who commits any offense against the laws of the United States; but no person shall be arrested without process for any offense not committed in the presence of the marshal or his general or special deputies, or either of them, or of the supervisors of election, or either of them, and, for the purpose of arrest, or the preservation of the peace, the supervisors of election shall, in the absence of the marshal's deputies, or if required to assist such deputies, have the same duties and powers as deputy marshals; nor shall any person, on the day of such election, be arrested without process for any offense committed on the day of registration.

SEC. 2023. Whenever any arrest is made under any provision of this title, the person so arrested shall forthwith be brought before a commissioner, judge, or court of the United States for examination of the offenses alleged against him; and such commissioner, judge, or court shall proceed in respect thereto, as authorized by law in case of crimes against the United States.

SEC. 2024. The marshal or his general deputies, or such special deputies as are thereto specially empowered by him, in writing, and under his hand and seal, whenever he or either or any of them, is forcibly resisted in executing their duties under this title, or shall, by violence, threats, or menaces, be prevented from executing such duties, or from arresting any person who has committed any offense for which the marshal or his general or his special deputies are authorized to make such arrest, are, and each of them is, empowered to summon and call to his aid the bystanders or *posse comitatus* of his district.

SEC. 2025. The circuit courts of the United States for each judicial circuit shall name and appoint, on or before the first day of May, in the year eighteen hundred and seventy-one, and thereafter as vacancies may from any cause arise, from among the circuit court commissioners for each judicial district in each judicial circuit, one of such officers, who shall be known for the duties required of him under this title, as the chief supervisors of elections of the judicial district for which he is a commissioner, and shall, so long as faithful and capable, discharge the duties in this title imposed.

SEC. 2026. The chief supervisor shall prepare and furnish all necessary books, forms, blanks, and instructions for the use and direction of the supervisors of election in the several cities and towns in their respective districts; he shall receive the applications of all parties for appointment to such positions; upon the opening, as contemplated in section two thousand and twelve, of the circuit court for the judicial circuit in which the commissioners so designated acts, he shall present such applications to the judge thereof, and furnish information to him in respect to the appointment by the court of such supervisors of election; he shall require of the supervisors of election, when necessary, lists of the persons who may register and vote, or either, in their respective election districts or voting precincts, and cause the names of those upon any such list whose right to register or vote is honestly doubted to be verified by proper inquiry and examination at the respective places by them assigned as their residences; and he shall receive, preserve, and file all oaths of office of supervisors of election, and of all special deputy marshals appointed under the provisions of this title, and all certificates, returns, reports, and records of every kind and nature contemplated or made requisite by the provisions hereof, save where otherwise herein specially directed.

SEC. 2027. All United States marshals and commissioners who in any judicial district perform any duties under the preceding provisions relating to, concerning, or affecting the election of Representatives or Delegates in the Congress of the United States, from time to time, and, with all due diligence, shall forward to the chief supervisor in and for their judicial district, all complaints, examinations, and records pertaining thereto, and all oaths of office by them administered to any supervisor of election or special deputy marshal, in order that the same may be properly preserved and filed.

SEC. 2028. No person shall be appointed a supervisor of election or a deputy marshal, under the preceding provisions, who is not, at the time of his appointment, a qualified voter of the city, town, county, parish election district, or voting precinct in which his duties are to be performed.

SEC. 2029. The supervisors of election appointed for any county or parish, in any congressional district, at the instance of ten citizens, as provided in section two thousand and eleven, shall have no authority to make arrests, or to perform other duties than to be in the immediate presence of the officers holding the election, and to witness all their proceedings, including the counting of the votes and the making of a return thereof.

SEC. 2030. Nothing in this title shall be construed to authorize the appointment of any marshals or deputy marshals, in addition to those authorized by law, prior to the tenth day of June, eighteen hundred and seventy-two.

SEC. 2031. There shall be allowed and paid to the chief supervisor, for his services as such officer, the following compensation, apart from and in excess of all fees allowed by law for the performance of any duty as circuit court commissioner: For filing and caring for every return, report, record, document, or other paper required to be filed by him under any of the preceding provisions, ten cents; for affixing a seal to any paper, record, report, or instrument, twenty cents; for entering and indexing the records of his office, fifteen cents per folio; and for arranging and transmitting to Congress, as provided for in section two thousand and twenty, any report, statement, record, return, or examination, for each folio, fifteen cents; and for any copy thereof, or of any paper on file, a like sum. And there shall be allowed and paid to each supervisor of election, and each special deputy marshal who is appointed and performs his duty under the preceding provisions, compensation at the rate of five dollars per day for each day he is actually on duty, not exceeding ten days; but no compensation shall be allowed, in any case, to supervisors of election, except to those appointed in cities or towns of twenty thousand or more inhabitants. And the fees of the chief supervisors shall be paid at the Treasury of the United States, such accounts to be made out, verified, examined, and certified as in the case of accounts of commissioners, save that the examination or certificate required may be made by either the circuit or district judge.

ELECTION OF SENATORS.

SEC. 14. When Senators to be elected.
" 15. Mode of election.
" 16. Vacancy occurring before meeting of legislature.
" 17. Vacancy occurring during session of legislature.
" 18. Election of Senators certified.
" 19. Countersign of certificate.

SEC. 14. The legislature of each State which is chosen next preceding the expiration of the time for which any Senator was elected to represent such State in Congress shall, on the second Tuesday after the meeting and organization thereof, proceed to elect a Senator in Congress.

SEC. 15. Such election shall be conducted in the following manner: Each house shall openly, by a viva-voce of each member present, name one person for Senator in Congress from such State, and the name of the person so voted for, who receives a majority of the whole number of votes cast in each house, shall be entered on the journal of that house by the clerk or secretary thereof; or if either house fails to give such majority to any person on that day, the fact shall be entered on the journal, At twelve o'clock meridian of the day following that on which proceedings are required to take place as aforesaid, the members of the two houses shall convene in joint assembly, and the journal of each house shall then be read, and if the same person has received a majority of all the votes in each house, he shall be declared duly elected Senator. But if the same person has not received a majority of the votes in each house, or if either house has failed to take proceedings as required by this section, the joint assembly shall then proceed to choose, by a viva-voce vote of each member present, a person for Senator, and the person who receives a majority of all the votes of the joint assembly, a majority of all the members elected to both houses being present and voting, shall be declared duly elected. If no person receives such majority on the first day, the joint assembly shall meet at twelve o'clock meridian of each succeeding day during the session of the legislature, and shall take at least one vote, until a Senator is elected.

SEC. 16. Whenever on the meeting of the legislature of any State a vacancy exists in the representation of such State in the Senate, the legislature shall proceed, on the second Tuesday after meeting and organization, to elect a person to fill such vacancy, in the manner prescribed in the preceding section for the election of a Senator for a full term.

SEC. 17. Whenever during the session of the legislature of any State a vacancy occurs in the representation of such State in the Senate, similar proceedings to fill such vacancy shall be had on the second Tuesday after the legislature is organized and has notice of such vacancy.

SEC. 18. It shall be the duty of the executive of the State from which any Senator has been chosen, to certify his election, under the seal of the State, to the President of the Senate of the United States.

SEC. 19. The certificate mentioned in the preceding section shall be countersigned by the secretary of state of the State.

THE ELECTION OF REPRESENTATIVES.

(THE FOLLOWING ARE THE MATERIAL PORTIONS OF THE ACTS OF CONGRESS IN FORCE UPON THIS SUBJECT.)

SEC. 22. Should any State deny or abridge the right of any of the male inhabitants thereof, being twenty-one years of age, and citizens of the United States, to vote at any election named in the amendment to the Constitution, article fourteen, section two, except for participation in the rebellion or other crime, the number of Representatives apportioned to such State shall be reduced in the proportion which the number of such male citizens shall have to the whole number of male citizens twenty-one years of age in such State.

SEC. 23. In each State entitled under this apportionment to more than one representative, the number to which such State may be entitled in the Forty-third and each subsequent Congress shall be elected by districts composed of contiguous territory, and containing as nearly as practicable an equal number of inhabitants, and equal in number to the number of Representatives to which such State may be entitled in Congress, no one district electing more than one Representative; but in the election of Representatives to the Forty-third Congress in any State to which an increased number of Representatives is given by this apportionment, the additional Representative or Representatives may be elected by the State at large, and the other Representatives by the districts as now prescribed by law, unless the legislature of the State shall otherwise provide before the time fixed by law for the election of Representatives therein.

* * * * *

SEC. 25. The Tuesday next after the first Monday in November, in the year eighteen hundred and seventy-six, is established as the day, in each of the States and Territories of the United States, for the election of Representatives and Delegates to the forty-fifth Congress; and the Tuesday next after the first Monday in November, in every second year thereafter, is established as the day for the election, in each of said States and Territories, of Representatives and Delegates to the Congress, commencing on the fourth day of March next thereafter.

SEC. 26. The time for holding elections in any State, District, or Territory, for a Representative or Delegate to fill a vacancy, whether such vacancy is caused by a failure to elect at the time prescribed by law, or by the death, resignation, or incapacity of a person elected, may be prescribed by the laws of the several States and Territories respectively.

SEC. 37. All votes for Representatives in Congress must be by written or printed ballot; and all votes received or recorded contrary to this section, shall be of no effect. But this section shall not apply to any State voting otherwise whose election for Representatives occurs previous to the regular meeting of its legislature, next after the twenty-eighth day of February, eighteen hundred and seventy-one.

ORGANIZATION OF MEETINGS OF CONGRESS.

SEC. 28. Oath of Senators.
" 29. Oath of President of the Senate.
" 30. Oath of Speaker, members and Delegates.
" 31. Roll of Representatives-elect.
" 32. When roll made by Sergeant-at-Arms.
" 33. When by Door-keeper.
" 34. When President may change the place of meeting.

SEC. 28. The oath of office shall be administered by the President of the Senate to each Senator who shall hereafter be elected, previous to his taking his seat.

SEC. 29. When a President of the Senate has not taken the oath of office, it shall be administered to him by any member of the Senate.

SEC. 30. At the first session of Congress after every general election of Representatives, the oath of office shall be administered by any member of the House of Representatives to the Speaker; and by the Speaker to all the members and Delegates present, and to the Clerk, previous to entering on any other business; and to the members and Delegates who afterward appear, previous to their taking their seats.

SEC. 31. Before the first meeting of each Congress the Clerk of the next preceding House of Representatives shall make a roll of the Representatives elect, and place thereon the names of those persons, and of such persons only, whose credentials show that they were regularly elected in accordance with the laws of their States respectively, or the laws of the United States.

SEC. 32. In case of a vacancy in the office of Clerk of the House of Representatives, or of the absence or inability of the Clerk to discharge the duties imposed on him by law or custom relative to the preparation of the roll of Representatives or the organization of the House, those duties shall devolve on the Sergeant-at-Arms of the next preceding House of Representatives.

SEC. 33. In case of vacancies in the office of both the Clerk and the Sergeant-at-Arms, or of the absence or inability of both to act, the duties of the Clerk relative to the preparation of the roll of the House of Representatives, or the organization of the House shall be performed by the Door-keeper of the next preceding House of Representatives.

SEC. 34. Whenever Congress is about to convene, and from the prevalence of contagious sickness, or the existence of other circumstances, it would, in the opinon of the President, be hazardous to the lives or health of the members to meet at the seat of Government, the President is authorized, by proclamation, to convene Congress at such other place as he may judge proper.

CONTESTED ELECTIONS.

SEC. 105. Notice of intention to contest.
" 106. Time for Answer.
" 107. Time for taking testimony.
" 108. Notice of depositions, service.
" 109. Testimony taken at several places at same time.
" 110. Who may issue subpœnas.
" 111. What the subpœna shall contain.
" 112. When justices of the peace may act.
" 113. Depositions, by consent.
" 114. Service of subpœna.
" 115. Witnesses need not attend out of the county.
" 116. Penalty for failure to attend or testify

SEC. 105. Whenever any person intends to contest an election of any member of the House of Representatives of the United States, he shall, within thirty days after the result of such election shall have been determined by the officer or board of canvassers authorized by law to determine the same, give notice, in writing, to the member whose seat he designs to contest, of his intention to contest the same, and, in such notice, shall specify particularly the grounds upon which he relies in the contest.

SEC. 106. Any member upon whom the notice mentioned in the preceding section may be served shall, within thirty days after the service thereof, answer such notice, admitting or denying the facts alleged therein, and stating specifically any other grounds upon which he rests the validity of his election; and shall serve a copy of his answer upon the contestant.

SEC. 107. In all contested-election cases the time allowed for taking testimony shall be ninety days, and the testimony shall be taken in the following order. The contestant shall take testimony during the first forty days, the returned member during the succeeding forty days, and the contestant may take testimony in rebuttal only during the remaining ten days of said period.

SEC. 108. The party desiring to take a deposition under the provisions of this chapter shall give the opposite party notice, in writing, of the time and place, when and where the same will be taken, of the name of the witness to be examined and their places of residence, and of the name of an officer before whom the same will be taken. The notice shall be personally served upon the opposite party, or upon any agent or attorney authorized by him to take testimony or cross-examine witnesses in the matter of such contest, if, by the use of reasonable diligence, such personal service can be made; but if, by the use of such diligence, personal service cannot be made, the service may be made by leaving a duplicate of the notice at the usual place of abode of the opposite party. The notice shall be served so as to allow the opposite party sufficient time by the usual route of travel to attend, and one day for preparation, exclusive of Sundays and the day of service. Testimony in rebuttal may be taken on five days' notice.

SEC. 109. Testimony in contested election cases may be taken at two or more places at the same time.

SEC. 110. When any contestant or returned member is desirous of obtaining testimony respecting a contested election, he may apply for a subpœna to either of the following officers who may reside within the congressional district in which the election to be contested was held:

First. Any judge of any court of the United States.

Second. Any chancellor, judge, or justice of a court of record of any State.

Third. Any mayor, recorder, or intendent of any town or city.

Fourth. Any register in bankruptcy or notary public.

SEC. 111. The officer to whom the application authorized by the preceding section is made, shall thereupon issue his writ of subpœna, directed to all such witnesses as shall be named to him, requiring their attendance before him, at some time and place named in the subpœna, in order to be examined respecting the contested election.

SEC. 112. In case none of the officers mentioned in section one hundred and ten are residing in the congressional district from which the election is proposed to be contested, the application thereby authorized may be made to any two justices of the peace residing within the district; and they may receive such application, and jointly proceed upon it.

SEC. 113. It shall be competent for the parties, their agents or attorneys authorized to act in the premises, by consent in writing, to take depositions without notice; also, by such written consent, to take depositions (whether upon or without notice,) before any officer or officers authorized to take depositions in common law, or civil actions, or in chancery, by either the laws of the United States, or of the State in which the same may be taken, and to waive proof of the official character of such officer or officers. Any written consent given as aforesaid shall be returned with the depositions.

SEC. 114. Each witness shall be duly served with a subpœna, by a copy thereof delivered to him or left at his usual place of abode, at least five days before the day on which the attendance of the witness is required.

SEC. 115. No witness shall be required to attend an examination out of the county in which he may reside or be served with a subpœna.

SEC. 116. Any person who, having been summoned in the manner above directed, refuses or neglects to atttend and testify, unless prevented by sickness or unavoidable necessity, shall forfeit the sum of twenty dollars, to be recovered, with costs of suit, by the party at whose instance the subpœna was issued, and for his use, by an action of debt, in any court of the United States; and shall also be liable to an indictment for a misdemeanor, and punishment by fine and imprisonment.

SEC. 117. Depositions of witnesses residing outside of the district and beyond the reach of a subpœna may be taken before any officer authorized by law to take testimony in contested election cases in the district in which the witness to be examined may reside.

SEC. 118. The party notified as aforesaid, his agent or attorney, may, if he see fit, select an officer, (having authority to take depositions in such cases,) to officiate with the officer named in the notice, in the taking of the depositions; and if both such officers attend, the depositions shall be taken before them both, sitting together, and be certified by them both. But if only one of such officers attend, the depositions may be taken before and certified by him alone.

SEC. 119. At the taking of any deposition under this chapter, either party may appear and act in person, or by agent or attorney.

SEC. 120. All witnesses who attend in obedience to a subpœna, or who attend voluntarily at the time and place appointed, of whose examination notice has been given, as provided by this chapter, shall then and there be examined on oath by the officer who issued the subpœna or, in case of his absence, by any other officer who is authorized to issue such subpœna, or by the officer before whom the depositions are to be taken by written consent, or before whom the depositions of witnesses residing outside of the district are to be taken, as the case may be, touching all such matters respecting the election about to be contested as shall be proposed by either of the parties or their agents.

SEC. 121. The testimony to be taken by either party to the contest shall be confined to the proof or disproof of the facts alleged or denied in the notice and answer mentioned in sections one hundred and five and one hundred and six.

SEC. 122. The officers shall cause the testimony of the witnesses, together with the questions proposed by the parties or their agents, to be reduced to writing in his presence, and in the presence of the parties or their agents, if attending, and to be duly attested by the witnesses respectively.

SEC. 123. The officer shall have power to require the production of papers; and on the refusal or neglect of any person to produce and deliver up any paper or papers in his possession pertaining to the election, or to produce and deliver up certified or sworn copies of the same in case they may be official papers, such person shall be liable to all the penalties prescribed in section one hundred and sixteen. All papers thus produced, and all certified or sworn copies of official papers, shall be transmitted by the officer, with the testimony of the witnesses, to the Clerk of the House of Representatives.

SEC. 124. The taking of the testimony may, if so stated in the notice, be adjourned from day to day.

SEC. 125. The notice to take depositions, with the proof or acknowledgment of the service thereof, and a copy of the subpœna, where any has been served, shall be attached to the depositions when completed.

SEC. 126. A copy of the notice of contest, and of the answer of the returned member, shall be prefixed to the depositions taken, and transmitted with them to the Clerk of the House of Representatives.

SEC. 127. All officers taking testimony to be used in a contested election case, whether by deposition or otherwise, shall, when the taking of the same is completed, and without unnecessary delay, certify and carefully seal and immediately forward the same, by mail, addressed to the Clerk of the House of Representatives of the U. S., Washington; and shall also indorse upon the envelope containing such deposition or testimony, the name of the case in which it is taken, together with the name of the party in whose behalf it is taken, and shall subscribe such indorsement. Upon the written request of either party the Clerk of the House of Representatives shall open any deposition at any time after he shall have received the same, and he may furnish either party with a copy thereof.

SEC. 128. Every witness attending by virtue of any subpœna herein directed to be issued shall be entitled to receive the sum of seventy-five cents for each day's attendance, and the further sum of five cents for every mile necessarily traveled in going and returning. Such allowance shall be ascertained and certified by the officer taking the examination, and shall be paid by the party at whose instance such witness was summoned.

SEC. 129. Each judge, justice, chancellor, chief executive officer of a town or city, register in bankruptcy, notary public, and justice of the peace, who shall be necessarily employed pursuant to the provisions of this chapter, and all sheriffs, constables, or other officers who may be employed to serve any subpœna or notice herein authorized, shall be entitled to receive from the party at whose instance the service shall have been performed, such fees as are allowed for similar services in the State, wherein such services may be rendered.

SEC. 130. No payment shall be made by the House of Representatives, out of its contingent fund or otherwise, to either party to a contested election case for expenses incurred in prosecuting or defending the same.

(The following are the provisions of an act of Congress, approved March 2d, 1875, being chapter 119, acts second session, 43d Congress:)

Be it enacted by the Senate and House of Representatives of the United States of America, in Congress assembled.

That so much of section one hundred and twenty-seven of the Revised Statutes, as requires the Clerk of the House of Representatives to open, upon the written request of either party, any deposition in cases of contested election, after he shall have received the same, and prior to the meeting of Congress, be, and the same is hereby repealed.

Sec. 2. That section one hundred and seven of the Revised Statutes of the United States shall be construed as requiring all testimony in cases of contested elections to be taken within ninety days from the day on which the answer of the returned member is served upon the contestant.

PRESIDENTIAL ELECTIONS.

Sec. 131. Except in case of a presidential election prior to the ordinary period, as specified in sections one hundred and forty-seven to one hundred and forty-nine, inclusive, when the offices of President and Vice-President both become vacant, the electors of President and Vice-President shall be appointed, in each State, on the Tuesday next after the first Monday in November, in every fourth year succeeding every election of a President and Vice-President.

Sec. 132. The number of electors shall be equal to the number of Senators and Representatives to which the several States are by law entitled at the time when the President and Vice-President to be chosen come into office; except, that where no apportionment of Representatives has been made after any enumeration, at the time of choosing electors, the number of electors shall be according to the then existing apportionment of Senators and Representatives.

Sec. 133. Each State may, by law, provide for the filling of any vacancies which may occur in its college of electors when such college meets to give its electoral vote.

Sec. 134. Whenever any State has held an election for the purpose of choosing electors, and has failed to make a choice on the day prescribed by law, the electors may be appointed on a subsequent day in such manner as the legislature of such State may direct.

Sec. 135. The electors for each State shall meet and give their votes upon the first Wednesday in December, in the year in which they are appointed, at such place, in each State, as the legislature of such State shall direct.

Sec. 136. It shall be the duty of the executive of each State to cause three lists of the names of the electors of such State to be made and certified, and to be delivered to the electors on or before the day on which they are required, by the preceding section, to meet.

Sec. 137. The electors shall vote for President and Vice-President respectively, in the manner directed by the constitution.

Sec. 138. The electors shall make and sign three certificates of all the votes given by them, each of which certificates shall contain two distinct lists, one of the votes for President, and the other of the votes for Vice-President, and shall annex to each of the certificates one of the lists of the electors which shall have been furnished to them by direction of the executive of the State.

Sec. 139. The electors shall seal up the certificates so made by them, and certify upon each that the lists of all the votes of such State given for President, and of all the votes given for Vice-President, are contained therein.

Sec. 140. The electors shall dispose of the certificates thus made by them in the following manner:

One. They shall, by writing under their hands, or under the hands of a majority of them, appoint a person to take charge of and deliver to the President of the Senate, at the seat of Government, before the first Wednesday in January then next ensuing, one of the certificates.

Two. They shall forthwith forward by the post-office to the President of the Senate, at the seat of Government, one other of the certificates.

Three. They shall forthwith cause the other of the certificates to be delivered to the judge of that district in which the electors shall assemble.

Sec. 141. Whenever a certificate of votes from any State has not been received at the seat of Government on the first Wednesday of January, indicated by the preceding section, the Secretary of State shall send a special messenger to the district judge in whose custody one certificate of the votes from that State has been lodged, and such judge shall forthwith transmit that list to the seat of Government.

Sec. 142. Congress shall be in session on the second Wednesday in February succeeding every meeting of the electors, and the certificates, or so many of them as have been received, shall then be opened, the votes counted, and the persons to fill the offices of President and Vice-President ascertained and declared, agreeably to the constitution.

Sec. 143. In case there shall be no President of the Senate at the seat of Government on the arrival of the persons intrusted with the certificates of the votes of the electors, then such persons shall deliver such certificates into the office of the Secretary of State, to be safely kept, and delivered over as soon as may be to the President of the Senate.

Sec. 144 Each of the persons appointed by the electors to deliver the certificates of votes to the President of the Senate shall be allowed, on the delivery of the list intrusted to him, twenty-five cents for every mile of the estimated distance, by the most usual road, from the place of meeting of the electors to the seat of Government of the United States.

Sec. 145. Every person who, having been appointed, pursuant to subdivision one of section one hundred and forty, or to section one hundred and forty-one, to deliver the certificates of the votes of the electors to the President of the Senate, and having accepted such appointment, shall neglect to perform the services required from him, shall forfeit the sum of one thousand dollars.

Sec. 146. In case of removal, death, resignation, or inability of both the President and Vice-President of the United States, the President of the Senate, or, if there is none, then the Speaker of the House of Representatives, for the time being, shall act as President until the disability is removed or a President elected.

Sec. 147. Whenever the offices of President and Vice-President both become vacant, the Secretary of State shall forthwith cause a notification thereof to be made to the executive of every State, and shall also cause the same to be published in at least one of the newspapers printed in each State.

Sec. 148. The notification shall specify that electors of a President and Vice-President of the United States shall be appointed or chosen in the several States, as follows:

First. If there shall be the space of two months yet to ensue between the date of such notification and the first Wednesday in December then next ensuing, such notification shall specify that the electors shall be appointed or chosen within thirty-four days preceding such first Wednesday in December.

Second. If there shall not be the space of two months between the date of such notification and such first Wednesday in December, and if the term for which the President and Vice-President last in office were elected will not expire on the third day of March next ensuing, the notification shall specify that the electors shall be appointed or chosen within thirty-four days preceding the first Wednesday in December in the year next ensuing. But if there shall not be the space of two months between the date of such notification and the first Wednesday in December then next ensuing, and if the term for which the President and Vice-President last in office were elected will expire on the third day of March next ensuing, the notification shall not specify that electors are to be appointed or chosen.

Sec. 149. Electors appointed or chosen upon the notification prescribed by the preceding section, shall meet and give their votes upon the first Wednesday of December, specified in the notification.

Sec. 150. The provisions of this title, relating to the quadrennial election of President and Vice-President, shall apply with respect to any election to fill vacancies in the offices of President and Vice-President, held upon a notification given when both offices become vacant.

Sec. 151. The only evidence of a refusal to accept, or of a resignation of the office of President or Vice-President, shall be an instrument in writing, declaring the same, and subscribed by the person refusing to accept or resigning, as the case may be, and delivered into the office of the Secretary of State.

(THE FOLLOWING IS THE TWENTY-SECOND JOINT RULE OF THE TWO HOUSES OF CONGRESS REGULATING THE MANNER OF COUNTING THE ELECTORAL VOTE, AND OF RECORDING AND DECLARING THE RESULT.)

---

22. The two Houses shall assemble in the hall of the House of Representatives, at the hour of one o'clock p. m., on the second Wednesday in February next succeeding the meeting of the electors of President and Vice-President of the United States, and the President of the Senate shall be their presiding officer; one teller shall be appointed on the part of the Senate, and two on the part of the House of Representatives, to whom shall be handed, as they are opened by the President of the Senate, the certificates of the electoral votes; and said tellers having read the same in the presence and hearing of the two houses thus assembled, shall make a list of the votes as they shall appear from the said certificates; and the votes having been counted, the result of the same shall be delivered to the President of the Senate, who shall thereupon announce the state of the vote and the names of the persons, if any elected, which announcement shall be deemed a sufficient declaration of the persons elected President and Vice-President of the United States, and, together with a list of the votes, be entered on the journals of the two houses.

If, upon the reading of any such certificate by the tellers, any question shall arise in regard to counting the votes therein certified, the same having been stated by the presiding officer, the Senate shall thereupon withdraw, and said question shall be submitted to that body for its decision; and the Speaker of the House of Representatives shall, in like manner, submit said question to the House of Representatives for its decision. And no question shall be decided affirmatively, and no vote objected to shall be counted, except by the concurrent votes of the two houses; which being obtained, the two houses shall immediately reassemble, and the presiding officer shall then announce the decision of the question submitted; and upon any such question there shall be no debate in either house. And any other question pertinent to the object for which the two houses are assembled may be submitted and determined in like manner.

At such joint meeting of the two houses seats shall be provided as follows: for the President of the Senate, the "Speaker's chair;" for the Speaker, a chair immediately upon his left; for the senators, in the body of the hall upon the right of the presiding officer; for the representatives, in the body of the hall not occupied by the senators; for the tellers, Secretary of the Senate, and Clerk of the House of Representatives, at the Clerk's desk; for the other officers of the two houses, in front of the Clerk's desk and upon either side of the Speaker's platform.

Such joint meeting shall not be dissolved until the electoral votes are all counted and the result declared; and no recess shall be taken, unless a question shall have arisen in regard to counting any of such votes, in which case it shall be competent for either house, acting separately in the manner hereinbefore provided, to direct a recess not beyond the next day, at the hour of one o'clock p. m.—*February* 6, 1865.

RESIDENCE.

House of Representatives, 42d Congress, 2d Session, Report No. 11.

JOHN CESSNA *vs.* BENJAMIN F. MEYERS.

FEBRUARY 7, 1872.—Laid on the table and ordered to be printed.

Mr. Hoar, from the Committee on Elections, made the following

REPORT:

THE COMMITTEE ON ELECTIONS, TO WHOM WAS REFERRED THE MEMORIAL OF JOHN CESSNA, CLAIMING TO BE ADMITTED TO THE SEAT FROM THE SIXTEENTH CONGRESSIONAL DISTRICT OF PENNSYLVANIA, RESPECTFULLY REPORT:

The case has required the consideration of many very interesting questions of law, and an examination, by itself, of the evidence in regard to the right to vote of each of several hundred persons. The committee have given it patient and thorough study.

The majority for the sitting member according to the returns, when correctly added, is fourteen. The contestant has shown that more than fourteen illegal votes were cast for his antagonist, and would have established his claim to the seat, were it not for illegal votes which were cast for the contestant himself, the evidence of which, so far as appears, first came to his knowledge when introduced in the case. The questions of law which have arisen are, some of them, exceedingly doubtful, and there are statements of the law in the reports of previous cases which would be quite likely to induce an expectation on the part of the contestant of a different result in the whole matter. He seems, therefore, to have been well warranted in the belief that his duty to the people required him to claim the seat. The whole case has been conducted with entire propriety on both sides.

The majority for the sitting member, as found by the return judges, is fifteen. There is a mistake in the footing, and one should be deducted, leaving fourteen. The contestant claims that three hundred and twenty-eight illegal votes were cast for the sitting member; that two lawful votes which were cast for himself were not counted, and that eight legal votes which were offered for him were rejected. The sitting member, joining issue on these allegations, claims also that three hundred and forty-one votes were illegally thrown for contestant. Of these contestant admits that eighty-one have been proved to be illegal.

The provisions of the constitution of Pennsylvania, concerning the qualification of voters, are as follows:

"Article III, Section 1: In elections by the citizens every (white) freeman of the age of twenty-one years, *having resided* in this State one year, and in the election district where he offers to vote ten days immediately preceding such election, and within two years paid a State or county tax which shall have been assessed at least ten days before the election, shall enjoy the rights of an elector. But a citizen of the United States who had previously been a qualified voter of this State, and removed therefrom and returned, and who shall have resided in the election district and paid taxes as aforesaid, shall be entitled to vote after residing in the State six months: *Provided*, That (white) freemen citizens of the United States between the ages of twenty-one and twenty-two years, and having resided in the State one year and in the election district ten days as aforesaid, shall be entitled to vote, although they shall not have paid taxes."

The contestant claims, first, that he received a majority of the votes cast at the election by lawfully qualified voters; and, second, that the votes of certain other persons, lawfully qualified, who desired to vote for him, were excluded, either from the box or the count, by the mistake or misconduct of the election officers. The result to which an examination of the first claim has brought us renders it needless to consider the second.

The questions which it is material to consider relate either to the qualification of voters under the clause in the constitution of Pennsylvania just cited, or to the rules of evidence which should govern the House in election cases.

Under these constitutional provisions, the burden of proof, when either party insists that a vote should be deducted from those cast and returned for his competitor, is upon that party to show that the person whose vote is in question voted; that the vote was for the competitor; that the voter lacked some one of the following qualifications, viz; citizenship of the United States; the age of twenty-one; residence in the election district for ten days just previous to the election; residence in the State one year just previous to the election, or for six months, if previously a qualified voter; payment, within two years, of a State or county tax, assessed at least ten days before the election, or, in lieu thereof, being between twenty-one and twenty-two years old.

It is claimed by the contestant that a considerable number of those who voted for his competitor lacked the qualification of residence in the election district. The largest number to whom this objection applies came into the election district for the purpose of working npon a railroad in process of construction therein, were employed in building said railroad, and were not proved to have formed any intention to reside in the district after its completion. The length of time which the completion of the road would be likely to occupy was not distinctly proved, but it was shown that persons who were in fact at work upon it continued in the district for a longer period than eighteen months. The committee have carefully considered the legal question which is thus raised.

The word "residence" used in the constitution of Pennsylvania in describing the qualification of voters is equivalent to "domicile," not in the sense in which a man may have a commercial domicile or residence in one country, while his domicile of origin and of allegiance is in another, but in the broadest sense of the term. As it is upon the meaning of this word that the case chiefly turns, it will be well to consider it a little more fully.

The word "domicile," or "residence," as used in law, is incapable of exact definition. Inquiries into it are very apt to be confused by taking the tests which have been found satisfactory in some cases and attempting to apply them as inflexible rules in all. Probably the definition which is most expressive to the American mind is that a man's domicile is "where he has his home." Two or three rules, however, are well established. A man must have a domicile somewhere; a domicile once gained remains until a new one is acquired; no man can have two domiciles at the same time. With these exceptions, it will, we believe, be found that nearly every rule laid down on the subject in the books, even if generally useful, fails to be of universal application, and would be opposed to the common sense of mankind if extended to some states of fact that may arise. For instance, Vattel defines domicile to be "*a fixed residence in any place with an intention of always staying there.*" On this Judge Story (Conflict of Laws, Sec. 43,) well remarks: "This is not an accurate statement. It would be more correct to say that that place is properly the domicile of a person in which his habitation is fixed, without any present intention of removing therefrom." But certainly Judge Story's definition is not much better. A man's domicile remains after he forms the intention of removing therefrom, and sometimes even after he removes, until he gets another. A man may acquire a domicile, if he be personally present in a place and elect that as his home, even if he never design to remain there always, but design at the end of some short time to remove and acquire another. A clergymen of the Methodist church who is settled for two years may surely make his home for two years with his flock, although he means, at the end of that period, to remove and gain another. So of the principle upon which the contestant most relies in the present case.

He claims—and many expressions can be found used by commentators and in judicial decisions which seem to support the claim—that personal presence in a place with intent to remain there only for a limited time and for the accomplishment of a temporary purpose, and to depart when that purpose is accomplished, will not constitute a residence. This is true as a general rule. It is true of those persons, probably the greater number, who, while so present and engaged in business, have some other principal seat of their interests and affections elsewhere. Most men have some permanent home, the claims of which outweigh those of a place of temporary sojourn. The place where a man's property is, where his family is, the place to which he goes back from time to time whenever no temporary occasion calls him elsewhere, the domicile of his origin, where the permanent and ordinary business of his life is conducted—that is to the ordinary man the place of his home. But we are now dealing with a class of persons who have no property, who have no family, or whose family moves with them from place to place, who have no place to return to from temporary absences, the domicile of whose origin is in another country, and has been in the most solemn manner renounced, and the ordinary business of whose life consists in successive temporary employments in different places.

Suppose a man, single, with no property, to come from Ireland and be employed all his life on railroads or other like works in different places in succession. If he does not acquire a residence he can never become a citizen, because he never would reside in this country at all. It seems to us that to such persons the general rule above stated does not apply, where a man who has no interests or relations in life which afford a presumption that his home is elsewhere, comes into an election district for the purpose of working on a railroad for a definite or an indefinite period, being without family, or having his family with him, expecting that the question whether he shall remain or go elsewhere is to depend upon the chances of his obtaining work, having abandoned both in fact and in intention all former residences, and intends to make that his home while his work lasts—that will constitute his residence, both for the purpose of such jurisdiction over him as residence confers, and for the purpose of exercising his privileges as a citizen. Of course the intent above supposed must be in good faith, and an intent to make such district the home for all purposes. The party's intent to vote in the district where he is, he knowing all the time that his home is elsewhere, will not answer the law.

The rule is stated by Chief Justice Shaw, in Lyman vs. Fiske, (5 Peck. 234,) as follows: "It is difficult to give an exact definition of habitancy, In general terms, one may be designated as an inhabitant of that place which constitutes the principal seat of his residence, of his business, pursuits, connections, attachments, and of his political and municipal relations. It is manifest, therefore, that it embraces the fact of residence at a place with the intent to regard it his home. The act and the intent must occur, and the intent may be inferred from declarations and conduct. It is often a question of great difficulty, depending upon minute and complicated circumstances, leaving the question in so much doubt that a slight circumstance may turn the balance. In such a case the mere declaration of the party, made in good faith, of his election to make the one place rather than the other his home, would be sufficient to turn the scale."

The article in the appendix to vol. 4 of Dr. Lieber's Encyclopædia Americana, title Domicile, written by Judge Story, is, perhaps, the best treatise on this subject to be found. He says: "In a strict and legal sense, that is properly the domicile of a person where he has fixed his true, permanent home and principal establishment, and to which, whenever he is absent, he has the intention of returning." It is often a mere question of intention. If a person has actually removed to another place, with an intention of remaining there for an indefinite time, and as a place of present domicile, it becomes his place of domicile, notwithstanding he may have a floating intention to go back at some future period. A *fortiori* would this be true if his "floating intention" were to go elsewhere in future, and not to go back, as in such case the abandonment of his former home would be complete.

In the Allentown election case (Brightly's Lead. Cases on Elections, 475,) it is said: "Unmarried men, who have fully severed the parental relation, and who have entered the world to labor for themselves, usually acquire a residence in the district where they are employed, if the election officers be satisfied they are honestly there pursuing their employment, with no fixed residence elsewhere, and that they have not come into the district as 'colonizers,' that is, for the mere purpose of voting, and going elsewhere as soon as the election is held. The unmarried man who seeks employment from point to point, as opportunity offers, and who has severed the parental relation, becomes a laborer, producing for himself, and thus adds to the productive wealth of the community in which he resides, being willing not only to enjoy political privileges, but also to assume and discharge political and civil duties." A *fortiori* would this reasoning apply to the married laborer who takes his family with him.

The habits of our people, compared with many other nations, are migratory. To persons, especially young men, in many most useful occupations, the choice of a residence is often experimental and temporary. The home is chosen with intent to retain it until the opportunity shall offer of a better. But if it be chosen as a home, and not as a mere place of temporary sojourn, to which some other place, which is more truly the principal seat of the affections or interests, has superior claim, we see not why the policy of the law should not attach to it all the privileges which belong to residence, as it is quite clear that it is the residence in the common and popular acceptation of the term.

The case of Barnes vs. Adams, (3 Con. El. Cas., 771,) does not, when carefully examined, conflict with these rules. The passage cited from that case is not a statement of the grounds on which the House or even the committee determined the case, but is a concession to the party against whom it was decided. It therefore, if it bore the meaning contended for, would not be authority in future cases. But the language, taken together, it seems to us, means only that going into an election precinct for a temporary purpose, with the intent to leave it when that purpose is accomplished, no other intent and no other fact appearing, is not enough to gain a residence. In this view, it is not in conflict with the opinion here expressed.

It is true that, as was remarked in the outset, a former residence continues until a new one is gained. But in determining the question whether a new one has been gained, the fact that everything which constituted the old one—dwelling house, personal presence, business relations, intent to remain—has been abandoned is a most significant fact.

5. We have, then, to apply these principles to the evidence in the case.

The contestant claims that three principal classes of persons who voted for the sitting member were disqualified by reason of non-residence, viz: persons who came into the district for the purpose of working on the railroad; students at the university, who came from other districts solely for the sake of pursuing their studies, and paupers supported in a poor-house common to all the districts in the county, who came to the poor-house from another district, and voted in the district where it is situated.

The cases of the railroad laborers and contractors should be disposed of by the following rules:

1st. Where no other fact appears than that a person, otherwise qualified, came into the election district for the purpose of working on the railroad for an indefinite period, or until it should be completed, and voted at the election, it may or may not be true that his residence was in the district. His vote having been accepted by the election officers, and the burden being on the other side to show that they erred, we are not warranted in deducting the vote.

2d. Where, in addition, it appears that such voter had no dwelling house elsewhere, had his family with him, and himself considered the voting place as his home until his work on the railroad should be over, we consider his residence in the district affirmatively established.

3d. On the other hand, where it appears that he elected to retain a home, or left a family or a dwelling place elsewhere, or any other like circumstances appear negativing a residence in the voting precinct, the vote should be deducted from the candidate for whom it is proved to have been cast.

The principles applicable to the students are not dissimilar. The law, as it applies to this class of persons, is fully and admirably stated by the Supreme Court of Massachusetts, in an opinion given to the legislature, and reported in 5th Metcalf, and which is cited with approbation in nearly all the subsequent discussions of the subject. Under the rule there laid down, the fact that the citizen came into the place where he claims a residence, for the sole purpose of pursuing his studies at a school or college there situate, and has no design of remaining there after his studies terminate, is not necessarily inconsistent with a legal residence, or want of legal residence, in such place. This is to be determined by all the circumstances of each case. Among such circumstances, the intent of the party, the existence or absence of other ties or interests elsewhere, the dwelling place of the parents, or, in the case of an orphan just of age, of such near friends as he had been accustomed to make his home within his minority, would of course be of the highest importance. See Putnam vs. Johnson, 10 Mass., 488.

The case of the paupers presents greater difficulty. Under the laws of Pennsylvania it is conceded they may be entitled to vote. In several contested election cases cited by the contestant, it is stated by the committee that, in the absence of statute regulations on the subject, a pauper abiding in a public almshouse, locally situated in a different district from that where he dwells when he becomes a pauper, and by which he is supported, away from his original home, does not thereby change his residence, but is held constructively to remain at his old home.

Monroe vs. Jackson, 2 Elect. Cas., 98.

Covode vs. Foster, forty-first Congress.

Taylor vs. Reading, forty-first Congress.

And there are some strong reasons for this opinion. The pauper is under a species of confinement. He must submit to regulations imposed by others, and the place of his abode may be changed without his consent. Having few of the other elements which ordinarily make up a domicile, the element of choice also, in his case, almost wholly disappears. There are also serious reasons of expediency against permitting a class of persons who are necessarily so dependent upon the will of one public officer to vote in a town or district in whose concerns they have no interest. On the other hand, the pauper's right to vote is recognized by law. It can practically very seldom be exercised except in the near neighborhood of the almshouse. In the case of a person so poor and helpless as to expect to be a life-long inmate of the poor house, it is, in every sense in which the word can be used, really and truly his residence—his home. And it is important that these constitutional provisions as to suffrage should be carried out in their simplest and most natural sense, without the introduction of artificial or technical constructions. It will, however, be unnecessary to determine this question, as will hereafter appear.

TABLE OF CASES CITED.

A.

B.

L.

EXPLANATORY.

"Cases of contested elections in Congress from 1789 to 1834 inclusive, by "Clark and Hall," cited as "Cl. & H.," or as "Clark and Hall."

"Cases of contested elections in Congress from 1834 to 1865 inclusive, compiled by D. W. Bartlett, clerk of the committee of elections," cited as "1 Bartlett."

"Cases of contested elections in the House of Representatives from 1865 to 1871 inclusive, compiled by D. W. Bartlett, clerk" &c., cited as "2 Bartlett."

INDEX.

(THE REFERENCES ARE TO SECTIONS UNLESS OTHERWISE STATED.)

A.

G.

PRACTICE IN CONTESTED ELECTION CASES (Continued)

Q.

QUALIFICATIONS OF VOTERS (Continued)

S.

TIME, PLACE AND MANNER OF HOLDING ELECTIONS (Continued)

www.ingramcontent.com/pod-product-compliance
Lightning Source LLC
LaVergne TN
LVHW020922110826
845150LV00004B/745

* 9 7 8 1 4 2 5 5 5 4 8 3 5 *